A DANCING PEOPLE

A DANCING PEOPLE

PEOPLE

Powwow Culture
on the
Southern Plains

Clyde Ellis

University Press of Kansas

Published by the
University Press of
Kansas (Lawrence,
Kansas 66049),
which was organized
by the Kansas Board
of Regents and is
operated and funded
by Emporia State
University, Fort Hays
State University,
Kansas State
University, Pittsburg
State University, the
University of Kansas,
and Wichita State
University

Library of Congress Cataloging-in-Publication Data

Ellis, Clyde, 1958–

    A dancing people : powwow culture on the southern Plains /
Clyde Ellis.

        p. cm.

Includes bibliographical references and index.

    ISBN 0-7006-1274-2 (alk. paper)

    1. Powwows — Great Plains.   2. Indians of North
America — Great Plains — Social life and customs.   I. Title.

    E98.P86E55   2003

    793.3´1´08997078—dc21   2003006868

British Library Cataloguing in Publication Data is available.

Printed in the United States of America

10 9 8 7 6 5 4 3 2 1

The paper used in this publication meets the minimum
requirements of the American National Standard for
Permanence of Paper for Printed Library Materials z39.48-1984.

Contents

Acknowledgments

Many people made this work possible, but none more so than the Indian people in Oklahoma and North Carolina who helped me write this book. In Oklahoma, Jessie and the late Harry Tofpi, Sr., took me in during the summer of 1989 after a chance meeting with their son, Harry, Jr., at — of all things — a powwow in Meeker, Oklahoma. Since then the Tofpis have been unfailingly supportive. Jessie and her sisters Pawnee, Shalah, Edith, and Delo and their families have been good friends, great consultants, and excellent traveling companions — especially when we were headed to Denny's or Braum's. Ron and Jennie Bemo constantly remind me that my room is ready any time I'll be in Oklahoma. Their friendship and help over the years are a gift that I can never adequately repay. Jennie's sisters — Jimmie Lee Tofpi Blanchard and Dru Tofpi Ponkilla — and their families also are a constant source of inspiration and support. Harry Tofpi, Jr., took me to powwows all over Oklahoma and proved to be a good friend.

Ralph Kotay introduced me to people in southwest Oklahoma, arranged interviews, put me up at his house, taught me to sing Kiowa hymns, took me to church, and patiently answered my questions about everything under the sun. Ralph also eagerly traveled to North Carolina and New Hampshire to speak with my students about our work on this and other projects, and he always had a good word to say to them about knowing your own history. Emily Satepauhoodle and Kenneth Murphy opened their home to me on many trips to Anadarko, Oklahoma, and always went out of their way to see that I had a place to sleep and food to eat. Jim Anquoe, Dennis Zotigh, Judy Carter, Danieala Vickers, Mac Whitehorse, the late Cy Hall Zotigh, the late Scott Tonemah, the late Vincent Bointy, Cornelius Spottedhorse, Pete Coser, Bill and Erin Bemo, Earl and Dianne Plumley, Sandy Rhoades, Elmer Sugar Brown, and Madeline Hamilton spoke to me about powwows in one context or another.

L. G. Moses, Luke Eric Lassiter, Dan Gelo, Colin Calloway, Jim Charles, David Rich Lewis, William Meadows, Emily Greenwald, Celeste Ray, Brian Hosmer, Colleen O'Neil, and Laura Roselle read all or part of the manuscript and saved me from as many missteps, mistakes, and dumb blunders as they could spot. After listening to early drafts of several chapters in sessions at the Western History Association's annual meetings, Margaret Connell-Szasz, Elizabeth A. H. John, and Susan Miller encouraged me to pursue this book. Anne Butler at the *Western Historical Quarterly* was instrumental in getting this project started when she solicited and subsequently published a version of chapter 1. In acts of generosity for which I remain deeply grateful, Jim Charles, Emily Greenwald, Jethro Gaede, John Troutman, and William Meadows shared their research and unpublished work with me. Todd Leahy took time from his doctoral studies to track down several newspaper accounts at the Oklahoma Historical Society, and Barbara Landis provided me with copies of the Carlisle School student newspaper.

At the Oklahoma Historical Society, Bill Welge, Judy Michener, Chester Cowen, Rodger Harris, Mary Jane Warde, Phyllis Adams, and Dennis Zotigh showed me innumerable kindnesses. An invitation to speak at the Buffalo Bill Center's 2002 Plains Indian Seminar honed my ideas about dance revivals. At Dartmouth College, Dr. Colin Calloway arranged a stint as the Gordon Russell Visiting Associate Professor of Native American Studies during the 2002 winter quarter and put me in the company of gifted students who offered interesting and provocative opinions about this work. Fifty-two of them suffered through a course in powwow history that will be better the next time around as the result of their probing critiques. At Elon University, Dr. Steven House, dean of the College of Arts and Sciences, funded three trips to Oklahoma late in the project. The committee that oversees Elon's eccentric sabbatical program approved a one-semester leave.

At the University Press of Kansas, Nancy Scott Jackson has been unfailingly and enthusiastically supportive from the moment I first pitched this book to her standing in a Portland, Oregon, hotel lobby during the annual meeting of the Western History Association. L. G. and Margaret Moses kept the porch light on, fed me, and gave me a room to call my own every time I was in Stillwater, Oklahoma. In more than a decade of driving Oklahoma's back roads, sitting at the drum together, and trying unsuccessfully to convince him of the merits of gas station coffee, Luke Eric Lassiter has been a good friend. Laura Roselle has been the companion we all hope for.

"We're a dancing people, always have been."

For one weekend every August, the Tulsa Fairground teems with thousands of people attending the Intertribal Indian Club of Tulsa's annual powwow, known as the IICOT Powwow of Champions. There's big money on the line in every category, and champion dancers from across the Southern Plains are there. They are joined by a large contingent of dancers from other regions who stop over at IICOT as part of the powwow-circuit that hits its peak in the summer months. Billed as the second largest powwow in Oklahoma after Red Earth, and voted the top large powwow for four consecutive years by *Native American Times* readers, the IICOT dance has gained a reputation as one of the region's best. For a small admission fee ($5 for the 2002 powwow — the club's twenty-fifth), visitors can take in some of the finest singing and dancing on the Southern Plains (as well as the tastiest funnel cake in northeast Oklahoma) at an event that captures every bit of the contemporary powwow's power and spectacle. Best of all, you do it in the air-conditioned comfort of a 10-acre indoor arena.[1]

Inside, visitors can browse several dozen booths whose sponsors offer everything from arts and crafts to information on bone marrow transplants in Indian country. Afternoons and evenings become a jumble of events filled by hours of dancing, giveaways, and contests. Neighboring tribes sponsor afternoon Gourd Dance sessions; visiting princesses and other powwow royalty are introduced and given prominent seats at the head of the arena; families ask for time to hold giveaways to acknowledge friends and relations with goods and monetary gifts; and dancers of all ages rush back and forth from the bathrooms to check their look. Elders open each dance session by praying over the assembled throng in their native languages, sometimes slipping in the English words "Intertribal Indian Club of Tulsa," "Jesus Christ," and "weekend." Some of Oklahoma's most prominent powwowers serve as head dancers and head singers and lend status to a dance that despite its prominence must compete with other powwows for participants. A tag-team of informative and entertaining emcees — also stars on the circuit — keeps the pace up. In between contest rounds and intertribal dance sessions, the emcees announce upcoming powwows, encourage spectators to visit the vendors, tell an endless array of mostly bad jokes, and plug IICOT's bingo hall, golf tournament, dance troupe, and scholarship fund. Meanwhile, powwow staffers work the crowd selling raffle tickets for Pendleton blankets, art, jewelry, and the always popular 50/50 raffle in which the winner takes home half of the money generated by ticket sales (and instantly becomes the best friend of everyone in sight).

The crowds ebb and flow as the dance sessions run their course, but when the contest finals roll around during the evening sessions on Friday, Saturday, and Sunday, thousands of spectators, friends, and participants jam the arena to take it all in. "For me, IICOT is what powwowing is all about," one dancer told me while we waited between contests for a round of intertribal songs during which everyone could participate. "The family's here, we have a good time, and if we're lucky one of us will take home some money. My folks have been here from the start [1977], and one day maybe my kids will come back." And besides, he added with a smile, "Mom gets to go to the mall while we're here."[2] When it's over, the participants pack up and head home before striking out for another dance the following weekend.

Drive four hours to the southwest corner of the state and you can take in a powwow that is markedly different, but equally powerful. In a copse of cottonwood trees on an allotment south of Carnegie, the Kiowa Tiah-Piah Society (pronounced tie-pay) hosts its annual Gourd Dance and powwow during the July 4 holidays. There are no admission fees, no hassles with city traffic, and parking is free. Not surprisingly, there are considerably fewer amenities than at the IICOT dance: no indoor air-conditioned dance arena, no flush toilets, and no grandstands. On a good day, the road to the encampment is equal parts thin gravel and mud hole, and the parking lot is a grass field that often resembles Indian country's version of gridlock. IICOT's air-conditioned comfort is replaced by the humid blast furnace that settles over the Southern Plains like a sodden blanket every summer. The heat can be brutal. Tipis, nylon tents, and all manner of campers compete for the limited shade, and groups of friends and relatives wait out the afternoon heat under tarps and small brush arbors before the dancing begins. Children play in the small creek that wanders through the grounds, and teenagers occasionally slip off to the car and sit in the air conditioning, or make the short drive up to the Sonic drive-in at Carnegie.

As at similar powwows, many families have camped for years in the same sites, where they have erected permanent picnic shelters and cooking areas. Visitors looking for one camp or another are pointed in the right direction by people who know the camps as well as they know their own neighborhood streets.

Because it's held a short drive from the nearest town, Carnegie (which barely qualifies as a crossroads in some folks' opinion), the Tiah-Piah dance ground evokes an older time for many participants who remember when dances were held out in the country, away from the hustle and bustle of city life. Like IICOT, the Tiah-Piah Society's dance is notable for its easy familiarity and welcoming atmosphere. Extended families use the occasion to reconnect, and there is a sense of camaraderie that is unique to such gatherings.

Many people eagerly await the week of the dance, arranging vacation days in order to spend as much time at the camp as they can. Some will arrive a day or two early, and then linger another day or so after the dance is over before packing up for the drive home. Participants spend considerable time visiting other camps; the overall mood is less hurried than at large contest powwows. Moreover, the camp is knit together physically and emotionally by a sense of shared purpose that some say is different from the feeling they get at, say, IICOT or Red Earth. This sense of fellowship is partly because a great many of the participants come from a handful of local communities dominated by a relatively small number of tribes, most notably Kiowas, Comanches, and Apaches. Too, the host organization draws the participants together in a number of ways. On the evening of the first dance session, for example, the entire camp is invited in groups of twos and threes into a large tipi where several men from the Tiah-Piah Society bless participants with cedar smoke and gifts of sage picked that morning from the surrounding hills. Visitors are welcomed, too, often finding themselves invited to camps for meals and invariably commenting on how well they're treated.

The powwow arena is a modest, relatively small circular affair in an open field surrounded by dozens of parked cars, trucks, and vans. A plywood speaker's stand dominates the western side, and benches for the dancers mark the arena's outer dimension. A more or less reliable lighting system cranks up after dark and lights the way to the dozen or so portable outhouses, parking areas, and camps in the immediate vicinity of the arena. Otherwise, as one Kiowa woman told me with a smile when I returned a folding chair that I'd borrowed one night, "It's flashlight country, unless you LIKE wandering around in the woods. Ayyy."[3] Unlike IICOT, where as many as ten drum groups sing, the Tiah-Piah dance has a single drum under the control of an invited head singer and anywhere from a dozen to twenty men and women who come out to sing. A trader or two might set up a table, but the area around the dance ground quickly fills with dozens of folding chairs. There are no contests unless a family or individual sponsors one to honor friends or relatives.

Like most powwows, this dance is intertribal and draws heavily from communities in and around Carnegie, Anadarko, and Lawton. There's always a large and welcomed contingent of non-Indians, mostly from south of the Red River — "Texicans" to their friends in the Kiowa community. In fact, this dance was established partly because of infighting among several Kiowa-dominated Gourd Dance associations concerning the appropriateness of allowing non-Kiowas and non-Indians to participate. Here, as in Tulsa, people gather to celebrate shared experiences through song and dance that maintain preciously guarded ways of life. There are no contests, no public throngs. But as at the IICOT powwow, the sense of a community gathering is palpable. "Here," one Kiowa woman told me, "I remember what it means to be a member of this family, this tribe of people. I wouldn't miss this for the world."[4]

On any given weekend, if you take I-40 east out of Oklahoma City to the Kickapoo Tribal Complex near the small town of McCloud, just north of Shawnee, there's a good chance you'll find a powwow being held for one cause or another. One Saturday it's a fund-raiser for the Kickapoo Powwow Club's annual dance; another day it's a birthday dance, a memorial dance, or a wedding anniversary dance. On one particularly memorable occasion in 1994, several families hosted a dance on short notice and raised money to fend off the foreclosure of the property on which the Kickapoo chapter of the Native American Church holds its meetings. The sponsors raised several thousand dollars, saved a sacred place, and fed dinner to nearly two hundred people in the bargain. It was a good day's work by any measurement.

A cook shack out back is always busy by the time dances begin at mid-afternoon or early evening, and a small concession stand in the community building/gymnasium/multipurpose room where many dances are held does a brisk business in soda pop and candy bars. Inside, three or four concentric circles of chairs ring the benches around a dance arena that on most nights is barely 30 feet wide. By the time the singers set up in the middle of the room, it's a tight fit all around. When a crowd fills the room, as it does for most dances, the cranky exhaust fans don't usually keep up with the heat and cigarette smoke.

When the crowds will be large, the dancing moves outdoors to a small field. The Kickapoo Powwow Club's annual dance in August, for example, is held outdoors, weather permitting, and resembles a cross between the IICOT and Tiah-Piah events. At the 2002 dance, almost no one camped overnight, for example, but several camp areas were set up where families ate, changed into dance clothes, and visited with friends. One small refreshment stand raising funds for a high school drama club did a steady business selling drinks, hot dogs, and frito pies (a concoction of fritos and chili smothered with soft cheese that's a dietary disaster worth every penny). Renowned Pawnee silversmith Bruce Caesar had the lone crafts booth (cash and checks, please — no plastic). The emcee, Orville Kirk, a well-known figure on the circuit, reminded the crowd time and again that the big news this year was "We got permanent lights! Can you believe it? No more lining up all those Indian cars and turning on the high beams after dark. Some guy today said he thought we'd put up Sun Dance poles, ayyyyyyy."[5]

Not as large as IICOT, or as rurally located as Tiah-Piah, powwows at the Kickapoo complex are nonetheless cut from the same cultural fabric as those other powwows. Oriented around songs, dances, and events that have significance for all in attendance, powwows at McCloud are intensely meaningful, perhaps because, as at Tiah-Piah, participants and spectators are more or less tightly knit by kinship and a sense of community that is expressed daily in numerous ways outside of the powwow. Indeed, some people believe that the smaller the dance, the better, in which case McCloud serves as the perfect environment. It's not that IICOT doesn't have an equally powerful effect. To be sure, it does; but many people who go to both kinds of dances often comment on how different the effect can be. At many small community dances, for example, singers and onlookers often outnumber the dancers (sometimes by three or four to one), and it's at dances like these that visitors can begin to discern the complexities of such gatherings.

The dancing itself is only part of what goes on, and for many of those who attend these events, dancing is meaningful *only* because it is one component among many that go into every powwow. "You know, I like to go and see Red Earth," a Sac and Fox woman told me during a conversation at the 2002 Sac and Fox annual powwow in Stroud. "But Red Earth's a different kind of powwow from something like Stroud, or Otoe, or Ponca powwow. It's a powwow as far as having the drums and dancers, but you don't get the same feeling there as you do here, at Stroud. If I want to go to a big powwow, I'll go to Stroud, where I'm still surrounded by my family. There are contests, for sure, and we got all of them people who are on the circuit looking to win, but we also have our traditional dances and our families. They sing our songs and we do those things that keep us tight with our tribal ways." By any measure, Stroud is a big dance; the Saturday night crowd for the 2002 powwow was estimated at four thousand.

From Oklahoma City's huge Red Earth celebration to the local school's Indian club fund-raising dance, powwows are a vital element in the creation and maintenance of contemporary Indian culture on the Southern Plains. Since the post–World War II era the powwow has become one of the most popular and visible expressions of the dynamic cultural forces at work in Indian country. Folklorist Barre Toelken, whose daughter is an accomplished dancer, describes the powwow as "one of the most rapidly growing expressions of ethnic awareness and identity to be found in the world today." "In the fullest sense of the word," he continues, "dance *embodies* cultural attitudes which cannot readily be articulated today in other ways."[6]

Clearly linked to pre-reservation societies, institutions, and practices, but also molded by modern values and needs, powwow culture reflects a considerable fund of cultural capital. It is a deeply complicated institution, simultaneously binding people from different communities, tribes, and traditions together even as it enforces social and cultural codes and relationships that are connected to tribally specific practices. Angela Wilson, a Dakota, says that "while I don't have an overly romantic view of powwows (I grew up on the powwow trail as my father emceed powwows during our summers), I do know they are places where senses of family and community are enriched. In the twenty-first century they offer one of the few places we can take our kids and let them run around knowing they will be safe. This is not to suggest that anything mystical occurs there . . . indeed, political disagreements are prevalent as are gossip and jealousy."[7]

As Wilson observes, it is important to note that powwows are not uncontested events. Power, knowledge, and status are at stake, and for many people the powwow is a way to assert a claim to one form or another of those things. Powwow people readily, even eagerly, comment on the disagreements and struggles that are common in the powwow world. Song knowledge, for example, is hotly contested, for singing carries considerable prestige and power. Head singers exercise tangible authority at the drum and in their communities, as do emcees and other leading figures on the powwow circuit. Not surprisingly, some of the disagreements are not all that earth shaking, as in the case of a Sac and Fox woman who told me she was skipping the 2002 Kickapoo Powwow because she believed one of the singers had treated her children disrespectfully at another dance. "He don't need my help," she said. Other times, the divisions signal more deeply felt fault lines, as when powwow associations or drum groups split due to internal disagreements and disputes. Such was the case in the 1980s, for example, when rival Gourd Dance associations appeared in Kiowa country, driven in part by personal rivalries and also by disagreements concerning who should be allowed to participate in the dance.[8]

Yet, for the most part, observers and scholars alike tend to view the powwow in a very uncritical way, seeing it as an event that downplays hierarchy and power. The irony of this position, as Luke Eric Lassiter and I point out in an essay on the complexities of powwow culture, is that powwows often tend to do exactly the opposite. Nonetheless, scholars and others continue to embrace curiously one-dimensional interpretations of the powwow's core meanings. Benjamin Kracht, for example, has employed Victor Turner's communitas theory to argue that Kiowa powwows erase hierarchy and ease rivalries and disagreements. In Kracht's estimation, these dances encourage a "'timeless condition' created by rituals bringing together people from different social strata . . . [who] are worshiping in a social environment where the participants are social and cultural equals." This notion of the powwow as an institution that levels social and cultural distinctions has a long history. Writing two decades prior to Kracht, Jack Campisi suggested that at powwows "a strong appeal to brotherhood . . . at least for the few hours of the ceremonies, acts thematically to draw the assemblage together."[9]

As Mark Mattern notes, "The powwow is often cited for its importance in contemporary Indian life as a constituent of tribal and Indian identity, and as a unifying force in Indian life. Although each of these testimonies may be true, each tells an incomplete story. Each downplays or ignores entirely the disagreements and conflicts that occur within the powwow grounds and that swirl around powwow performances. Each erases the multiple differences among Indians and implies that Indian identity and commitments are simply reinforced and reproduced through powwow practices, rather than debated, negotiated, and changed. Each also erases the constitutive presence of power and politics within the powwow arena."[10] This debate runs like a thread through the history of the powwow. Some Indians, for example, criticized their kin who danced in the Wild West shows, others objected to what they perceived as the powwow's challenge to Christianity, and still others thought that powwows were relics of a past best left behind. Today, some critics are disdainful of powwow people who, in their estimation, spend an awful lot of time building elaborate dance outfits and chasing contest dollars instead of devoting their time and energy to more serious things like political activism. Clearly, the powwow does as much to divide Indian people as it does to unite them, and in this sense it is no different from any number of other contemporary social, cultural, religious, and political institutions in Indian country. Gaming, for example, and peyote, also tend to prompt passionate debates about what constitutes legitimately "Indian" expressions.

Yet, as this book suggests, whether understood as a pan-Indian or tribally specific event, dancing often satisfies needs and obligations that are not adequately met in any other way. Indeed, such is its power that to this day many Southern Plains Indian people organize their lives around dancing and all that it represents. "We're a dancing people, always have been," the late Harry Tofpi, Sr., once told me. A Kiowa, Harry grew up in the 1930s in Carnegie, Oklahoma, where he began attending dances at an early age. "God gave us these ways," he told me. "He gave us lots of ways to express ourselves. One of them is these dances. When I go to them, whatever they are — powwow, gourd dance, Black Legs, whatever — I'm right where those old people were. Singing those songs, dancing *where they danced*. And my children and grandchildren, they've learned these ways, too, because it's good, it's powerful."[11] Many Indian people on the Southern Plains agree with Harry's assessment.

As Loretta Fowler has noted, because dance is a cultural construction, it has been "invented, discarded, reinterpreted . . . [and] adapted to new social realities."[12] That dynamism has been one of its most enduring qualities. As they have done since the late nineteenth century when reservations wrought great changes, Southern Plains Indian people have used dancing to negotiate new social and cultural realities and protect tribal and community values. Seeking to ameliorate what many Indian people saw as the corrosive effects of unbridled individualism, industrialization, and capitalism, tribes turned again and again to practices that had sustained them for generations. In many cases, Indian people appealed to dancing, for it often captured in a unique way the practices, relationships, and beliefs with which they were reluctant to part. Historically crucial for its role in pre-reservation tribal political economies, by the twentieth century dance emerged as a kind of permeable boundary in the search for stability and cultural continuity. It proved resilient and adaptable, and was capable of reinforcing important ideals and values even as the context and expression of those things shifted.

The powwow's role in maintaining old ways and introducing new ones is compelling and clear. Whether as social, cultural, psychological, economic, or political statements, powwows have become one of the most powerful expressions of identity in the contemporary Indian world. Gloria Alese Young, whose unpublished dissertation on Oklahoma powwows has been the standard source for nearly two decades, writes that "the powwow is an event built on an overarching philosophy of 'Indianness' which serves to (1) integrate the members of many disparate cultures into, at a supratribal level, one identity based on a set of previously established stereotypes, (2) establish symbolic boundaries between kinds of people (Indian/non-Indians, conservative/modern) and geographical regions, and (3) raise the quality of life of its participants through improved mental health and social contacts."[13]

Although scholars often mention powwow culture in discussions of twentieth-century Indian life, there have been relatively few attempts to trace its history and evolution. Given the enormous importance that powwow people attach to these events, the relative lack of attention to powwow history is curious. As Toelken notes, however, the reasons for such lapses are not especially surprising. Ritual and ceremonial dances have often been topics for research, he writes, but vernacular dance traditions like the powwow have been taken less seriously. Toelken suggests that contemporary powwows probably contradict popular notions about "authentic" Indian culture and non-Indians are therefore tempted to think of them as "a mishmash of leftover ideas no longer seriously functional in the world of the Indians."[14]

While the literature on Southern Plains tribes has added much to our understanding of contemporary powwows, its coverage has tended to be fairly narrow, often focusing on single events or groups. Yet as Kenneth A. Ashworth, Daniel J. Gelo, Thomas Kavanagh, Luke Eric Lassiter, William Meadows, Benjamin Kracht, Jethro Gaede, Morris Foster, Loretta Fowler, and Stephanie Anna May suggest, Southern Plains powwow culture is bound up in a complicated set of negotiations. Ashworth's dissertation makes provocative suggestions about the economic impetus that he believes drives many powwows; Gelo's work on Comanche songs and the role of powwow emcees has helped to broaden our understanding of the importance of song traditions and powwow leaders; Kavanagh has made important contributions to our understanding of the relationship between pan-Indian and tribal traits; Lassiter's ethnography of the Gourd Dance is important both for its deeply collaborative spirit and its community-centered discussion of song; Kracht has interesting ideas about a Kiowa community dynamic revealed by the powwow, and he has charted the development and evolution of contemporary dance culture; Gaede has begun to unravel the story of the all-important American Indian Exposition; Meadows has written the definitive work on Kiowa, Comanche, and Apache warrior societies; Foster has written a compelling ethnography of the Comanche community in which he discusses, among other things, the changing contours of dance; Fowler situates Cheyenne-Arapaho dance culture in her insightful discussion of social and cultural issues; and May has written a fascinating dissertation on the intersection between powwowing, tourism, performance, and everyday life among the Alabama-Coushattas.[15] Standing on the shoulders of these scholars, and thankful for the vantage point that such a perch gives me, I hope to extend the scope of their works into a broadly based history of Southern Plains powwow culture that tells us something about why and how it happened, and what it means.

It is a story of generous proportions that encompasses determined resistance movements, relentless suppression, internal disputes, and the fluorescence of truly powerful and moving song and dance traditions. And as the chapter headings suggest, a history of powwow culture includes discussions of events and issues that take us farther afield than some readers might anticipate. Trained as a historian, I make no claims as an ethnographer or cultural anthropologist. Lassiter's determined lessons during a decade of friendship and fieldwork in Oklahoma notwithstanding, I have never quite broken free of the lessons I learned from W. David Baird and L. G. Moses fifteen years ago as a doctoral student in history. But after two decades of reading the work of the anthropologists noted above, and of others who led the way to what used to be called the

"New Indian History" (a movement now on the verge of venerable middle-age), it is clear that a collaborative approach is the best way to do this work.

So, with apologies to my intellectual and methodological betters, I make several ventures into collaborative ethnography in the belief that doing so makes this account more revealing and more complete. I am guided by the advice that the late Harry Tofpi, Sr., gave to me each summer as a graduate student and later as a professional academician. As I packed my things to leave Oklahoma for my home in North Carolina, we'd sit on the front porch of his daughter's home in Shawnee and Harry would ask me what I'd learned that summer. When I was finished, he'd take my hand, give it a shake, and say, "Remember, son, don't forget to put *us* in the story. We want to be heard. And do what you can to get it right."[16]

I follow a chronological approach with a couple of sidetrips that are more topically framed. Let me say a word on what this study doesn't do. There is little in this book on dance styles and clothing. These are topics that have been repeatedly written about, and I have little to add that would change our understanding of those things. My interest here is less with dance clothes than with the cultural and historical roots of the powwow. I want to know where it came from, what connections it has to traditional practices, and what its innovations have to tell us about the contours of contemporary Indian identity and belief. Readers will quickly discern a certain Oklahoma bias; in some ways my title is a bit misleading, for much of what follows is based on the experience of Oklahoma tribes and their people. While I would agree that there's more to the Southern Plains than Oklahoma, I would argue that in the search for both the historic and contemporary roots of Southern Plains powwow culture, Oklahoma is where the search inevitably leads. It is both the generally acknowledged center of the powwow world and the place where the contemporary powwow took its familiar form (although some folks in the Dakotas, Montana, and Wyoming might have something to say about that). Moreover, with one of the highest concentrations of tribes and native people in the United States, Oklahoma has a kind of critical mass that makes it uniquely powerful in the powwow world. Finally, there is little in the book on the arena shows that appeared in the 1970s and 1980s, like Red Earth, Denver March, and Gathering of Nations. In omitting them I am not suggesting that these aren't powwows, for surely they are. But as powwow people told me time and again, these huge contest powwows are very different from even the largest contest powwows in Oklahoma like IICOT, Ponca Powwow, or the Sac and Fox Powwow. Indeed, I would argue that they are a phenomenon unto themselves and deserve a book of their own.

Chapter 1 is an overview of the issues and events that form the core of powwow culture, as well as of the book itself. I include the role of traditional society dances, attempts by federal officials to suppress dances, the rise of resistance movements and adaptive strategies, the appearance of new dance forms at fairs and expositions, and finally, the emergence by the 1940s of a full-blown powwow culture. Subsequent chapters develop these topics in turn, but the heaviest emphasis is on the formative years of roughly 1890–1950. In chapter 2, I examine the influence of nineteenth-century society dances and rituals on the development of the powwow and try to make connections between those earlier dances and the newer forms of dance that were increasingly popular by the turn of the twentieth century. Chapter 3 addresses the attempts to suppress dance across the Southern Plains. In a story whose outline is broadly familiar to many readers, federal policymakers forbade to one degree or another nearly every kind of dance. Yet as this chapter suggests, the campaign was never entirely successful, and ironically prompted a number of accommodations and concessions that later became components of the powwow, including a performative tradition and an increasingly secularized but deeply meaningful dance culture that flourished across the Southern Plains by the 1920s.

Chapter 4 examines how some Southern Plains people gravitated toward the emerging performative context of dances as paid entertainers. This is a topic that has gotten surprisingly little attention, but in the context of the powwow's larger history it suggests important issues about the agency of native people in determining their own livelihoods. Moreover, the connections between these performers, the shows for which they worked, and the powwow are compelling; collectively they tell us something about the performative, public aspects of powwow culture. Chapter 5 turns to the formative era of the powwow as we now know it. After briefly examining the revival of warrior societies and dances during the first decades of the twentieth century, this chapter considers how the changing legal contours of the 1920s, along with a determination by many communities to maintain dancing, led to the dramatic growth of dances. By the mid-1920s, large powwows were becoming increasingly common, as were smaller family and community dances. Large intertribal powwows were appearing all over Oklahoma, most notably at White Eagle, where the Poncas were laying claim to the first true intertribal powwow and the dance styles and contests that came to typify it.

Chapter 6 continues this discussion by taking up the Craterville Indian fair that ran between 1924 and 1933 and the Anadarko American Indian Exposition, which began in 1934 and continues to this day. These were followed by the rise during the 1940s, 1950s, and 1960s of large urban powwows in places like Tulsa, Oklahoma City, Wichita, and Dallas. The combination of large urban Indian populations, renewed interest in Indian culture, and relatively high levels of mobility hastened and influenced this growth. But there was more going on here besides popularity and opportunity, and I would argue that powwow culture by this time was also beginning to assume real importance in the construction and negotiation of post-war cultural and social institutions and values. Chapter 7 concludes the book with a series of conversations and interviews with powwow people across Oklahoma in which I try to suggest some of the ways that Native people think about powwows by asking them to comment on why they go to dances, and on what they mean to them as Indian people.

CHAPTER ONE

"It's our way of life. It goes with us all the time, every day."

An Overview of the Powwow's History

On a Saturday evening in August 1996, at a dance arbor near Meeker, Oklahoma, the evening session of an annual community powwow was briefly delayed as a local Sac and Fox family brought its teenaged son into the arena dressed in dance clothes for the first time. The audience listened patiently as relatives spoke on the boy's behalf and watched as an uncle walked him around the arena. One of his grandfathers roached him, called to the drum for the family song, and asked us to dance with the family to commemorate the boy's decision to pay for his seat. The family then held a giveaway to mark the occasion, and urged the audience to bear witness to the fact that this young man had accepted the powwow culture that plays an integral role in the maintenance of cultural identity in many Indian communities on the Southern Plains. "It's your *right* to have this way," said one man on behalf of the boy. "But you have to be careful with it."[1] The decision of that family to bring its son out in his dance clothes publicly affirmed the importance of the songs and rituals that frame contemporary powwows on the Southern Plains. Song and dance are expressions of belief and action that, despite decades of adaptation and change, have remained a forum for expressing values not always adequately or appropriately expressed through other means. Part ceremony and part public show, with roots in Indian and non-Indian worlds, the modern powwow has become an arena for maintaining and reinterpreting cultural practices that might otherwise disappear.

Southern Plains powwow people say that dancing is about more than what can be seen. "We have to take care of it, to pass it on to our children. It's our way of life," says Billy Evans Horse, a Kiowa. "It goes with us all the time, every day." Whether through the acknowledgment of kinship ties, the naming of children, or the appointment of ceremonial leaders, in many communities powwows are the central vehicle by which Indian people negotiate a shared identity and a common cultural fabric. Although hardly the only activity Indians use to address these issues, dance is widely perceived as particularly potent and emotionally satisfying for those who embrace it. "Music and dance are integral parts of the social and cultural life of the native peoples of the Southern Plains," writes Thomas Kavanagh, and constitute "the dynamic and creative expressions of Indian identity and pride, both for individuals and communities."[2]

For Theresa Carter, a Kiowa, powwow music is such a central part of her life that she cannot "imagine being without it. . . . It's part of our everyday life . . . I get *tired* sometimes, and I *gripe.* . . . But, I need that music." She is not alone. At the 1996 Kiowa O-ho-mah ceremonial, one man recounted publicly between sobs how his most precious memories were of his mother "who sang O-ho-mah songs to us kids while she did housework. I'll *always* protect these ways. My mom, my dad, all those old ones from a long time back — I can't ever forget how they loved this dance." For others, expressions of kinship and community define the powwow as an event that draws Indian people together in a profoundly meaningful way. Richard West, a Southern Cheyenne, writes that dance is "among the most profound cultural expressions — for me personally — of what it is to be Cheyenne." For Haddon Nauni, a Comanche, powwows reflect a larger sense of Comanche social order: "Here you are with all of your people, your family. . . . If you do it in the right way, it'll be a blessing in your life." The late Ron Harris, a Sac and Fox, saw powwowing as a vital cultural current: "The simplest way to keep the fires strong is to keep within the sound of the drums." The late Harry Tofpi, Sr., a Kiowa, told me that *Daw-K'ee,* or God, had given him this way. He was obligated to protect it, he said, "the best way I know how."[3]

Yet, protecting and practicing these ways has not always been easy to do. During the reservation era the Indian Office vigorously opposed societies and their rituals as vestiges of an uncivilized way of life. Breathlessly denouncing dances as lurid spectacles promoting everything from sexual licentiousness to pagan worship, government officials energetically attempted to suppress them. The campaign reached its end in the 1920s when the Indian Office made one last run at ending dances. By then it was far too late to hope that dancing could be ended by official dictates; nevertheless Cato Sells, the commissioner of Indian affairs from 1913 to 1921, and Charles Burke, who served in that capacity from 1921 to 1928, were undeterred. Sells queried agency superintendents in 1920 about the corrosive effects of what he termed the "old Indian dances," and wished to know to what "extent such dances tend to retard the advancement of the Indians and what effect it has on their morals." Acting with knowledge of "The Secret Dance File," a collection of reports on dance practices considered so obscene that it could not be openly circulated, Burke issued Circular 1665 on April 26, 1921, in which he excoriated dances for their "acts of self-torture, immoral relations between the sexes, the sacrificial destruction of clothing or other useful articles, the reckless giving away of property, the use of injurious drugs or intoxicants, and frequent or prolonged periods of celebration which bring the Indians together from remote points to the neglect of their crops, livestock, and home interest."[4]

Two years later Burke issued a supplement to 1665 in which he assured Indians that he did not intend to deprive them "of decent amusement or occasional feast days." But he added that "no good comes from your 'give-away' custom and dances and it should be stopped. It is not right to torture your bodies or handle poisonous snakes in your ceremonies. . . . You do yourselves and your families great injustice when at dances you give away money or other property, perhaps clothing, a cow, a horse or a team and a wagon, and then after an absence of several days go home to find everything going to waste and yourselves with less to work with than you had before." Burke wanted dances limited to one a month "in the daylight hours of one day in the midweek," abolished completely in April, June, July, and August, and off-limits to anyone under the age of fifty. Responding to complaints in 1924 stemming from Burke's policies, Secretary of Interior Hubert Work said he intended no suppression of "any dance that has a religious significance, or those given for pleasure and entertainment which are not degrading," but went on to declare that "certain practices . . . are against the laws of nature, or moral laws, and all who wish to perpetuate the integrity of their race must refrain from them." Urging Indians to resist those things "which appeal to lower animal emotions only," Work stood his ground.[5]

Despite concerted attempts to prevent the spectacle of what reformers deemed prurient ritual, the fact of the matter is that government officials failed to end dancing. "Even at the height of the Ghost Dance," notes L. G. Moses, "agents were unable to suppress every performance." Dances, he writes, "continued to be performed on citizen allotments, free from interference by the agents."[6] The immediate problem lay in the very system designed to root out the old ways. The Indian Office, a sinkhole of influence peddling, was captive to bald-faced political intrigue so thinly veiled that even career bureaucrats winced at its practices. Senator James H. Kyle observed in 1894, for example, that federal employees often considered Indian work "a license to filch and rob the Indian," and General Henry Heth concluded that the bureau was little more than "the dumping ground for the sweepings of the political party that is in power." Reformer Herbert Welsh wrote in 1891 of a governor "who laughingly admitted that for party workers fit for nothing else, he usually found jobs in the Indian Service." It was little wonder that Secretary of the Interior Carl Schurz once described "a thoroughly competent, honest, and devoted Indian agent" as "a rare jewel." Supervised in turn by an Interior Department that one scholar suggests was charged with so many disparate tasks that it ought to have been called "the Department of Miscellany," it is not surprising that talk often turned to despair when the Indian Question arose. "For the weak and dishonest," writes Robert H. Keller, Jr., "it was a wide-open opportunity for quick wealth; for the honest man it was an impossible job."[7]

Conditions at many Southern Plains agencies corroborate William T. Hagan's assertion that the government's interests lay not in assimilating the tribes but in giving "the stamp of legitimacy to United States efforts to concentrate the Indians and open the region to white exploitation." "Government practice," observes Keller, "depended on white society, promoted white expansion, reflected white values, and protected white frontiersmen." Thus the assimilation agenda of the era rested on three contradictory ends: "protecting Indian rights, promoting westward expansion, and protecting American citizens."[8]

Not surprisingly, the reservation system on the Southern Plains teetered on the edge of failure from the beginning. Often staffed by hacks and incompetents, many agencies suffered repeated episodes of fraud and near collapse. The Kiowa-Comanche-Apache Reservation, observed one inspector in 1885, was little more than an "asylum for relatives and friends who cannot earn a support elsewhere." The tribes endured five agents in eight years, one of whom had been a grocer, and another a lumberyard manager. A third had no experience with Indians or the West, but was described by a friend as "entirely free of bad habits (never drank liquor in his life)." One would-be agent listed his prior applicable experience as "hotel owner." Methodist missionary John Jasper Methvin, who characterized one agent as "a great man in ruins on account of drink," described the agency in 1886 as "chaotic" and its employees as "a crude and crusty crowd."[9] This was hardly the bunch that could be trusted to end dancing on the Southern Plains.

At the same time that government agents were generally failing to suppress dances, a series of outside forces began to shape dance by actively encouraging Indians to sing and perform. The various Wild West shows and traveling carnivals popular at the turn of the century are a case in point. "Persons in the Indian service continued to rail against the shows," notes L. G. Moses, "but, when pressed, nevertheless cooperated in the contracting of Indians." Beginning in 1883 with Buffalo Bill Cody's Wild West Show, by 1890 fifty different shows toured the United States, Canada, and Europe. Hiring hundreds of Indians precisely because they could dance, showmen such as Cody and the Miller Brothers eagerly sought out Indians who would, as Commissioner of Indian Affairs Thomas Morgan dourly expressed it, parade "with [their] war dances, paint, and blanket." Show Indians, he lamented in 1889, were "the lowest type of Indian." In Oklahoma, the Miller Brothers 101 Ranch Real Wild West employed hundreds of Poncas, Osages, Kiowas, and Comanches between 1908 and 1916, while dozens of small-time sideshows and carnivals criss-crossed the region hiring Indians to do everything from dancing to bullfighting.[10]

The arena shows Cody popularized appeared to be little more than Hollywood-style extravaganzas, but their influence on the powwow was significant in several ways. The Wild West's grand entry parade, for example, complete with galloping Indians and gun-toting cowboys, was a crowd-pleaser that quickly found its way, in modified form, into powwows. No powwow worth its salt these days opens without a grand entry, often referred to as "the parade in." There is also evidence that modern contest powwows have roots in the auditions held by the Wild West shows and in how winners were paid for their performances and rewarded with contracts. Yet, as Moses has observed, the Wild West shows had deeper significance. Indians need not be dragooned into the shows; many of them eagerly signed on for reasons that included "money, travel, and adventure." Black Elk, reveals Moses, enjoyed "the adventure of it all, in performing re-creations of brave deeds, and in getting paid for it." Walter Battice, a Sac and Fox who worked for the 101 Ranch Real Wild West, was more blunt about the attractions of working with a Wild West show. About the travel he commented, "You can bet I saw all the law would allow me."[11]

It is also quite clear that the chance to perform songs and dances for themselves encouraged many Indians to join. Show Indians knew that performing was neither a culturally moribund act nor a clear-cut case of victimization. One Pine Ridge agent noted in 1899 that "school boys speak longingly of the time when they will no longer be required to attend school, but can let their hair grow, dance the Omaha, and go off with the shows." Moses remarks that Show Indians "did more than play supportive roles in the victory tableau of 'pioneer' virtue triumphing over 'savagery.' " Wild West Indians "were spokespersons for the right of Indians to be themselves. They survived the contest. . . . They were never destroyed." Joe Rockboy recalled that he joined a Wild West show because it gave him a chance "to get back on a horse and act it out again." Rockboy and others knew that "ethnic identity need not be preserved through isolation; it may also be promoted through contact [with whites]." And as Mark G. Thiel has noted, the shows became a kind of surrogate for older forms of gathering. "Reminiscent of pre-reservation warrior customs," he writes, "the commencement and conclusion of many show seasons became a time of celebration when contenders for employment, performers, and their friends and relatives gathered." Indeed, Cody paid Indians to be Indians, an unwittingly efficient encouragement in the maintenance of traditional institutions. ("The Indians had only to be themselves," affirms Moses.) What was entertainment for eager audiences turned out to be something much more important for the Indians who put the shows on.[12]

By the mid-1930s Commissioner of Indian Affairs John Collier inaugurated what he intended to be a radical departure from previous policy. Committed to reversing the attack on tribal culture, Collier issued Circular 2970 on January 3, 1934, calling for the "fullest constitutional liberty, in all matters affecting religion, conscience, and culture" and requiring the Indian Office to show an "affirmative, appreciative attitude toward Indian cultural values." It further stated, "No interference with Indian religious life or ceremonial expression will hereafter be tolerated. The cultural liberty of Indians is in all respects to be considered equal to that of any non-Indian group."[13]

But there was more than this going on, and leaving the matter in Cody's hands, or in Collier's, ignores much deeper and important actions in Indian communities. ("They didn't need a white man to tell them they could dance," recalled Harry Tofpi.[14]) At the same time that the reservation system was failing Indians across the Southern Plains pushed the limits of acceptable behavior. While in many places they willingly adapted dances to less confrontational modes, in others they engaged in clandestine meetings. Whatever they did, Lassiter contends that across the region Indian people "continually thwarted the goals of the Indian office." And as Carol Rachlin points out, "even at the worst period of federal suppression," no ceremony was interrupted for more than two years. "Indian culture in western Oklahoma," she concludes, "never died. . . . Indians remained Indians." Aided by isolation, inept agency officials, and most importantly, by a keen determination to maintain control of their ritual and ceremonial institutions, Indians kept dancing. For the Apaches, writes Clifford Coppersmith, "always there was the Mountain Spirit Dance." In its various forms, Thiel reminds us, dance remained "perhaps the most viable surviving pre-reservation activity."[15]

In some cases there was open and defiant resistance to government dictates, as in the case of the Kiowa O-ho-mah Lodge, a warrior society whose members simply refused to stop dancing. Along with the Kiowa Ton'konga, and Tiah-Piah societies, O-ho-mah members continued to meet and dance despite intense pressure. Indeed, the Kiowa calendars record the *revival* of the Taipego (an earlier name for the Tiah-Piah Society) and Ton'konga in 1912 following the suppression of the Sun Dance and the issuing of individual allotments where, ironically, advocates found remote locales for dances beyond the immediate reach of agents. O-ho-mah members mounted an especially determined resistance to government bans. One Kiowa woman recalls her great-grandfather's testimony: "If you want me to give up my Ohomo ways you'll have to kill me. Death is the only thing that will keep me from Ohomo." An O-ho-mah song composed during this time tells O-ho-mah dancers, "Do not hesitate to dance; Go ahead and be arrested/jailed."[16]

Because resistance often left dancers and their relatives in harm's way, however, many responses were less confrontational. Thomas Kavanagh observes that on the Southern Plains the Omaha Dance (also called the Grass Dance or Crow Dance), which played a key role in the development of the powwow, emerged among the Poncas, Kaws, Omahas, Kiowas, and Pawnees in the late nineteenth century at about the same time as the Ghost Dance. The Ghost Dance waned in most places by the late 1890s, but the Omaha Dance — from whence comes the contemporary term "war dance" — became increasingly important among the Southern Plains warrior societies. Originally led by officers who wore regalia linked to society practices and offices, the dance included "ceremonial and ritual acts involving the heroism of war deeds, and an accompanying feast."[17] When the martial ethos of warrior societies began to fade in the late nineteenth century, the immediate societal purpose of the Omaha Dance eroded and its practice took on a more secular form and meaning. Among the Pawnees, Omahas, Poncas, and Osages, notes Kavanagh, the dance "dispensed with the crow belt while retaining much of the ritual and many of the officers of the Inloshka societies." Subsequently referred to as "Straight Dance," the new dance showed elements of the Midewiwin, also called the Drum or Dream Dance, and was notable for a revitalization ethos similar to that prophesied by the Ghost Dance.[18]

Western Oklahoma Indians were also transforming the Omaha Dance. When government policies prevented young Kiowas and Comanches from earning war honors, and thus denied them the social and ritual prestige associated with such honors, many dances and ceremonies underwent a period of significant change. However, submission was not surrender, and all across the Southern Plains societal dances began to reflect new cultural realities. When dance advocates could not follow the example set by the O-ho-mah, other alternatives became more attractive. Among other things, "the exclusive right of the men's societies to participate was abandoned," notes Kavanagh, "and the ceremony was opened to all, including women." Moreover, the Kiowas and Comanches introduced elaborate new dance clothes and styles with bustles worn not only on the back but also on the arms and neck. Color-coordinated beadwork harnesses, dyed long johns, long strips of bells, and large feather crest headdresses completed the ensemble that shortly came to be called "fancy dance."[19]

In a similar way, Morris Foster contends, by the early twentieth century radically changing conditions in Comanche communities constrained the people's ability to associate in traditional ways and necessitated new arrangements regarding "the public social occasions used for the purpose of community maintenance." Because public gatherings like dances constitute "a history of the organization and maintenance of the Comanche community," states Foster, they are crucial in the negotiation of public and private codes of conduct that reflect ongoing change.[20] One kind of response began in the summer of 1906, with annual summer encampments that featured traditional dances. Quanah Parker, for example, is known to have hosted a series of such encampments at Cache in the years between 1903 and 1908. These were often held at isolated allotments and were attended by fairly small numbers of participants. "Mostly, just the elders took part [that is, danced]. Just a few selected men, maybe five or six," recalled Tennyson Echawaudah. These encampments shortly became the locus of a revived Comanche dance tradition.[21]

Importantly, although the summer encampments were an attempt to revive pre-reservation rituals, in time they gave way to a new social and cultural order inside the Comanche community that was increasingly based on evolving forms of dance gatherings. By the second decade of the twentieth century, annual encampments reflected a growing generational and ritual schism in the community. Previously restricted from participating (probably due to the lack of warrior status), young Comanches gained prominence in the dance crowd as well as in the Native American Church by the 1930s as the pre-reservation generation began to decline in numbers and influence. Dancing and the use of peyote, Foster notes, had once been "elements of the same belief system." Rising generations of younger Comanches, however, now assigned powwows a distinctly spiritual power, and thus fostered the rise of "two distinct 'religions'" in the Comanche community. As a result, "powwows provided these younger Comanches with their first opportunity to participate actively in a Comanche-derived . . . form of gathering. . . . Dance gatherings, which previously had had a carnival atmosphere, became more solemn occasions in the late 1930s."[22]

Two simultaneous events seemed to be occurring. On the one hand, pre-reservation warrior societies and their dance rituals maintained some of the power and utility that had previously made them so important. On the other hand, as dance traditions responded to new realities, the momentum that was helping to revive warrior society dances also produced a new kind of secular social event increasingly referred to during the post–World War II years as the powwow. "Powwows are not unchanging continuations from the depths of time," writes Thomas W. Kavanagh. For that matter, neither were nineteenth-century dance traditions. Change kept these dances meaningful and relevant, and it was not long before they became the source of new cultural practices responding to new needs. "We don't do dances the same way as a long time ago," a Cheyenne man told me, "but we hold on to the ideas, the thoughts that those old people taught us." When the Kiowas revived the Tiah-Piah in 1958, for example, it was not as a veterans' society, but as a dance open to all Kiowas — men and women, young and old. Dances remained important by evolving in response to new social, cultural, spatial, and ritual realities.[23]

Scott Bradshaw, an Osage-Quapaw, declares that even if his great-grandfather could not recognize all of the elements of the contemporary Osage I'n-Lon-Schka, he would nevertheless understand its function. "The sense of family, the pride of heritage, the seriousness of the occasion, the humor of the moment," says Bradshaw, "are the same as they have always been when Indians gather."[24] The annual Ponca Powwow, held every year in early August at White Eagle, Oklahoma, is clearly not the same thing as the Ponca Helushka, which meets and dances on other occasions. Yet it is clear that Ponca Powwow is a psychologically and culturally vital part of contemporary Ponca life. That it is also "secular" does not in any way lessen its profound role in the Ponca community.

One of the most important influences in the evolution of dance on the Southern Plains is modern warfare. As noted above, martial valor was a critical factor during the pre-reservation era for the attainment of status and prestige. The erosion of such opportunities rippled through the entire cultural fabric of tribes. Largely denied opportunities for warfare by the end of the nineteenth century, many warrior societies languished. Ironically, modern warfare helped to provide the impetus for the creation of a new, yet traditionally inspired, warrior ethic. In the opinion of many powwow people, twentieth-century warfare is the critical link in the revival of many dances and rituals from the pre-reservation period. Indeed, the world wars dramatically influenced both the form and purpose of dance across the Southern Plains. Drawn to the martial ethos that defined a great deal of their past, Southern Plains people saw participation in the nation's wars as both an obligation to be borne by loyal citizens and a validation of their continued allegiance to specific and honorable traditions. As a result, the utility of dances, songs, and rituals previously associated with warfare reemerged with even greater force. Ralph Kotay, a Kiowa, told me "this powwow thing really got going when our boys came home from overseas in World War II. Those service clubs got going and sponsored dances for those boys, and then it just took off."[25]

Presented with an opportunity to celebrate in ways denied them since the late nineteenth century, Indian people used twentieth-century warfare to create a context in which traditional rituals assumed new and useful meaning. Unlike the pre-war years when many older Indians were ambivalent about the need to pass on knowledge with limited relevance for post-allotment, post-reservation generations, the war years confirmed that traditional martial rituals could be revived to serve the needs of a new generation of warriors. "Many aspects of traditional Indian cultures gained renewed importance and vigor during World War I," writes Thomas Britten, "allowing young people to witness, perhaps for the first time, aspects of their cultures about which they had only heard from elders."[26]

Alerted to the appearance of such celebrations, the Bureau of Indian Affairs saw World War I as a turning point in the assimilation campaign and kept up the assault on dances by insisting that they were "acts of disloyalty and an attempt to subvert the will of the government." Kiowa-Comanche Agency officials announced on the eve of the war that "both the Indians and the public should be made to realize that these old customs retard the march of civilization." Once again agents withheld annuities from dancers, including, with some irony, returning Indian veterans. Unable to prevent homecoming dances, Commissioner of Indian Affairs Cato Sells skeptically commented in 1919 on the Indians' insistence that "by reviving the native costume and some form of old war-time dances they can best express complete approval of those who enlisted under the banner of American freedom."[27]

Undaunted by bureaucratic meddling, Indian communities enthusiastically sponsored dances and celebrations to honor servicemen. They also inaugurated a flurry of celebrations that became the first wave of a revivified dance culture across the Plains that coalesced, by the 1940s, in the modern intertribal pow-wow. In Oklahoma, Indian communities sent their young men to Europe with appropriate songs, rituals, and dances widely used in the pre-reservation era. Although not all tribes held military society dances per se, the treatment accorded veterans undoubtedly established a connection between pre-reservation military societies, their dances, and the honor traditionally accorded their members. Between 1917 and 1919, for example, Apaches and Pawnees hosted scalp and victory dances that included the use of German helmets and uniform parts taken from captives and those killed in combat. A 1919 Cheyenne scalp dance in Canton, Oklahoma, reportedly included the use of an actual German scalp. And at a 1919 Pawnee victory dance, dancers wore traditional dance clothes and modern military uniforms.[28]

Other Indian peoples also revived pre-reservation warrior society practices with surprising vigor. A Cannon, North Dakota, 1918 victory dance featured a mock attack on an effigy of Kaiser Wilhelm that became the focal point of the event. "Warriors crept forward and shot at the effigy until it fell down. Afterward, four children previously selected for the purpose counted coup on the Kaiser. Next, four men counted coup, the first of whom rode the horse of a Sioux soldier killed in World War I." War songs appeared with the words "German" and "kaiser" prominently featured, the Lakotas going so far as to refer in one song to the Germans as "crying like women." In the Kiowa community, the return of World War I veterans sparked numerous victory and scalp dances at which veterans received new names, engaged in old warrior society practices, and generally enjoyed the same status and prestige as nineteenth-century warriors. Following the war, the Kiowas began to reestablish warrior societies and gave them contemporary names, such as the Victory Club and the Purple

Heart Club. These and other societies vigorously sponsored dances, to the never-ending irritation of government agents.[29]

World War II and Korea proved decisive in the continued use and revival of many society songs and dances. The late George Watchetaker, a Comanche, recalled that "after World War II those veterans were considered warriors, just like a long time ago." Jim Anquoe, a Kiowa, chuckled that after World War II he saw so many honor dances for Pawnees that "I thought every Pawnee ever born was in the military." Gus Palmer, Sr., a Kiowa who was instrumental in the resurgence of the Kiowa Ton'konga, or Black Legs Society, remembered that "the old people said, you younger men are entitled to carry it on. You men today are just like the men in the old days — warriors. You fought for your people." Kracht observes that unlike World War I, when only fourteen Kiowas served, World War II "produced numerous veterans who kept alive the Kiowa warrior spirit related to *dwdw,* the 'power' assisting success in warfare." The veterans' service thus necessitated the use of song and ritual previously associated with warrior societies. Kiowas proclaim that "on battlefields throughout the twentieth century many Kiowas have fought and died without giving ground, as if the Sacred Arrow also held their sashes," a reference to the old Ton'konga practice of staking a sash to the ground in the face of an attacking enemy, obligating the owner to "remain and die at his post."[30]

During the 1940s and 1950s, dances historically used to honor such service enjoyed renewed importance, and, in several cases, were revived after lengthy periods of dormancy. Leonard Riddles, a Comanche, commented that "with WW II, you got a change with these boys going and coming back from the services. Every week they'd have it [a dance] somewhere, someone's relative coming in on furlough or leaving, and they'd honor him." On the Southern Plains, two especially notable renewals occurred when, in the late 1950s following the Korean War, the Kiowas brought back the Tiah-Piah, or Gourd Dance Society, and the Ton'konga. When he returned from Korea, Harry Tofpi, Sr., remembered being welcomed home "just like in the old days — songs, dances, prayers. They had a big Gourd Dance for me. I talked about what I had done in combat, just like those guys did a long time ago." Scott Tonemah recalled that the revived Gourd Dance reminded Kiowas of the importance of warriors and their obligation to protect and defend their people.[31]

In the Kiowa community this willingness to embrace United States military institutions and values also reveals how women came to take new and active roles in powwow culture. In October 1927, Kiowa women organized a chapter of the American War Mothers, an association of women whose sons and daughters have served in the armed forces and who have been honorably discharged. "To the Kiowa tribe," notes one account, "this was a unique organization in that ninety-eight percent of its charter members were non-English speaking." Formally chartered in February 1944, the Kiowa War Mothers not only embraced the organization's official goals, which included assisting "patriotic works," but also used the chapter to express explicitly Kiowa cultural values through song and dance. It was one of six all-Indian chapters in Oklahoma.[32]

Moreover, the War Mothers honored the service of their children with specific song traditions and dances. "In a sense," according to Lassiter, "they were reviving warrior societies, but did so along gender lines. There were women's organizations prior to this, but this is new, this is not a revival, per se, it's a fashioning of older ideals modified to reflect the twentieth century."[33] A new song tradition called War Mothers' Songs confirmed the deliberate combination of traditional forms of recognition with more contemporary ones. During World War II, for example, numerous War Mother songs appeared with words like these: "Our sons and daughters went overseas. They fought the Germans, they returned safely together." As Jim Anquoe put it, "Those songs, they were made to soothe those women. When your son is in combat, you don't know whether he's going to survive or not. You can't help him. So what you can do is pray. It's the only tool you got. And they prayed hard. Those songs were like that." A Kiowa woman told me matter-of-factly, "Those songs brought my brother home from World War II and Korea, just like when my grandma sang for my grandpa way back there when he went away to fight the cavalry."[34]

The War Mothers are one example of a gender-specific response to contemporary powwow culture that acknowledges the importance of women. As Meadows explains it, such organizations became "culturally significant because they serve as the primary enculturative arena that belongs to and focuses upon women and continues to enculturate younger generations in traditional Kiowa women's roles. Direct participation in these activities . . . assures the survival of traditional dances, martial ideology, and the use of Kiowa language in songs. Participation further serves as a traditional form of maintaining and enhancing women's roles."[35]

Many women saw the emerging powwow as one way to assert influence in their communities. Loretta Fowler notes that during World War II, for example, Cheyenne and Arapaho War Mothers were the "chief organizers" of dances held to honor those tribes' servicemen. More recent participants suggest that this line of action remains firmly in place. Tina Parker Emhoolah, a Comanche, told Lassiter that women are "the most committed participants" in the Comanche Gourd Clan, while Florene White Horse, a Kiowa, told him that "if it wasn't for women . . . there would be no men at this dance. . . . All of the members know that they are incapacitated if they do not have a woman — a wife, sister, whatever. . . . A woman plays a very integral role in what is going on out there. . . . That's reality. Who is the best person that they [the men dancers] would want to back them up. Who stands there behind them in that 104 degrees and gives out the most beautiful tremolos in honor of that man? No one else can do this but a woman. No one else in the world can perform that task."[36]

By the mid and late 1940s the modern powwow complex was beginning to take on a clear form. Although revived warrior society dances continued to gain momentum as well, they did so as part of a more diversified dance culture. Encouraged by the burgeoning urban Pan-Indianism of the post-war years, annual intertribal powwows (often located in urban places) appeared with increasing frequency by the early 1950s. Commenting on why intertribal powwows gained popularity in the post-war era, Ralph Kotay, who has been singing at powwows since the 1940s, said, "Well, after 1950, powwows began to spread out and it caught on all over. People in town helped to organize it in Oklahoma City, Wichita, and Tulsa." For Kotay, as for most powwow people, intertribal powwows — even big contest dances — are no less important and meaningful than community dances, or even ceremonies. "This was given to us," he says. "It's all the same, even though maybe we don't do it just like we did way back there. All tribes like to dance. These are still our traditional ways: our people have been doing this all our lives."[37]

A good example of this new powwow movement occurred among the Comanches, whose homecoming dance for Korean veterans in 1952 led to a new powwow tradition. Kavanagh writes of the dance that came to be known as "Comanche Homecoming": "While its immediate origins date to an event held in honor of Korean War veterans, it has antecedents in events held after both World Wars in tribute to returning soldiers." Comanches acknowledged connections between the older practices of military societies and more contemporary forms of dance, but as Foster and Kavanagh note, these post-war dances assumed new and different roles in the Comanche community. Kavanagh writes that Comanche Homecoming, for example, is the "high point of the social year for Comanche powwow people." Indeed, it wasn't until the 1970s that Comanches reformed their veterans' societies; in the interim, powwows became "the consensus form of public gathering Comanches . . . used to organize their community."[38]

Kiowas, too, witnessed a similar evolution in their dances, with the O-ho-mah being cited as a prime example of this adaptation. As early as 1949, John Gamble argued that the appearance of new dance styles at the O-ho-mah suggested an important transition marked by "the steady decline of O-ho-mo ceremonialism." Lassiter contends that after 1900 O-ho-mah dances became increasingly linked to a new context in which the ceremony "began to develop as a social rather than a warrior society's dance." Attracted to the new and flashy fancy war dance style that had previously spun out of the Omaha complex, the Kiowa O-ho-mah took on a new look. Although important vestiges of its original purpose remained in place (the honoring of returning veterans, for example), as the dance grew in popularity it came to be used in new ways, most notably for "community social dances (i.e., community-wide, intertribal dances not framed by society ceremonials), and in Indian shows and fairs." Lassiter observes that, while clearly linked to the past, the emerging powwow complex "neither followed an unchanging set of rules nor unfolded in a predictably patterned way; instead, it evidenced the unique intersection of individual lives with tradition."[39] Like the revived society dances, the O-ho-mah dance thus assumed a broader social and community purpose during and after World War II by serving as a vehicle to balance convention against context. Its new songs and revived dance continued to serve specific O-ho-mah needs, but Lassiter notes that after 1940, the war dance's popular form was distinctly different from the old O-ho-mah dance. Yet the relationship between O-ho-mah and the emerging powwow complex was clear, and Lassiter concludes that the "O-ho-mah Lodge was a major catalyst for . . . framing the so-called powwow era in southwestern Oklahoma."[40]

Today, dance flourishes on the Southern Plains in a variety of forms. Lassiter describes four dominant expressions of the old Omaha Dance: "First, the original dance ceremony maintained by men's societies like the O-ho-mah Lodge; second, powwows that emerged from the Omaha Dance's popular expression *within* Plains communities . . . ; third, Plains contest powwows like Oklahoma City's Red Earth; and finally, contest and other powwows outside the Plains." Some dances, like the Kiowa Tiah-Piah, Ponca Helushka, and Osage I'n-Lon-Schka remain important as tribally specific men's societies. Adapted to meet contemporary needs, such dances help to maintain cultural boundaries.[41]

On the Southern Plains, few things seem more suited to mediating cultural and community identity than the powwow. Although it is true that powwows reflect complicated and contested interpretations of social memory and action, it is also true that such debates notwithstanding, powwows remain extraordinary for their power to mold and express identity. As David Rich Lewis reminds us, Indian people "define themselves, their experience and significance every day in hundreds of variations."[42] That was the message conveyed that evening in 1996 in Meeker. "Being Indian is a hard way," said one man on behalf of his grandchild, "but this arena will help you in life, it will help you find the strength to meet your problems." It is a sentiment expressed often and with great emotion on the Southern Plains. On the last night of the 1996 O-ho-mah, an elderly Kiowa man told the story of how as a young boy he had seen his grandfather cornered by the Indian agent at an O-ho-mah encampment in the 1910s. The agent denigrated the event, describing it as a heathen ritual, unfit for a people trying to civilize themselves. Determined to cut off the Kiowas's gathering, the agent announced that if the tribe would stop dancing, he would send rations to the entire camp. The man telling the story paused. An uncomfortable murmur could be heard in the seats all around me as Indian people reacted to yet another story of how their relatives had been persecuted for believing in traditional ways. Savoring the moment, the man uttered several words in Kiowa and finished his story: "My grandpa looked back at the agent, looked him square in the face and said, 'We don't want your rations. We want this dance.' "[43] It was a desire that would be repeated many times in the years to come.

CHAPTER TWO

"The sound of the drum will revive them and make them happy."

Nineteenth-century Plains Society Dances and the Roots of the Powwow

Although the contemporary Southern Plains powwow is a relatively recent phenomenon, its roots stretch back more than two centuries to the various military, social, and religious society dances practiced by Plains tribes. Like the powwow culture they influenced, those tribal societies and their dances played crucial roles in social, cultural, political, and martial affairs, and their influence reached to every corner of life. Like the powwow, publicly performed society dances acknowledged shared experiences and values and were powerful markers of membership, prestige, and status. Morris Foster has observed that such public social occasions were and remain peculiarly important in many Indian communities. "A social identity is by definition a public identity by which one is known in the community at large," he writes. "Simply by being present at a powwow, a Comanche communicates a strategic choice that may have long-term consequences for his or her social identity within the community." Haddon Nauni, one of Foster's consultants, expressed an opinion that echoed back to the society dances that his people practiced decades ago: "That arena is your people, your society."[1] Such sentiments are as applicable today as they were in the nineteenth century.

Though some societies might meet and dance only once a year, the importance of such events was unmistakable. James H. Howard believed that "ceremonial activity and dancing occupied most of a Plains Indian's spare time. Probably a third or more of a 19th-century Ponca's year was taken up with preparing for or participating in such activity, and even today such activity looms large for many adult Southern Ponca."[2] This was true for many reasons. Societies and their dances often reflected deep ties of fictive and biological kinship, and thus helped to knit together families, bands, and moieties. These societies also undertook a wide variety of functions from mutual aid to warfare, and as with the contemporary powwow, were avenues by which young men and women alike aspired to prominence and respectability. Society dances are significant examples of how cultural institutions changed and diffused over time, just as the powwow has.

Because they used dance and its associated rituals to celebrate and publicize their importance, Plains societies had performative, ritual, and cultural qualities that remained recognizable and meaningful when their dances gained new life in both the revived ceremonials that appeared in the early and mid twentieth century and in the powwow culture that was derived in part from those earlier dance traditions. A careful look at the relationship between the contemporary powwow and these society dances reveals a complicated story that ties action and belief together across a significant period of time. Indeed, the links are so compelling that it is impossible to fully appreciate the evolution, structure, and meanings of the contemporary powwow without understanding society dances; for not only did they influence the physical form and style of early powwow culture, they imparted values and ideals that continue to shape it. Beginning with a topical discussion of some core values and ideals that connect earlier Plains dance societies to the powwow, this chapter will conclude with a look at how the Omaha Dance and Drum Dance complexes formed a crucial point of departure in the evolution of a new form of dance that ultimately came to be known as the powwow.

While there were numerous and important differences among societies, it is also true that many of them had widely shared values, practices, and ideals. The so-called soldier, or warrior, society was the most important and widely shared of these societies. In his 1898 calendar history of the Kiowas, for example, James Mooney explained that the tribe had "an elaborate military organization . . . known as . . . 'Warriors.' A similar organization is found among most of the prairie tribes, and is commonly known to the whites as the Dog-soldier society, from an imperfect rendering of the name of one of the principal bands. The Kiowa organization consists of six orders, each having its own dance, songs, insignia, and duties." Nearly two decades later, Clark Wissler commented on the Pan-Plains nature of these associations, saying, "Many societies can be traced along first to last, leaving no room for doubt but that we are here dealing with the same organizations." In case after case, native informants assisting anthropologists at the turn of the twentieth century provided evidence of the commonalities of these societies. The Plains Indians' use of society dances (especially the all-important Omaha or Grass Dance complex, which will be discussed at the end of this chapter) is important for our discussion, for it suggests a Pan-tribal ethic based on common values and ideals that came to characterize the contemporary powwow. In that sense, the emergence of the powwow is a logical, evolutionary step in a history of dances and societies that were present among, and deliberately shared by, many Plains tribes.[3]

Mooney was struck by the fact that late nineteenth-century Kiowa society dances often attracted visiting delegations from other tribes' societies, including those of the Dakota, Comanche, Southern Cheyenne, Arapaho, and Nez Percé. Like other observers, Mooney found that these societies and associations shared general forms, functions, and purposes that crossed tribal lines. In the definitive work on Southern Plains military societies, William Meadows notes that dozens of Indian consultants confirmed this universality in interviews conducted in Oklahoma during the 1930s. These interviews, he writes, "indicate that certain societies of other tribes were regarded as equivalents of the Kiowa organizations. This is significant in that it demonstrates the similarity among many of the types of military societies found across the Plains." Commenting on the Kiowas' use of ethnonyms to describe other tribes' societies (in this case, the Apaches), Meadows writes that "the Kiowa recognized the similarity of Apache societies to their own. Similar intertribal societal associations existed among the Mandan, Hidatsa, and Arikara." According to Kiowas interviewed in 1935, "the Cheyenne and Arapaho were considered to have equivalents of the top five Kiowa societies. . . . When members from these tribes attended a Kiowa Sun Dance, they also participated in their associated society's activities." Guy Quoetone, a Kiowa, put the matter a bit more bluntly in a 1967 interview when he answered a question about Kiowa warrior society dances by saying "our people copied them" from the Sioux.[4]

In addition to the warrior societies, which were important in varying degrees in Plains political economies, other types of societies and dances were well-developed across the Plains as well, and they, too, exerted considerable influence on the powwow's evolution. Alanson Skinner, for example, discussed twenty-three Iowa societies and dances that he grouped into three categories: societies and social dances (predominantly warrior society dances), animal and mystery dances, and recent religious organizations, by which he meant the Ghost Dance and the Native American Church. Of the dances he described, twelve were societal and social in nature, eight were animal and mystery dances, and three had religious motifs.[5]

In his work on the Poncas, Skinner listed eighteen men's and women's dance societies divided into three broad categories: sacred, bravery and war, and social pleasure. Eleven of the dance societies came from men's warrior and social associations, four from women's groups, and three from mystery cults. Robert H. Lowie identified eighteen Eastern Dakota societies and divided their dances into five categories: medicine dances, military society dances, dances by associations of individuals having the same vision, dances sponsored by individuals, and social. Lowie described nineteen society dances found among the Comanches, Wind River Shoshones, and Utes, while James R. Murie described twenty-seven

Pawnee societies and their dances and divided them between three categories: bundle societies, private organizations, and medicine men's societies. Among the Oglalas, Clark Wissler found twenty-six societies divided between the *akicita,* or police societies, headsmen, war societies, and feast and dance associations. His work on the Blackfoot people covered thirty-four such organizations divided between men's and women's groups, religious societies, and dance associations.[6] Clearly, dancing was important, and it was associated with a wide variety of purposes and practices. In thousands of pages of closely detailed discussions of everything from dance clothing to membership requirements, these scholars turned out dozens of essays chronicling the form, function, and history of societies and their dances.

Concentrating on the three cardinal characteristics of police and soldier functions, age-graded membership, and the "no flight" pledge in battle, Wissler and his contemporaries studied the history, purpose, and diffusion of societies and their rituals, convinced they were keys to understanding earlier Plains political economies, especially during the tumultuous late nineteenth and early twentieth centuries when many observers assumed (and occasionally hoped) that the disappearance of such rituals — if not the tribes themselves — was only a matter of time. Accordingly, those scholars were determined to collect as much firsthand information as possible before the living tableaux of the reservations vanished. Indeed, most observers agreed that the survival of all but the remnants of those earlier societies, tribes, and cultures was impossible in a rapidly industrializing world. This supposed fate made the need to salvage as much information as they could a self-evident fact for anthropologists, ethnologists, historians, and government officials alike.

As it turned out, neither the tribes nor all of their societies and dances disappeared, and further, a great deal of what those scholars described survived through adaptation, revival, or resistance. Wissler and others could not have known it, but their work remained important for other reasons, not the least of which is that it formed a bridge between the twilight of the old societies and their dances and the new forms of dance that appeared during and after the reservation era. Yet, even when it became apparent by the mid-twentieth century that this material had direct relevance for understanding contemporary cultural institutions in Indian country, it got surprisingly limited use, especially where the evolution of the modern powwow is concerned. James H. Howard, for example, thought the importance of dances and ceremonies on the Plains had been both "greatly underestimated" and routinely passed over in favor of studies "going into great detail concerning the political, social, legal, and economic systems of a particular group." When studies did mention dances, it was not always in a culturally or historically sophisticated context, as when Ernest Wallace and E. Adamson Hoebel wrote in 1952 that the Comanche war dance "in some respects compares to the modern college pep rally."[7]

Curiously, a century after Wissler and his contemporaries (most notably Robert H. Lowie, James Mooney, George Dorsey, A. L. Kroeber, Pliny Earle Goddard, Alanson Skinner, Alice Fletcher, and Francis La Flesche) published their accounts of Plains ceremonies and rituals, scholars have given relatively little attention to the relationship between those earlier dances and societies and the evolution of the contemporary powwow. It is unfair to say authors have ignored the relationship completely, but much of the published work on powwow culture pauses only long enough to establish a broad connection between traditional societies and the powwow before moving quickly to a discussion of clothing, dance styles, and the spirituality of powwow dancing.[8]

At the other end of the spectrum, some scholars insist that there are no tangible connections between society dances and the contemporary powwow. Aaron Fry, for example, believes that this approach cannot explain "any of the supposed changes from Grass Dance to powwow etiquette," and concludes that "the idea that Grass Dance societies somehow magically transformed into powwows does not explain the current coexistence of Grass Dance/Hethuska societies on both the northern and southern Plains." Fry is ignoring the role of change and adaptation over time when he says that dance cultures existing simultaneously is evidence that they are *not* connected. Indeed, the logical explanation of the dances' coexistence is, as Abe Conklin suggests and as dozens of powwow people told me, that the Grass Dance influenced new forms of dance even while it survived as a society dance. Evolution is a self-evident fact, for example, in the case of the Kiowa O-ho-mah Society, which was unquestionably the site of a new and flourishing powwow culture in the early twentieth century *and* the site of a renewed devotion to O-ho-mah ways. Other tribes had similar experiences as the context of dance culture changed. New dances differed from their predecessors, but the relationship between traditional society dances and the emerging powwow was clear."[9]

Fry is not alone. Tara Browner dismissed the early literature generally, and Wissler specifically, arguing that the idea of a deliberately diffused, Pan-Plains dance complex based on the all-important Omaha Dance was a fiction concocted by uninformed and culturally insensitive scholars who, social Darwinists that they were, can hardly be trusted to have gotten anything right.[10] The weight of the evidence, however, clearly confirms connections between the older societies and the burgeoning powwow culture of the early twentieth century. Wissler and his contemporaries discerned those connections, Indian people who were participants in early twentieth-century dance culture pointed them out, and the overwhelming majority of powwow people today regard the connections as not only obvious but also as evidence of the powwow's ties to earlier, revered traditions.

The consequences for our discussion are several-fold. Because most works on the contemporary powwow summarize rather than examine the details of pre-reservation society dances, they downplay the relationship between them and unduly narrow the powwow's cultural and historical contours. Ignoring these early sources also tends to mask the adaptation and diffusion of Plains society dances in a process central to the evolution of the contemporary Southern Plains powwow. As a result, powwow culture often appears to have only a nominal connection to the society dances that preceded it, an approach that isolates historically important assumptions, values, and practices that frame the contemporary powwow. But, as Gloria Young has pointed out, at least six dance traditions were precursors to the contemporary powwow: War, Scalp, Calumet, Omaha, Drum, and Stomp. The objections of Fry and Browner notwithstanding, the relationship between these society dances and the powwow is much more substantive and important than many sources generally suggest. As Kavanagh has succinctly put it, "The pow-wow is the modern version of the Grass Dance, a secular dance which diffused widely across the Plains in the late 1800s."[11]

Typically, the complex cultural and historical underpinnings of the contemporary powwow are passed over in favor of detailed narrative descriptions of dance styles and the importance of dance as a spiritual event. Without denying that these are interesting and important matters, it is also generally true that they tend to get most if not all of the attention, especially in the popular press. In Howard's words, most accounts "gloss over" the details of ceremonial life "in a few paragraphs."[12] Yet, as Jim Charles, Luke Eric Lassiter, and R. D. Theisz have suggested in their works on powwow songs, emphasizing the performative qualities of dancing and dance clothing can unwittingly obscure values and practices with deep roots in the society dances that were precursors to the contemporary powwow.[13]

Before considering society dances, a distinction should be made about the difference between older dances, their continuing or revived forms, and the contemporary powwow. As subsequent chapters make clear, the powwow and society dances are not the same thing, but they do share some important and common practices, formats, and clothing. Moreover, as dance events they share a sense of purpose and power. The distinction between the powwow and society dances is complicated by the fact that even as some of the society dances were being revived in the first decades of the twentieth century, they were simultaneously providing some of the inspiration for the contemporary powwow.

A good example of the mingling of traditional and contemporary dances occurs at the Kiowa O-ho-mah ceremonials in Anadarko, Oklahoma, each summer. Active on a continuous basis since 1884, O-ho-mah dances were conspicuous examples of Kiowa resistance to forced assimilation. "We *never* stopped dancing," was how one member put it at the 1996 O-ho-mah encampment. Yet, it was also at annual gatherings like the O-ho-mah that more secular forms of dance known popularly as fancy war dancing began to appear in the early twentieth century, when Plains dance culture was in a state of enormous change. The new dances, notes Lassiter, were clearly influenced by O-ho-mah dances, but were "community-wide intertribal dances not framed by society ceremonials."[14] There is no doubt that these new dances were part and parcel of the era's burgeoning powwow culture.

For those who doubt that society dances like the O-ho-mah were a template for powwows, it is worth remembering that what was happening was the logical extension of society dance culture into new areas and audiences. The phenomenon wasn't new, and it wasn't an either/or choice; O-ho-mah members maintained their traditions and dances according to time-honored conventions even as they allowed new dance styles to make inroads. The pattern remains in place to this day. At O-ho-mah meetings today, afternoons are taken up with dances conducted according to the society's protocols. Evenings are often given over to social powwow dancing, but even then many sessions are dominated by songs with direct links to O-ho-mah families and traditions. Visitors, however, sometimes find the distance between the two dance events difficult to gauge because the same arena and emcee are used, many of the same singers are present for both sessions, most of the dancers attend both sessions wearing the same dance outfits, and there is a similar regard paid in both sessions to matters of community, family, and culture. Both events use dance to affirm and celebrate tribally specific forms of identity, but they are quite different in matters of detail.

This blurring is true at many other society dances across the Southern Plains where time is split between sessions devoted to society and powwow dancing, or where the society dancing bears such a close resemblance to powwow events — at least outwardly — that there seems to be little substantive difference between the two. As Abe Conklin, the now deceased Nudahonga (headman) of the Ponca He-thus-ka Society, observed in 1994, the relationship between powwows and society dances is not open to debate. "The powwow was held in the ways of the He-thus-ka," he wrote. "It kind of resembled the He-thus-ka."[15] Interestingly, the relationship goes both ways. Because both kinds of events share large numbers of the same participants, powwow culture exerts its own influence on society dances in terms of songs, regalia, and tradition. Readers should keep in mind that this discussion will navigate between these two related yet different dance traditions and will make some generalizations in order to contextualize larger points.

Although Wissler and his colleagues focused on three central characteristics shared by many Plains societies, a host of other institutions and values were associated with those societies that touched on a wide variety of issues, including power, status, order, and public comportment. In time, ideas associated with all of these issues were grafted in one form or another onto the contemporary powwow, which, like its dance predecessors, became one way by which Indian people created and maintained important boundaries of identity. This integrating of ideas is as true on the Southern Plains as it is elsewhere in the Indian West. Indeed, societies so widely shared their practices that it serves little purpose at this point in the discussion to focus solely on Southern Plains tribes.

I am not implying the absence of tribally specific traits and practices, but am suggesting that in the context of a Pan-tribal phenomenon like the powwow, the shared aspects of society dances are as important as their differences. As with society dances, regional and tribal differences in powwow gatherings became apparent, of course, and in their revived or sustained form society dances remained important boundaries of tribally specific identity. From its beginnings, however, the powwow, by virtue of its broader sense of inclusion, has often served as a vehicle for celebrating widely shared institutions and values. But I am not siding completely with scholars who have argued that the powwow has or will ultimately obliterate tribally specific dance cultures. Rather, I mean only to suggest that the powwow is clearly linked to, among other things, Plains society dances, some of which by design or accident shared strikingly similar purposes, clothing, and ritual. As I state in the conclusion, I do not believe that the powwow has become a wholly Pan-Indian expression.

Because the warrior society complex that ultimately became one of the inspirations for the powwow was a Pan-Plains phenomenon, it makes sense to place the Southern Plains tribes and their society dances into as broad a context as possible, making specific reference to them where appropriate and applicable. Also, though early powwow culture on both the Northern and Southern Plains took a great deal of its form, protocol, and accoutrement from the well-known and widely diffused Omaha Dance (often referred to as the Grass Dance), this dance was among the last to appear in the late nineteenth century and was but one among a host of society dances whose influence can be clearly discerned in both the formative and contemporary powwow.

As throughout the Plains, a web of societies, dance groups, and various associations helped to establish order and control in various aspects of life on the Southern Plains. In this, all kinds of societies played important roles, but some of the most notable examples come from the soldier societies (also widely referred to as warrior societies). As James Mooney noted in 1912, such groups were common across the Plains:

> Throughout the plains from N[orth] to S[outh] there existed a military organization so similar among the various tribes as to suggest a common origin, although with patriotic pride each tribe claimed it as its own. . . . Each society had its own dance, songs, ceremonial costume, and insignia, besides special taboos and obligations. . . . At all tribal assemblies, ceremonial hunts, and on great war expeditions, the various societies took charge of the routine details.[16]

In his work on Southern Plains military societies, Meadows reveals that by the nineteenth century these groups had sophisticated organizational and ritual matrices connecting them to a wide number of other functions and duties that were not limited to war and policing. These societies, writes Meadows, "(1) often were much more structured than previously noted, (2) shared many general similarities yet varied significantly in detail from one population to another, (3) functioned in a variety of social and political contexts . . . , (4) differed in their individual roles within their respective communities and . . . (5) current societies often exhibit a high degree of cultural continuity from their antecedents." Moreover, he continues, such associations had "a common and collectively shared ideology, ethos, and associated symbols" that was Pan-Plains in scope.[17] From a tribal perspective, then, such societies were powerfully integrative agents that cut across bands and families. J. Gilbert McAllister emphasized this integrative role in his work on Plains Apache societies, writing that the "only clearly defined segments among these Apaches are the adult dancing societies, composed of all important and prominent men or women. All families were represented and bound into a sort of brotherhood or sisterhood. Thus, these groups cut across family lines and unified the tribe as a whole."[18]

Observers of and participants in nineteenth-century Plains societies rarely failed to point out that a great many of those societies and their dances were associated with enforcing codes of conduct and comportment. Whether during the movement of camp, buffalo hunts, or the Sun Dance complex shared by many Plains tribes — to name only three especially important events in the lives of Plains people — society members were conspicuous by their prominence as arbiters of control. Moreover, their ceremonials and dances helped to establish and maintain cultural institutions and practices that were not limited to societal or ceremonial events, or even to warfare, characteristics that remain present in the powwow today.

Wissler noted that Oglala *akicita* societies were responsible for a wide range of duties, and that their authority was not to be taken lightly no matter the circumstance. His consultants described akicita members as "those who see that there is general order in camp when traveling from one place to another; those who attend to the duties of overseeing the buffalo hunt. . . . They also see that no one kills another, but in case one does, they either kill him or destroy all his property, kill his horses, destroy his tipi, etc." Pliny Earle Goddard's Sarsi consultants reported that during the Sun Dance and at their own society dances, members of the Dog, Police, and Preventer societies "pulled down and cut up the tipis of any who dared to disobey their orders." The Preventers had a particularly harsh reputation, and Goddard's consultants told him, "All the people were much afraid of this society. They had to do whatever its members directed." Conversely, Meadows reports that Comanche military societies did not play so central a role in events like buffalo hunts, and that when they did intervene because of fractious behavior or danger, their actions were often less coercive and relied instead on shaming members into proper behavior.[19]

Among the Iowas, authority was expressed by men who were simultaneously leaders of the Mawatani and Tukala dance societies and headsmen of their sub-gentes, a deliberate combination of offices that ensured that "outside of the organization, their prestige in the society was supposed to lend prestige and make for order." Those Iowa men who were "bustle wearers" made a deliberate show of their status by walking through camp wearing their bustles, an act that "advertised their position in society." The ownership of bustles — or Crow Belts — was typically restricted to a small number of especially honored men. By the early twentieth century, such restrictions were eased and bustles came to be a nearly universal piece of dance regalia. Until then, however, those who owned them were treated with deference and respect. "Bustle wearers in the Ponca He-thus-ka Society," wrote Abe Conklin, were "the bravest and the strongest in the tribe. It was like the Congressional Medal of Honor today in the army."[20]

The Kiowas had an especially well developed ranking and status system in the six bands that made up the tribe by the late nineteenth century. Members belonged to one of four classes whose lines were most clearly established by the acquisition of war honors and material wealth in the form of pony herds with which to mount more raids, earn more honors, and thereby increase one's individual and familial status. This class structure was explicitly linked to "the existence of a formal set of social ranked military societies in regard to age and social status. . . . As an individual's social and war status increased so did his membership in the higher-status societies." Thus, members of the top two classes enjoyed a disproportionate share of leadership offices in the eight men's and two women's military societies of the era. As with other tribes, including the Sarsi, Ponca, Osage, and Kansa, many of the Kiowa organizations were restrictive about who could join, and in the case of Iowa societies under the control of leading men or their kin, "membership was denied to those not socially qualified."[21]

The connections between powwows and the emphasis on order, control, and hierarchy at society dances can be discerned at several levels. Though most descriptions of the powwow emphasize its role as a leveling device that unites participants in a nearly perfect if temporary sense of equality reminiscent of what Victor Turner called communitas, there is an equally strong case to be made that like the society dances preceding them, powwows also enforce a clearly articulated sense of status, prestige, and power.[22] Too, the Pan-Plains form and function of the powwow (acknowledging, of course, regional peculiarities) echoes the "collectively shared ideology, ethos, and associated symbols" to which Meadows calls attention. Just as there is a clearly identifiable continuity among societies that have survived to this day, there is a similar continuity between those societies, their traditional purposes, values, and practices, and the powwow they helped to inspire. While it is possible to make too much of this idea, it seems reasonable to suggest that in its form, function, and history as a shared Pan-Plains phenomenon, the contemporary powwow does not radically diverge from patterns and habits that were deeply established long before the powwow emerged in its contemporary form.

Even as contemporary powwow culture is a way for participants to express a shared sense of identity, it encourages (and occasionally imposes) status, prestige, and power. Powwows provide explicit examples of specific cultural boundaries to be defined and protected. As with the society dances that preceded it, powwow culture reminds participants that order and hierarchy are important, and that dance can create, maintain, modify, and revivify certain values and practices so that they stand fast as cultural mooring posts. Thus if the soldier societies themselves no longer operate in precisely the same ways as in the nineteenth century, the ideals they represented of orderliness and control continue to be felt in the contemporary powwow. As Forrest Kassanavoid, a Comanche, described in a 1990 conversation with me, "We don't have all of those old societies anymore. We have some of them, and we have new ones that have come about in our lifetime. And we have *lots* of other organizations that sponsor dances. So, to me, those organizations help to keep the ways of those societies that are gone alive and useful. I listen to what those committee heads say, because they're important people, they come from good families that have given a lot to our people. If we listen to them, go to the dances, do the things we ought to be doing as Indians, as Comanche people, then we'll be okay."[23]

In addition to their role as arbiters of order and continuity, society dances enforced other values that were easily modified to fit the new cultural contours of the powwow. For example, among the more commonly expressed sentiments about the contemporary powwow's importance are numerous variations on this statement: "As long as we dance, we shall know who we are." Or: "The power of the powwow is able to put into immediate grasp our wonderful spirituality, the love and respect of our homeland, the ready smile of our people and our unique culture." Or: "Powwows . . . interact with and support the most important traditional values of family, heritage, and parentage."[24] While these examples are taken from contemporary sources, they reflect long-standing (some would say "traditional") values that link powwows with earlier forms of dance in ways that participants readily recognize and appreciate. Generosity, familial loyalty, community, and spirituality were repeatedly noted by nineteenth-century observers and participants of society dances; in the twenty-first century, powwowers regularly invoke the same characteristics as counterweights to the encroachment of non-native institutions and values, doing so to make a point about the unique power of dance to shape and inform notions of identity.

Commenting on the Omaha Hethu'shka Society in 1911, Alice C. Fletcher and Francis LaFlesche stated that "the rules and influence of the society tended to enforce peace and harmony in the tribe," a task that was broadly applicable to every such warrior society on the Plains. But more than that, the Hethu'shka Society and its dances were charged with responsibilities that extended beyond enforcing order. "It is said," they remarked, "that the object in establishing the Hethu'shka Society was to stimulate an heroic spirit among the people and to keep alive the memory of historic and valorous acts." Edwin Thompson Denig wrote that the Assiniboine considered dancing "a characteristic mode of expressing popular opinion on most, if not all, occasions and is generally done with the view of swaying the multitude, and conforming their actions to certain measures. It is also one of their principal means of publishing and handing down to posterity the remembrance of their gallant actions, of inspiring the young with a desire for distinctions."[25] Indeed, the Kiowas' and Apaches' Rabbit societies trained youths in the martial prowess that would bring them distinction in later life. In the case of the Kiowas, the Rabbit Society's dances occurred in conjunction with those of at least two other adult warrior societies. In the case of the Apaches, these dances were events during which youngsters "were encouraged to emulate the martial ideology and actions of their elders, such as counting coup in battle and later reciting them, which would form an important part in their adult life as warriors and in their social status."[26]

The emphasis on martial prowess comes as no surprise, of course, for it was a sentiment that was widely expressed on the Plains. Many society dances were performed in anticipation of or in celebration after battles with the enemy. (It is an unfortunate fact of history that this practice inspired Wild West show owners to lump performances of these dances under the altogether regrettable label "war dances.") Murie's Pawnee consultants told him that the One Horn Society dance "was held to teach the men how to act during battle and to remind them that there was a being who watched over them and gave them courage." Iowa men about to go to war were guided by the same values. "Men went to war for many reasons," wrote Skinner, "but chiefly for fame. A father might say to his son, 'Go out and die so that I may hear of you till the end of my days. Increase your name. If you are shot in the back and fall on your face I'll be shamed, but if you are wounded in front and fall on your face, I'll be proud.'" Denig, however, reported that some Assiniboine took a more pragmatic view of such matters, telling him that "wounds behind are fully as honorable as those before. Running away where success is impossible is more commended than death or defeat by remaining."[27]

Many societies made similar demands on their members, expecting them to stand fast in battle (the well-known "no retreat" obligation) and if necessary to die without hesitation in defense of their people. Doing so earned a man great prestige. As among the Crows, those Fox Society members who stood fast enjoyed "a certain prestige and in some cases special privileges at feasts. They were said to be . . . 'doomed to die.'" A similar ethic prevailed among the Southern Plains tribes. Meadows notes that members of the Kiowa Koitsenko Society (variously spelled as Ka-itsenkop, Kaitsenko, and Qoitsenko, and translated as Real Dogs, Principal Dogs, Horses, and Sentinel Horses) had "more dangerous battle obligations" than the other societies, including being first into battle and last in retreat. In addition, ten members staked themselves to the ground with long sashes to face the enemy, a circumstance from which only death or the valorous aid of a society brother could release him. At least one Comanche band had a similar society, called Los Lobos, or the Wolves, whose members were obliged to stand fast in battle, as were four members of the Apache Klintidie, or Horsemen's Society.[28]

The sash worn by Kiowa men was an example of how society regalia would subsequently continue to symbolize martial heritage even when it was worn in secular powwow dances. Some Southern Plains dancers have suggested to me that the long dragger worn by Straight dancers from the back of the neck to the ground is a symbolic representation of the sashes worn by members of societies with a no-retreat order. In other cases there is no question that items previously associated with warfare made their way into the powwow in secularized forms open to all. The Crow Belt, porcupine hair roach, and otter-hide breastplate, for example, were clearly borrowed from warrior society dances across the Plains, and for a time in the early twentieth century they constituted core elements of the man dancer's basic dance kit. Recall that in societies some pieces of clothing were universally understood as badges of honor and prestige, especially Crow Belts and porcupine hair roaches, two items that showed up in many Plains warrior society dances.

The deeper meaning of such things was well known to those who had seen or participated in society dances, and the pieces would remain powerful reminders of that earlier heritage long after they became associated with the powwow. James R. Walker's consultants told him that members of various Oglala warrior societies "all have similar regalia with which to act. All the regalia are used in war; because of them, they try to perform deeds. . . . the regalia will help him to kill." Walker noted the use by Kit Fox members of bells strung from the waist to the ankles, for example, and commented that the bells they showed a member had fought the enemy and had danced to commemorate it. Other sources suggest that bells were used to indicate having been wounded in battle. Indeed, Walker goes on to discuss in the context of warrior society practices virtually every piece of what would become the prototypical early powwow dance kit for men.[29] A century later, these pieces of dance regalia maintain their symbolic power, especially in the powwow style called men's traditional in which dancers continue to wear the scalp feathers, hair roaches, bustles, and breastplates of an earlier era, as well as to carry the dance sticks, whips, whistles, and wing fans that in one society after another denoted membership, status, positions of office, and power.

In addition to these physical reminders of society influence, the tradition of using song texts to extol the bravery of individuals (or to celebrate the larger purposes of societies) continued to have relevance in the powwows that emerged after the reservation era. Indeed, songs were particularly potent vehicles for maintaining and transmitting stories of martial prowess and were implicitly linked with dances. In the case of Assiniboine war parties, they celebrated their victories according to a saying that went "they have killed, they are coming to sing." Kiowa elders recalled in 1935 that in former times the Black Legs Society would "sing that they are all going to die, that they are not coming back." Oglala Kit Fox songs often called attention to their members' oaths to defend their people, and if necessary, to forfeit their lives in battle. "I am a Fox, I am supposed to die," went one song. "If there is anything difficult, if there is anything dangerous, that is mine to do." The Blackfoot All Brave Dogs Society had a song that reminded members "it is bad to live to be an old man."[30]

Typical of this genre, one Ponca song called out the enemy, in this case the Sioux leader Spotted Tail: "Do you want to fight me? Spotted Tail, hurry and come with your group to fight. Get your shield; I'm not afraid to die." An Omaha He-thus-ka Society song from the nineteenth century made a similar boast: "When I come to the battle I shout, I shout as I stand in my place, I shout my command as I stand." These sentiments are recalled in dozens of powwow songs commemorating the bravery of Indian soldiers beginning with World War I and continuing down to the present time. Notable recent examples of this include both the Comanche and Kiowa Desert Storm songs, as well as dozens of songs composed during and after the Korean and Vietnam wars.[31]

This heritage is continually recalled in the contemporary powwow, where the bravery, sacrifice, and service of Indian people are unfailingly commemorated. Indeed, many people on the Southern Plains point to the numerous dances in honor of Indians in military service during World War II as one of the turning points in the evolution of the contemporary powwow in the region. Memorial Day and Armed Forces Day dances are common on the Southern Plains, as are large numbers of dances sponsored by various veterans' associations. Grand entries and parade-ins are invariably led by a color guard dressed in military clothing (that includes eagle feather bonnets, porcupine hair roaches, or scalp feathers) and carrying national, state, tribal, and organizational flags and staffs, including prominently displayed eagle feather staffs that were commonly used in earlier society dances to denote war leaders and society officers.

Memorial songs, veterans' songs, and flag songs typically follow the parade-in and are an acknowledgment of native peoples' military service. An appropriate tribal flag song is always sung, many of which were composed after the world wars. Because they were inspired in some cases by old scalp songs or war songs, they call attention to bravery and courage precisely as their nineteenth century precursors did. The flag song of the Apache Tribe of Oklahoma, for example, was composed in 1927 by a man named Captain Kosope. Like many other flag songs, it was based on an old scalp dance song. Meadows's consultants translated the song as saying this: "Our flag got saved. Our young men got saved. That is why we sleep good at night."[32]

In many cases a victory song is rendered after the colors have been posted (especially at Northern Plains powwows) and the color guard often dances out of the arena accompanied by other veterans or their relatives in the audience who have been invited to join them. It is not unusual for the color guard to retreat in the style of traditional battle dances, imitating movements on the battlefield while brandishing and occasionally firing weapons. In another practice reminiscent of nineteenth century warrior society dances, veterans are often asked to retrieve items dropped from dance outfits, especially eagle feathers.

The emphasis on courage, sacrifice, and service are clear echoes of older, traditional society practices that have survived to assume renewed importance in the powwow. (Recall Abe Conklin's comment that "the powwow was held in the ways of the He-thus-ka.") Indian people generally, and powwow people specifically, equate military service today with the selfless acts that typified pre-reservation warrior status. Just as their ancestors used dances to recount, commemorate, and celebrate martial prowess and sacrifice, contemporary powwow people use dances to honor men and women who they believe are worthy of respect if not awe. Commenting on Lakota dances, Powers writes, "Nowhere else do we witness the full significance of these persistent symbols of fearless deeds in battle and accolades to the returning heroes than in the songs, dances, and attendant ceremonies related to what I call the continuing warrior tradition."[33]

Yet if Plains dance societies were unabashedly associated with warfare, they placed a high premium on generosity and benevolence as well. Although he was perhaps overstating the case, Lowie observed that among the Crows, early twentieth-century dance clubs "must be conceived as being in large measure mutual benefit organizations."[34] Indeed, it was not enough that a man and his family should accumulate their share of war honors, political importance, or spiritual influence. Such notoriety, if it was to be more than an example of crass, material success, obligated leading men and their kin to become exemplars of generosity and kindness. Among the Sarsi Hair Parters dance society, for example, Goddard noted that the "possession of certain objects confers rank, duties, and power upon the individual," including an obligation to provide for his less fortunate kin. Leading Kiowa society members doctored the sick, named children, and arranged burials. Kansa warriors acted as go-betweens in marriage contracts and presided at naming ceremonies.[35]

In many cases this ethic necessitated that members maintain relatively unfettered access to material goods, something that imposed limits on who could join the most prestigious societies and thus aspire to the most prominent positions. It was partly for this reason that the Assiniboine Crazy Dance Society deliberately avoided men known to be misers. Wissler's consultants told him that initiates in the Oglala Kit Fox Society should be men of means, because membership required them to "give away horses and goods to the poor and needy . . . or just cast out property and let the public grab for it." Members (who were also expected to be good dancers; those "bashful" about it were "not in demand") were expected to demonstrate "bravery, generosity, chivalry, morality, and fraternity for fellow members." In addition, "they should not lie or steal (except to the enemy), and should set an example by complying with the recognized rules of the hunt and camp." For those willing and able to meet the society's requirements, membership was sealed with a dance. The same was true among the Kiowas. In a 1936 interview, one Kiowa man recalled that after a man was initiated into a society, "He has to dance. If he doesn't know how he must make the effort anyway. Then the leaders tell their brave deeds. Then he's a member, after he has once danced."[36]

Wissler's Oglala consultants told him that one of the most important obligations of akicita organizations "was to enhance social and fraternal relations among their members. We were told that poor men were never taken in because they had not the means to assist the needy and to make feasts and also because a man who had no personal ambition to rise in the world was not a likely person to carry out the ideals of an organization. . . . It is the ideal that members help both by word and deed the struggling poor man. . . . All this supports the Oglala conception that men's societies . . . are to promote the not altogether selfish social and philanthropic activities of their members." Likewise, Lakota consultants revealed to Walker that the Kit Fox Society "was originated by chiefs and headmen for the purpose of aiding the poor and helpless. . . . In time of war it was the duty of the Foxes to defend the old, weak, and helpless." Many Southern Plains organizations were bound by similar obligations, as with the Apache Manitidie, a society that policed encampments but also undertook notable acts of charity. "Throughout the history of the Manitidie," writes Meadows, "this has been one of their greatest functions and symbol of their sense of continuity with the past." Murie reported that Pawnee Crazy Dog Society members might remove their moccasins at a dance "and put them on a needy bystander."[37]

Skinner's Ponca consultants told him that their He-thus-ka Society "helps people mourn for their dead, and makes collections of gifts for bereaved people to help dry their tears. When other tribes come to visit these people, they entertain them, and also take up collections for outsiders who ask for help." Writing nearly a century later, Conklin noted that "the duty of the He-thus-ka, years ago, was to look after the elders, widows, orphans, and see that they were taken care of, that they were protected. They also protected the camp, years ago." In a 1968 interview, Sylvester Warrior, a Ponca, said that members of the He-thus-ka "were benevolent to their people. That was one way which they took care of their indigent people. People who were in need, the orphans and widows as they used to say . . . They practiced generosity. Everything that they did, was to help someone." Peter Le Claire characterized the larger purpose of the He-thus-ka like this: "it is said that anyone that is not well and feeling bad and anyone that is mourning, the sound of the drum will revive them and make them happy."[38]

Wherever they gathered, dance societies performed duties that placed them at the heart of their communities' needs. This ethic survived the reservation period. When other parts of the traditional Southern Plains tribal political economies underwent drastic change, many communities maintained societies, their dances, and the values bound up in them as not only links to a cherished past but also as bulwarks against a hostile contemporary world. Browner makes an interesting point about this bond when she asserts that "the spatial organization of contemporary Lakota pow-wows mirrors encampments of previous centuries." Similar patterns emerged on the Southern Plains. As Ed Red Eagle, Sr., an Osage, put it in a 1967 interview about the history of the Osage I'n-lon-schka, "This dancing of the ways of our people every spring has been going on, has been in this country since 1884. . . . It's my understanding . . . [we] have been dancing in the same manner and the same fashion ever since. And this dance is in the same fashion as it was in the very beginning with our great, great grandparents and they had received their dances from the Kaw Indians and the Ponca tribe."[39]

The existence of Pan-Plains dance complexes and their role as precursors to the contemporary powwow is beyond dispute. As Meadows writes, " 'Unafraid Of' (commonly called Dog Soldier) Societies appear to have been one of the earliest documented and most widespread forms of Plains societies." Dennis Zotigh, a Kiowa, notes, moreover, that their link to powwows is clear: "Once ceremonial songs, dances, and their significance were exchanged," he writes, they "created a foundation for the inception of the Inter-tribal powwow."[40] Yet the powwow did not simply emerge from a general set of influences that came out of these societies. In fact, while many societies and dances influenced the emergence of pow-wow culture, two dance traditions played especially important roles in the region's changing dance cultures. One was the Omaha Dance, also called the Grass Dance after the sheaves of long grass that dancers often put in their belts. Variously, the name is said to have derived from the practice of dancing over the tall prairie grass to flatten it in order to make a dance ground. The other tradition was the Drum Dance, also called the Dream Dance.

Like the Omaha Dance in its last incarnation, the Drum Dance appeared late in the nineteenth century. According to Gloria Young, the first eyewitness report of the dance came in 1893 by Reverend Clay MacCauley, who observed the dance among the Menominee at Keshena, Wisconsin, in 1880 or 1881. (Young further reports that MacCauley's comments were delivered during a lecture in Tokyo, Japan, of all places, and appeared in the *Japan Daily Mail* on March 21, 1893. James S. Slotkin believes the year was 1879. Of MacCauley's lecture, he writes, "MacCauley speaks of an 1880 'report to Washington' that the author has not been able to find in any of the government archives.")[41] Whatever its details, the Drum Dance spread quickly across the upper Midwest and Great Lakes region. In short order the Sioux, Potawatamis, Winnebagos, and Ojibways had the dance, and members of those tribes were "apparently the catalyst of an organized attempt . . . to spread the dance to other communities and tribes. The dance was transferred between groups in the same manner as the grass dance," writes Young. "One group manufactured a drum and took it, with the songs and other presents, to a receiving host group." Moreover, adds Young, "The grass or Omaha warrior societies which developed out of the old Iruska [the Pawnee form of the Omaha] met the Algonquian shamanism and Medicine Lodge among the easternmost Siouan tribes and created the environment out of which emerged the Drum Dance."[42]

Appealing to a desire for peace and the end of hostilities, its adherents considered the Drum Dance an outlet for prayerful reflection and peaceful cohabitation with whites and Indians alike. In his 1893 Bureau of Ethnology Report on the Menominees, Walter James Hoffman quoted a man named Red Eagle, who suggested that the dance was religious in character but should not be confused with the Ghost Dance. "We hope with our dance to break up by and by the old medicine dance, and all such things," said Red Eagle. "You saw the flag above us. That is to show that we are friends of the Great Father. You saw some men dancing and acting as though they were firing off guns. . . . They show that some of us helped the Great Father in the big war [the American Civil War], and we are ready to help him again. . . . We lifted our hands to the sky; that was for prayer. We held out our hands, palms downward; that was to receive the answers to our prayers."[43]

In 1885, the Potawatomi agent in Kansas submitted a report that confirmed much of what Red Eagle said. The dance had been introduced two years earlier and had spread to every tribe at the agency since that time. Its adherents, he wrote, displayed an "intense devotion" and "are chaste, cleanly [sic] and industrious. . . . They seem to have adopted the religion as a means of expressing their belief in justice and mercy of the Great Spirit." Then, in a statement that is extraordinary for its apparent endorsement of dancing, he concluded that the dance was not "an unmixed evil, as under its teaching drunkenness and gambling have been reduced 75 per cent, and a departure from virtue on the part of its members meets with severest condemnation. . . . I do not consider it a backwards step for the Indians."[44]

Young, Wissler, and Kavanagh all write that in the last decades of the 1800s the Drum Dance and the Omaha Dance combined in the Indian Territory. Young paraphrases Wissler, who apparently believed that "by the twentieth century they were so much alike that the Drum Dance was proclaimed a variation of the grass dance." As noted above, Young argues that the connection between the two dances was much older, with "the connection dates long before the grass dance revival of the 1860's." Using the word "powwow" as a reference to the Drum Dance, Stephen Riggs wrote in 1893 that "the Grass Dance seems to have been the base from which the Powwow developed," a point that Slotkin uses to assert that by the late 1870s "either the Sioux woman's variant of the Grass Dance, or modifications made by the Midwest tribes, constituted the Dream Dance or Powwow."[45]

Whatever the precise details ("We cannot reconstruct with confidence the development of the Powwow religion," wrote Slotkin in 1957), Young claims that this much is certain: "In the 1880s, the grass and Drum Dance met and intermingled in the variety of tribes in Indian Territory." Kavanagh notes that the Prairie tribes of Oklahoma and Nebraska — the Osages, Omahas, Poncas, and Pawnees, took the Omaha/Drum Dance complex in one direction while the Western tribes, the Kiowas, Comanches, and Cheyennes, for example, took it in another. Howard believed that for the former tribes the dance acquired a deeply religious nature reminiscent of the Drum Dance. He explained that after 1880 the Ponca Heluska "began taking on a religious flavor. Instead of the war speeches and coup-countings of the earlier dance there were long prayers for the benefit of the group. . . . Gift giving, rather than war honors, was the basis of admission. It was also about this time that women were admitted as dancers. Students of American ethnology will recognize this form of the dance as that which diffused from the Dakota tribe to the Central Algonquian groups as the 'Dream Dance' or 'Drum Religion.' "[46] According to Kavanagh, the Kiowas, Comanches, and Cheyennes "dispensed with the crow belt while retaining much of the ritual and many of the officers from earlier societies" when they transformed dance traditions. Even before it was combined with the Omaha Dance, writes Young, the Drum Dance was establishing patterns of dance and meaning that would ultimately find fertile ground in the powwow. "It restored some traditions such as wearing the accoutrements 'of our fathers,' " she notes, "but concentration was on adopting a moral code which would make its adherents conform more to the ideals of the wider non-Indian society while still embracing an Indian belief and ceremony system."[47]

Like the Drum Dance, the Omaha Dance was a link between older society dances and the appearance of a new kind of performative, public dance culture that ultimately produced the powwow. Because of its relatively late appearance, it was the Omaha Dance societies that were still meeting and dancing in the midst of the reservation era's forced federal assimilation campaigns. While it is true that other societies also survived, the Omaha was especially widespread, and its supporters were adept at molding it to fit new needs. Young maintains that, "the music, dance, and ritual of this society were flexible and changed with changes in Indian lifeways to survive at a time when more rigid ceremonies were being abandoned."[48]

Indeed, the Omaha Dance spread to some tribes *after* they had gone on to reservations, making it an important example of dancing's new forms being used to negotiate cultural boundaries. In this context, the Omaha Dance complex helped to fill the void left when other societies went out of existence. And as previously noted, in many cases, revived or sustained forms of the Omaha Dance, such as the Kiowa O-ho-mah, Ponca Heluska, or Osage I'n-lon-schka societies, became the locus not only of a revivified warrior society ethos, but of a newly emergent powwow ethos that took its inspiration and to some degree its form from those society dances. In all, the relationship between the Omaha Dance and the powwow is strikingly persuasive.

This is so for several reasons. Because it was widely shared in general form and function across the Plains, the Omaha Dance constituted an early Pan-tribal dance form. Its regalia, especially the bustle and hair roach, became trademarks of the dance and could be seen in one form or another at dances from Oklahoma to Montana. Mooney recounts that in the winter of 1889–1890, for example, a group of Comanches visited the Kiowas for a dance that he said "somewhat resemble[d] the Omaha dance," and that such dances were also found among the Wichitas and Pawnees. In fact the dance was the "Child Making Dance," hence the adoption. It was not the Omaha Dance, but the Kiowa version of the Calumet Dance received from the Pawnees. Yet if Mooney's analysis is off the mark in its details, he was nonetheless correct about the notion that what he was seeing was a diffused dance tradition.[49]

As Wissler put it in 1916, "Among all the tribes of the Plains area we have a series of societies with which the grass dance has something in common; at least there is a similarity in the generalities of regalia."[50] The Omaha's underlying purposes and forms were markedly similar from tribe to tribe, especially during the late reservation period when it became an increasingly secularized dance form itself, even when performed in a societal context. Its most important diffusion occurred late in the nineteenth century, making the Omaha Dance contemporaneous with the era's increasingly secular and widely shared dance culture, a culture that showed influences from earlier society traditions but which was coming into its own as the powwow. It was also the form of dance most widely popularized by the Wild West shows and other performative genres. Because Buffalo Bill Cody, the Millers, and their numerous imitators drew heavily from Northern Plains tribes for their Indian talent, and because almost all of the male dancers were devotees of the increasingly popular (and largely secularized) Omaha Dance with its distinctive bustle, hair roach, otter-hide breast plate, and long straps of bells, the style gained a distinction that might otherwise have eluded it. When the dance spread to other tribes, it sparked a war dance craze that soon took on a life of its own at fairs, exhibitions, intertribal visitations, and powwows.

The origin of the Omaha Dance is complicated, but the clearest information on its earliest forms begins with the Pawnees, whose Iruska Society and dance have been widely interpreted as the starting point for the dance's diffusion. In his 1914 discussion of Pawnee societies, Murie (himself a Pawnee) noted that the Dakota first learned the dance from the Omaha, but knew that it had begun with the Pawnees, who had also taught it to the Arikaras (fifty years before Murie's account), who then took it to the Crows. Described by Murie as "a very powerful medicine society," the Iruska Society was characterized by two things that were subsequently shared by numerous other tribes as the dance came to them. One concerned the society's ritual of taking pieces of boiling meat from a pot without suffering any injury. Iruska translated as "the fire is in me," and its members were said to have the power to " 'extinguish the life in the fire,' or . . . overcome the power of other medicines." Regarded as medicine men, not soldiers, Iruska members treated burns, and were believed to be immune from being burned themselves.[51]

The other notable influence of the Iruska came in its regalia, specifically the porcupine hair roach and Crow Belt or bustle, both furnished by animal helpers according to an origin story related by a man named Crow-feather. In his 1916 essay on dancing societies, Wissler called the Crow Belt and roach the "two striking objective features" of the dance and explained that they came into the Omaha ceremony "because the headdress and the Crow-belt were war honors and the participation of their owners would automatically bring them into the ceremony."[52] Across the Plains, these pieces of dance clothing would become universally used by adherents of the Omaha Dance. When the Omaha Dance was secularized and popularized as a new form of social dance, the regalia went with it and assumed a new life.

The evidence that the Iruska's central characteristics were shared across the Plains is overwhelming. What Wissler referred to as the ceremony's "fire trick" of handling fire and boiling liquids was reported among the Eastern Dakota, Iowas, Arapahos, Gros Ventres, Cheyennes, Oglalas, Hidatsas, and Mandan, for example. The name given to it by other tribes also indicates a clear link: The Omaha called it the Hethuska, the Iowas called it the Helocka, the Kiowas called it the Ohomo (O-ho-mah after about 1927), the Kansa called it the Helucka, and the Poncas called it Helocka (later Heluska). As Wissler declared, "The similarity to the Pawnee term is obvious."[53] The question of who got it when and from what source is not entirely clear, but Wissler's consultants related that the Ponca claimed to have gotten it from the Sioux, and in turn passed it on to the Kansa. But the story is complicated by the fact that as it was being spread, the Omaha Dance was also being transformed from a society dance into something that would become much more secularized. Young, for example, refers to a "new grass dance influence . . . introduced into Indian Territory in 1887 through . . . three Pawnee men, members of the Skidi band, who visited the Oglala Sioux in South Dakota" and brought back a version of the dance to their own tribe that, ironically, they had previously helped to diffuse.[54] Thus, there were two phases of the Omaha's diffusion: an early one in which the ceremonial aspects of fire handling were important, and a later, or "modern," one (after the 1860s) when the dance became more social in form and function. It is the latter form with which we are concerned.

Beginning around 1860, the Iruska began to undergo important changes that would ultimately give the dance new form and meaning. Wissler believed that the Teton Lakota were the first to take the more modern form of the dance up after the Omahas taught it to them "about 1860." From there it spread across the Northern Plains to the Arapahos, Blackfeet, and Assiniboine, Sarsi, Gros Ventres, and Crows, among others. On the Southern Plains, it found its way from the Pawnee to the Poncas, Kansas, Iowas, Osages, Otos, and Kiowas. The Kansa people recalled that they got it from the Poncas, who got it from the Sioux, and that the dance had once been called the "Sioux dance." Among the Kiowas, the lineage ran from the Omahas to the Lakotas to the Cheyennes and finally to the Kiowas. In their work on the Omaha, Fletcher and LaFlesche noted that "during the last century, the Hethushka has spread among other branches of the Siouan family; tribes differing in language and customs have adopted it, so to speak. Among these are the Pawnee." Indeed, this complicated transfer of the dance shows up in the Pawnee case more clearly than others. Having been the originators of the old Iruska, the Pawnees appear to have received the dance back in a new form from the Oglalas during an 1887 visit. "The origin of the modern form of this dance," wrote Murie, "lies between the Omaha and the Osage, but it was derived from an older ceremony which the Omaha, and possibly the Osage, borrowed of the Pawnee." The dance that Murie saw was "generally known among the Pawnee as a variation of their own Iruska, though in its present form it was introduced through Oglala influence." Wissler attributed the greatest role in all of this diffusion to the Dakota, although other tribes claimed priority (and still do). At any rate, regardless of who was responsible for spreading the dance across the Plains, by the end of the nineteenth century, Jimmy W. Duncan notes, "This complex was perhaps the most widely diffused ritual in North America."[55]

As the dance diffused in the late nineteenth century, it began to lose some of its ceremonial aspects. Part of this loss was explained by the fact that, because diffusion coincided with the reservation era, the new form of the dance existed in a cultural environment that was dramatically different from the one that had existed a generation earlier. As a result, the martial ethos that had influenced many societies and their dances began to erode. "With this new life," wrote Wissler, old "social ideals and machinery were decidedly out of joint," and "unusual conditions for the assimilation and diffusion of new traits" appeared. Commenting on the modern form of the dance, Wissler observed that "its function is everywhere chiefly social and its meetings are distinctly social gatherings.

This should not be taken as denying the existence of serious ceremonial elements, but as asserting one of the striking characteristics of the grass dance, in contrast to the iruska." In his work on the Oglalas, Wissler commented in 1912 that the Omaha Society "was very popular. It still exists but has become a mere social function." As evidence of this, Wissler reported that "after a time anyone could wear the regalia and little attention was paid to the rules." Skinner wrote that among the Kansa, the Omaha dance was still performed, "but has no ceremonial meaning, being only a social function. Many of the characteristic regalia and other paraphernalia are still found, but they have apparently lost their significance." Lowie wrote that the Utes' "modern social dance commonly called the War dance . . . apparently does not differ from the Grass dance as found among the Plains Indians, except that it lacks all the more serious features."[56]

It seems likely that Skinner and Lowie were overstating their cases, for people more intimately associated with these dances have suggested a more nuanced context for the dance's adaptation. In her insightful work on Lakota dance culture, Adriana Greci Green writes, "There is evidence the performance of Omaha Dances retained much of the ritual structure of the Omaha Society, even in its 'transformed' appearance. Most importantly, it maintained its essential and vital function: to express the microcosm of Lakota social and warrior structure and ethics, continuously through time, but especially as it related to the present."[57] Regina Flannery reached a similar conclusion in her 1947 essay on the Gros Ventre Grass Dance. The dance's martial emphasis had declined in the context of reservation culture, but its use as a persuasive display of status and prestige had been maintained. "As the younger men had no chance to show their prowess in warfare and hunting," Flannery wrote, "there was a change of emphasis to recognition of superior singing and dancing ability as one of the roads to public approval." Moreover, she continues, it was the Grass Dance "that seems to have filled the void left in social life. . . . In this way the Grass Dance provides occasion for group recreational outlets, while at the same time enhancing the feeling of social solidarity."[58]

Others have made similar observations. Callahan noted that while the function of the Osage I'n-lon-schka "is chiefly social, and its meetings are distinctly social gatherings, it still has serious ceremonial elements." Otis Russell, an Osage who was in his late 80s when he was interviewed in 1970, commented that when the Poncas and Kaws brought the Grass Dance to his people, its context was clearly different from its original warrior ethic. "They said they wished for us to have it 'cause we got to think about these little children coming up. While they're small, keep them from having mischief. They want them to come and watch 'em dance. They look on. Maybe when they grow [up] they'll be there too. Maybe some of 'em singing. So that's what they think about it. And they told our Indians that's where to take that." Powers's comments on the Oglala form of the dance attest to this generally shared idea. "The Omaha was designed for people who like to have a good time," he remarked, adding, despite changes in the dance over time, "Omahas of every era have had one thing in common: they have brought the people together, they have provided a reason for the people to gather, and during the present times have allowed the Indian people the right of self expression."[59]

Meadows, Kavanagh, Foster, and Lassiter have discussed in detail a similar set of circumstances among the Kiowas, Comanches, and Apaches. The Kiowa received their version of the dance, the O-ho-mah, from the Cheyennes in 1884 (who had previously received it from the Sioux), the same year that the Kaw people brought it to the Osages, who called it the I'n-lon-schka. In those cases, as in all others, a large number of horses changed hands as a sort of purchase price. In a 1967 interview, Bert Geikoumah, a Kiowa, recounted, "The Cheyennes give that organization to the Kiowas. And the Kiowas gave them horses. . . . [Cheyennes] let you join the Ohomo Dance and you have to give him a horse." Jim Anquoe, a Kiowa, related a story to me that he heard from an elderly Cheyenne man who said that the Cheyennes gave the dance to the Kiowas at Fort Marion, Florida, during the late 1870s when numbers of men from both tribes were incarcerated for their roles in the Red River War. "Whenever the Cheyennes were singing their Omaha Dance," said Anquoe, "Kiowas, if they were sweeping, or marching, they drop whatever they were doing and run over there and start kicking up [i.e. dancing]. They *loved* that." When Anquoe serves as a head singer, he always publicly thanks the Cheyenne people for bringing this dance to his people. Although other accounts put the Kiowas' acquisition of the dance later than the Fort Marion episode, a collection of ledger drawings at the Oklahoma Historical Society drawn by a Kiowa prisoner at Fort Marion includes a depiction of a Kiowa man dancing with a bustle, a practice that several Kiowas and Cheyennes told me they believe began only *after* the Kiowas received the O-ho-mah and its accoutrements, including the bustle that remains the society's most visible and powerful icon to this day.[60]

The Comanches received their War Dance from the Poncas, and Meadows characterizes the Quahada Band's version of that dance as representative of "a late-nineteenth-century diffused segment of the Grass Dance." The Apaches got the dance from a visiting contingent of Pawnees between 1885 and 1900, to whom they traded a number of horses in return for the dance and a drum. As a result of this exchange, the Apaches called the dance *Dahvashsahgootas,* or "Pawnee Dance." Like older forms of the Omaha Dance, Apaches initially considered their version a male warrior society dance, but by the turn of the century, such dances and their encampments "may have functioned as a surrogate for earlier tribal-level communal gatherings with the decline of the other Apache men's societies in the late nineteenth century."[61]

Foster describes a similar set of circumstances in the Comanche community. As early as 1906, Comanches were hosting summer encampments that revolved around traditional dances. Such dances, writes Foster, were "a move within the community to revive traditional rituals that had been abandoned during the reservation period. Their revival may have been inspired by local Anglo towns that hired Comanches to dance at their civic celebrations in the years immediately after allotment. Surviving members of prereservation military societies subsequently were asked by their Comanche neighbors to perform the dances in intracommunity contexts. While the military societies had ceased to function as social units, former members had not forgotten the cultural forms they used." Among the society dances revived in this way were the buffalo dance, spear dance, crow dance, scalp dance, and horse-stealing dance.[62]

So, by the time the twentieth century dawned, a dynamic set of forces was at work in Indian communities across the Plains. Their older societies forcibly suppressed, or less relevant in the new cultural context of the reservation, Plains people nonetheless continued to dance and celebrate, often through the newly adopted Omaha or Grass Dance. Secularized to fit new needs, the dance incorporated old values and maintained time-honored practices associated with communal meetings. At the same time, those older societies had hardly been forgotten, and their values and practices found revived importance in several ways, including their being transplanted into the public, performative dance culture that was becoming more and more popular as the century went on. The powwow wasn't on the horizon just yet, but it was getting closer with each passing year.

INDIAN DANCER
(KIOWA)

Kiowa fancy dancer, no date, but probably from the 1920s judging by the long underwear, skull cap, and fluffy bustles. His stylized pose suggests why the style was called "fancy dancing." (Denver Public Library, Western History Collection, photography unknown, x-32401)

Afternoon Gourd Dance Session with concession stand in foreground. Kiowa Tiah-Piah Society, south of Carnegie, Oklahoma, July 2000.

Typical family camp, Kiowa Tiah-Piah Society, south of Carnegie, Oklahoma, July 2000.

Giveaway, Sac and Fox Powwow, Stroud, Oklahoma, July 2002.

Campsite with permanent shelter, Sac and Fox Powwow, Stroud, Oklahoma, July 2002.

Veterans dancing the United States and tribal flags out of the arena after Grand Entry, Sac and Fox Powwow, Stroud, Oklahoma, July 2002.

Ledger drawing from Ft. Marion by the Kiowa artist Koba of a Kiowa dancer wearing a bustle, 1875–1878. Notable because it suggests that the Cheyennes who were imprisoned with Kiowas at Ft. Marion, Florida, gave them the O-ho-mah Dance several years sooner than other sources suggest. (Bertoia Collection, Oklahoma Historical Society)

Osage I'n-lon-schka dancers outside the dance hall in Gray Horse, Oklahoma, dressed in what would come to be called Straight Dance clothes. Probably early twentieth century. (Ruth Mohler Collection, Oklahoma Historical Society)

Cheyenne horse giveaway at Watonga, Oklahoma, powwow, 1947. Note the automobile in the background. Cars were pulled up to the arena so that their headlights could be used to illuminate the dance grounds after dark. (Tartoue Collection, Oklahoma Historical Society)

Shalah Rice Rowlen in a man's fancy dance outfit at the 1944 American Indian Exposition, Anadarko, Oklahoma. The dancer on the left is Chester Lefthand, who helped to popularize fancy dancing in the 1920s. (Tartoue Collection, Oklahoma Historical Society)

Fancy dancers at the 1942 Ponca Powwow. Note the feather headcrests, sometimes called "Zulu Hats." (Tartoue Collection, Oklahoma Historical Society)

Zack Miller of the Miller Brothers 101 Ranch Real Wild West Show rehearsing dancers for a World's Fair performance, year unknown. (Cracraft Collection, Oklahoma Historical Society)

Campsite at the 1947 Ponca Powwow. (Tartoue Collection, Oklahoma Historical Society)

Wynema Archanbault wearing a man's fancy dance outfit, 1948 American Indian Exposition, Anadarko, Oklahoma. This is an excellent example of fancy dance clothing during the 1940s. (Tartoue Collection, Oklahoma Historical Society)

Dance grounds, 1947 Ponca Powwow. Note the loudspeaker hanging in the tree. (Tartoue Collection, Oklahoma Historical Society)

CHAPTER THREE

"There is no doubt the dances should be curtailed."

*Indian Dances and Federal Policy on the
Southern Plains, 1880–1930*

Even if they didn't understand all of its details, federal Indian officials were certainly aware of the power that dancing had in many Indian communities. Eager to get control of the reservations, and to impose an orderly and disciplined assimilation program, policymakers confidently launched a series of campaigns in the late nineteenth century to suppress dancing and replace it with what reformers deemed more suitable kinds of gatherings. Imagine their consternation, then, when things didn't go according to plan. A case in point occurred in early August 1897, when Major Frank Baldwin, the agent at the Kiowa-Comanche-Apache Reservation in southwestern Oklahoma, received a letter from an Indian man named Squirrel asking permission to hold a dance. After reminding Baldwin that the Indians had obeyed an order the previous spring to suspend their dances, Squirrel wrote, "I know that you are willing to let these Indians have their pleasure when they do just as you wish them to do. . . . it has been a long time [since] I had my fun. All the other tribes of Indians been having their fun." Two months later he was at it again, asking for a written permit "so I can hold my dances . . . without running to you every month and interfearing [*sic*] with your business."[1]

Although Indians often queried agents for permission to do one thing or another, Squirrel's letter was unusual in that it revealed a gaping paradox in federal Indian policy at the end of the nineteenth century. As part of a clearly articulated assimilationist agenda designed to transform Indians, policymakers officially forbade the very dances for which Squirrel sought approval. It was all well and good that he politely asked, and then apologized for interfering with the agent's busy schedule; but according to federal policy, Squirrel should not have bothered to raise the issue. Bureaucrats considered dancing of any sort inimical to progress, and by definition something to be suppressed. But the situation was more complicated than such thinking implied. As it turned out, Indians not only felt comfortable asking for permission, they could fully expect to get it. Federal policies notwithstanding, officials at the nation's Indian agencies sanctioned dances even as they simultaneously disparaged them for their perceived depravity and licentiousness. As a result, a hotly contested debate emerged among policymakers, agents, Indians, and reformers about the merits of dances and the aims of federal policy.

How could this happen, and what were its consequences for the evolution of the Southern Plains powwow? In an era characterized by policy rhetoric that was nothing if not unambiguous, Indians across the Southern Plains continued to dance, and to attach deep meaning to such occasions. Despite reports from agents and reformers that dances and all they represented were withering away, Southern Plains Indians by their actions proved otherwise. But because they were rarely free to act without fear of reprisal, tribes modified culturally rich practices like dancing. Likewise, policymakers found themselves constantly revising their positions in light of the inability to impose uniform or systematic controls.

As a result, Indians and agents alike made concessions in order to maintain some semblance of order, thus Squirrel's letter. This was hardly unique in the context of the dance question. As numerous studies have shown, such maneuvering was typical of virtually every facet of reservation life, and officials regularly negotiated cultural, political, and economic concerns in response to the chaotic reservation system. But scholars have paid less attention to the complicated relationship between official attempts to suppress dances and the emergence of new dance traditions — and ultimately, the powwow — than they have to other topics. However, the topic is important given that dances constituted such an obvious target in the campaign to civilize Indians, and that the failure to eradicate dances led to new and powerful forms of gathering and expression. Certainly, the constantly evolving contours of dance culture on the Southern Plains reflected this new state of affairs. There is no question that whites and Indians alike recognized this matter as a crucial element in the contest to remold Indians' cultural identity. Policymakers intended to use the dance bans as part of a far-reaching campaign to reconceptualize tribal identities so that they reflected cultural models based on white, middle class, Protestant America. For reformers charged with the task, the campaign was especially urgent on the Southern Plains, a region once described by Robert Utley as "a crucible in which Grant's Peace Policy encountered its severest test," and where "high-minded theory shattered on hard cultural reality." The statements were as true for the dance bans as for policy directives in general.[2]

At the heart of the issue lay the fairs, exhibitions, and community gatherings that dominated Southern Plains dance culture between 1880 and 1930. While Indians used these occasions to maintain important cultural practices, federal officials used them to suppress or control such behavior. But a curious combination of forces complicated the situation. For every federal bureaucrat who issued policy as if it were holy writ, there was some poor agency official whose lot it was to make such pronouncements workable in a reservation world that was anything but manageable. For every reformer who thundered against the pagan excesses of dances, there was an Indian willing to make an accommodation if it meant being able to dance. And for every missionary who bemoaned the fair-going public's taste for savage spectacle, there was an entrepreneur with a Wild West show.

The campaign against dancing began in earnest in the 1880s when public pressure mounted for a solution to the so-called Indian Question. Noting in 1881 that the civilization of the tribes was "certainly the object and intention of our government," Commissioner of Indian Affairs Hiram Price (1881–1885) observed that nothing less than a cultural transformation would forestall the Indians' extermination. One year later, the Indian Office issued its "Rules Governing the Court of Indian Offenses," in which it took a stand against plural marriages, intoxication, and, of course, dances. In the years following the Civil War, a phalanx of determined reformers and bureaucrats rallied behind a campaign of forced assimilation, demanding what Commissioner of Indian Affairs Thomas Jefferson Morgan (1889–1893) described in 1889 as "the absorption of the Indians into our national life, not as Indians, but as American citizens."[3]

Convinced that dances and their associated rituals posed a fundamental threat to the government's assimilation goals, officials waged an intensive campaign between the 1880s and the early 1930s to suppress Indian dancing. In their determination to destroy dances, agents found especially eager accomplices in any number of places. Missionaries, local citizens, reformers, and philanthropists alike joined the chorus and placed their combined influence behind policies designed to destroy every ritual, ceremony, and dance that reinforced Indianness and, therefore, stood in opposition to federal aims. Not surprisingly, some of the most determined foes of dancing could be found at the mission stations that dotted the reservations.[4] Eugenia Mausape, a Kiowa, recalled in a 1967 interview that when she was a young girl attending the Methodist boarding school in Anadarko at the end of the nineteenth century, Reverend J. J. Methvin had counseled that dances were "a bad road to be going." She admitted, "I kept it in my heart. I don't go. I never did go. I never did dance. . . . I don't want to go to hell." In southwest Oklahoma, Baptist and Mennonite missionaries took a particularly strong stand on the matter. In September 1915, Kiowa-Comanche Agency field matron Mary Clouse (spouse of Reverend H. H. Clouse of the Rainy Mountain Kiowa Indian Baptist Church) sent a stinging indictment of the "dance element" to Agent C. V. Stinchecum in which she charged dancers with corrupting the morals of the young people and tearing down the work of the schools. "These dances are one of the breeding places of illegitimate children, which is becoming the shame of the tribe. Lust," she warned the agent, "is on the rise." Her husband commended Stinchecum in December 1916 "for the strong and noble stand you have taken against the dance question among the Kiowas. . . . These dances are a financial and moral curse; destructive of all that is noble and upbuilding. The dance element will be down on you and will talk against you…but you are right and we Indian missionaries are with you and will pray that you and your force will be strong and go on and break up this question."[5]

At the Mennonite Post Oak Mission near Cache, Reverend A. J. Becker and his wife Magdalena (who was also a part-time field matron) strenuously opposed Comanche dances. Reverend Becker refused baptism to dancers on the grounds that "they had not been saved from their heathenish ways. What would it profit if their names are put in the church rolls but are not written in heaven?" In August 1919, Magdalena wrote that the dances caused violent behavior and noted that "wiping [whipping] wifes [sic] was the fruit" of such occasions. Dances were "time and money wasted," she thought, so she spared no effort in her campaign against them. In 1920 she used her considerable influence to break up a large dance on the grounds that it not only disrupted her work but also encouraged immodest behavior among young Kiowas and Comanches as well. "These dances and large gatherings," she wrote, "are ruining our Indian boys and girls . . . they will be paupers before long and the hospitals filled with boys and girls infected by different decease [sic]."[6]

But not every missionary was so confident of being able to discourage Indians from dancing. After attending a Kiowa Ghost Dance in April 1896 near Saddle Mountain, Baptist missionary Isabel Crawford wrote with obvious distress in her diary of being told by several Kiowas "God had given the Book to the White People and taught them to read it, but He gave to the Indians the dance road and told us to hold on to it tight till He came back to earth with our dead and the buffalo." Yet Crawford was also aware of disputes between tribal members, and she wrote of her hope that the anti-dance crowd was gaining momentum. In December 1898, for example, she optimistically reported that a Kiowa named Domot had informed her "the Ghost Dance chiefs who are making all the trouble do not help anybody for they try to pull us all back to the old bad Kiowa roads." Odlepaugh, who was a Crawford supporter and a deacon in the Saddle Mountain congregation, confided to her that "there is one thing that gives us trouble. The Ghost Dance people are all abusing my brother Lucius very strongly because he is willing to let you build on his land. We do not like this, of course, but we can't help it."[7]

Taking a decidedly more antagonistic stance were the many local whites who disliked Indians, held low opinions of government agents, and scoffed at the army's ability to do much of anything except put on parades. In the spring of 1896, for example, a man named Brown wrote angrily to Cheyenne and Arapaho agent A. E. Woodson to report rumors of a large dance gathering of Kiowas, Comanches, Cheyennes, and Arapahos planned for early July on the Cheyenne and Arapaho Reservation. "Inasmuch as one Indian . . . boasts that they will drive out the whites . . . It would be well to put a stop to their gathering," wrote Brown, "as it is a fact . . . that they won't be drove onto their allotments . . . without making trouble for the whites." [8]

Brown spoke plainly of his disdain for federal and military authorities and their collective incompetence when it came to settling the Indian problem, but was convinced that he was wasting his breath. The impending dance was "a menace to the white settlers," he wrote, but Brown characterized the agency as a collection of idiots and incompetents who couldn't find their way indoors out of the rain.

> You with others drawing big saleries [sic] don't know anything and care less about the conduct of those sneaking redskins," he muttered, "your modest labor being to sign the pay role [sic]. If we are not entitled to the protection of the government we will try to protect ourselves and in doing so we are pledged the help necessary to make it quite unnecessary to have the same job done again. . . . We give you due notice what to expect though of course you with others of your set will be as usual in safety. Now consider this matter well and don't think we are joking. We are well aware you don't care to place yourself out here in danger and you are not caring to how the settlers are harassed.

Brown signed the letter "Yours, on guard." Agent Woodson sent a copy to Kiowa-Comanche-Apache agent Baldwin with assurances that "there is not truth . . . in this report so far as I can ascertain, but if your Indians have such a visit in view, I request you to prevent their coming at this time for such a purpose." It is instructive to remember that Brown's tirade, with its thinly veiled threats of murder and mayhem, was occasioned by *rumors* of a dance gathering. [9]

Missionaries, agents, and local citizens who made it their business to stop dances were speaking a language that policymakers understood, and no one spoke with more assurance or urgency on the matter than Secretary of the Interior Henry Teller, whose 1883 annual report captured official Washington's mood. Writing with the certitude that was the hallmark of nineteenth-century policymakers, Teller clearly identified the greatest threat to assimilation. A "few non-progressive, degraded Indians," he declared, "are allowed to exhibit before the young and susceptible children all the debauchery, diabolism, and savagery of the worst state of the Indian race." And although debauchery, diabolism, and savagery came in many forms, first on Teller's list was "the continuance of the old heathenish dances." Such occasions, Teller assured his readers, "are not social gatherings for the amusement of these people, but, on the contrary, are intended to stimulate the warlike passions of the young warriors," including theft, rape, and murder. In order to rescue the tribes from barbarism, went Teller's reasoning, reformers had to compel Indians "to desist from the savage and barbarous practices that are calculated to continue them in savagery."[10] And that meant an end to Indian dances.

Those tempted to dismiss the influence of dances had merely to recall the extraordinary alarm raised by the Ghost Dance phenomenon, or by various other gatherings inevitably described as "war dances." M. B. Louthin, a homesteader in Chickasaw Territory, remembered that in 1891 "the Comanches, who were blanket Indians out west of us, staged a big Ghost Dance which made us more or less nervous . . . before the United States Troops could be returned from the 'Wounded Knee' Agency, the Comanches had quieted down and everything was peaceful." And it wasn't only the Ghost Dance that raised the alarm. A Choctaw woman who participated in the WPA narratives project of the 1930s recalled that as a young woman she attended dances among the Creeks, Seminoles, Chickasaws, Choctaws, Osages, Iowas, Kickapoos, Shawnees, and the Comanches and Kiowas, whom she characterized as the "wild Indians." "In summing them all up," she confidently observed, "I would say that in every case it amounts to practically the same. . . . The most exciting dance among any of them is their War Dance, working themselves up to a fever heat and ready to do or die for what they think is right." This fear of violence was also a theme in Frank Gill's account of an encounter with Kiowas whom he met while rounding up stampeded cattle. The Kiowas brought Gill into their camp where "they all jumped up and began the war dance all around me after which they all sat down on their blankets again until about four o'clock when they all jumped up again and started their dancing around me again. The old chief came over to me and asked me if I was afraid of them and I said, 'No, why should I be afraid of you people.' (I was scared most to death. . . . I had not closed my eyes all night or hardly moved.)"[11]

Methodist minister J. J. Methvin recalled in a WPA interview that when military officials promised to forcibly prevent the 1890 Kiowa Sun Dance, Big Tree replied that "he would fight." Informed the next morning that "the Agency was full of soldiers," the Kiowas called off the dance and broke camp. Another participant in the WPA narratives remembered that when an agent intervened in an intertribal dance meeting near Fort Cobb attended by Comanches, Kiowas,

Apaches, Cheyennes, and Arapahos, the Indians announced "they were going to dance or fight." This prompted officials to summon the army, whereupon the officer in charge promised that if the dance was held "he would call out the soldiers and confiscate all of their belongings and make them prisoners for the rest of their lives." The threat was taken as a genuine expression of intent, and the camp shortly dissolved.[12]

Greer County Sheriff Sam Houston Tittle reported a similarly tense encounter in 1891 when a white boy named Jake Booher, who was running a herd of cattle, and a Kiowa man named Bob Poline "fell out over a steer." Afraid that the Indian was going to attack him, Booher shot first and killed Poline. "This caused a great commotion among both the whites on the Greer County side of the river and the Kiowa on the Territory side," remembered Tittle, and prompted fears that more violence was probably in the offing. Ominously, Tittle reported, the Kiowas went into camp, "had war dances, and said that they were going to fight the whites as they felt that the whites were imposing upon them." Settlers gathered their families and took refuge in the town of Mangum while a delegation of peacemakers had the shooter arrested and held a parlay with Kiowa headsman. In the end, cooler heads prevailed. "When we convinced them that Jake [the shooter] would be tried, they agreed they would not make any more trouble as Bob Poline had a bad record among his own people." What is striking about these accounts is that whites often perceived dance gatherings as "usually pretty noisy and also pretty exciting," as one man put it, as well as events associated with violence and threats of aggression. Indeed, the promise by one army officer to "call out the soldiers and confiscate all of their belongings and make them prisoners for the rest of their lives" suggests the depth of the fear that many whites felt when dances occurred.[13]

And, frankly, if the relationship between dancing and the appeal to violence was overplayed by whites, such gatherings did in fact underscore a determination to maintain practices that whites found troubling and bothersome. Anyone with lingering doubts as to the ability of dances to reinforce old values and to mediate the inequities and ennui of reservation life, for example, would have been well advised to read the 1899 Pine Ridge Reservation annual report, in which the agent wrote that "school boys speak longingly of the time when they will no longer be required to attend school, but can let their hair grow [and] dance the Omaha."[14] The idea that school boys intended to continue the dance nine years after the debacle at Wounded Knee, and more than two decades after the Omaha Society's final military victories, compelled observers to acknowledge its enduring influence. Eight years later, a missionary at Rosebud Agency wrote an even more startling account after attending the agency's annual July 4 celebrations. Ostensibly occasions for celebrating Americanism, on the Lakota reservations such events were especially worrisome to officials because they often featured performances of the Omaha Dance. If some whites enjoyed the dances for their sheer spectacle, Indians openly embraced the cultural capital that such occasions created, a point driven home with considerable clarity when one participant commented, "We need only the Sun Dance, and we have it all back."[15]

The Lakota who made that statement had like-minded friends on the Southern Plains. In 1920, for example, the superintendent of the Pawnee School nervously reported that some Pawnees apparently intended to hold yet another Ghost Dance, a revelation that must have worried even the most determined assimilationists. In fact, when such a dance had been held six years earlier, one observer commented it was "a reversion to old-time practices in every way." And as Squirrel told Major Baldwin, he meant to have his pleasure, but the dance in question constituted serious business. It was, wrote Squirrel, "just like your own religion [in] which you white people worship with our one great father." Because dances clearly allowed Indian people to shape the contours of reservation life, many communities and dance organizations refused to buckle in the face of threats, bribes, or restrictions.[16]

However, the campaign to halt dancing was prompted by more than recalcitrant Indians; the curiosity of whites also was a factor. The public's appetite for frontier nostalgia at the end of the nineteenth century made Indians a much sought-after form of entertainment; whites eagerly hired Indians and encouraged precisely the displays that officials so detested. Given the level of suspicion and fear associated with dances, this interest seems at first glance to be a curious inconsistency. But context was everything, and when dances were presented under the watchful gaze of white entrepreneurs and organizers, spectators could feel safe. It was rather like seeing animals at the circus: encountering the same animals in the wild would have been cause for panic; displaying them as exhibits under the control of white masters, however, released audiences from their fears and allowed them to trade their apprehension for a voyeuristic gaze. And so it was that only one year after Secretary Teller's fist-pounding announcement about the evils of dancing, Dr. H. A. Lewis of Wichita Falls, Texas, informed Kiowa-Comanche-Apache agent P. B. Hunt that "the Apaches want to come down here and have a dance for our people this year . . . at the anniversary of our town. . . . We will have some kind of celebration . . . and they will add to the attractions." To Hunt's unending discomfort, Lewis later reported that the enterprise had not only exceeded "all we could have expected," things had gone so well that he had hired sixty of the Apaches for a road trip to the upcoming New Orleans Exposition.[17]

High on the list of the government's complaints about these shows was their portrayal of Indians as exotic, primitive, and war-like. Although Squirrel assured Baldwin that proper decorum would be observed ("There is no guns, or anything towards war"), and Lewis promised that the Apaches would be well cared for, most shows and exhibitions celebrated images that brazenly contradicted official policy. Consider the case of Will Pyeatt, proprietor of the White Sulphur Inn in Sulphur, Indian Territory. In August 1899, Pyeatt wrote to the Kiowa-Comanche-Apache Reservation to recruit "the wildest blanket Indians to be had. . . . we want Indians that will eat raw meat and give the war and goast [sic] dance." Pyeatt planned exhibitions of old-time camp life and other frontier doings. But those things were largely beside the point; above all, he wanted Indians who would dance "just like they used to."[18]

In coming years, dozens of exhibitions, fairs, and Wild West Shows popularized Indian dancing by gleefully publicizing attractions to which a curious public flocked. Pawnee Bill, Buffalo Bill, Comanche Bill, Tiger Bill, Indian Bill, Texas Bill, Texas Bud, California Frank, Bronco John, Buckskin Joe, Cherokee Ed, Captain Ed, the Miller Brothers, the Dallas State Fair, the Louisiana Purchase Centennial, the Muscogee Indian International Fair, the Craterville Fair, the Anadarko American Indian Exposition, and a great many other individuals and events made Indian dancing a centerpiece of their shows. Seizing on the era's taste for exotic Indians, promoters eagerly satisfied the public's hankering for a taste of what one man called "the Red Man as he was." In 1920, for example, the promoters of the Hudson Bay Company's 250th anniversary celebration reminded the Canadian public that "in a few short years the opportunities for . . . a reconstruction of the costumes, manners and customs of former days will have passed away." As one official put it: "What an opportunity for films! As an object lesson, and an attraction for the public, it would be a superb show."[19]

Across the Southern Plains, there was no shortage of opportunists planning shows where the public could see "real Indians" doing what real Indians did best: dance. The Hobart, Oklahoma, Commercial Club was refreshingly blunt about plans for its 1902 July 4 celebration: "With other amusements we would like to have an Indian dance." In 1896, W. A. Husted had informed the Kiowa-Comanche-Apache agent that he was "contemplating going into the Indian show business," and planned "a regular series of dancing and ball playing, provided I can get the Indians." Five years earlier, another aspiring entrepreneur named W. F. Mull was convinced that dancing Apaches and Comanches were the perfect props to advertise his patent medicines. (No mere snake-oil salesman, Mull solemnly assured the agent he was a *regular Graduate in medicine.*) In 1905, another would-be Buffalo Bill politely requested "4 or 6 bucks and 3 or 4 squaws" for a small Wild West show.[20]

Driven by the twofold specter of Indians *and* whites conspiring to disrupt the government's assimilation program, the Indian Office broadened the bans to include virtually every kind of dance gathering when Commissioner of Indian Affairs Thomas Jefferson Morgan revised the rules for the Indian Courts in 1892 and added strong language against dancing. "Any Indian who shall engage in the sun dance, the scalp dance, or war dance, or any other similar feast," stated the regulations, "shall be deemed guilty of an offense." Dancers faced fines, imprisonment of up to thirty days, forfeiture of annuity payments, and assorted other punishments.[21]

Yet the lines were more or less clear even before Morgan gave official sanction to more stringent policies. Objecting specifically to the use of dancing Indians for public spectacle, the Indian Office promptly derailed Dr. H. A. Lewis's plan to take an Apache dance troupe to the 1884 New Orleans Exposition. Commissioner of Indian Affairs Hiram Price (1881–1885) informed Lewis that the government's official policy was "to induce the Indians to abandon their wild and roving habits and to become peaceable, industrious, and useful citizens." As Price observed, "This certainly cannot be done by allowing them to be paraded over the country and exhibited the same as wild animals." One Indian farmer, the commissioner intoned, "will do more to civilize and elevate the race . . . than one hundred Indians parading through the country for exhibition."[22] Price sent Lewis packing.

During the next decade the government moved aggressively to suppress dances. Commissioner Morgan, whose favorite targets were the Wild West shows that proliferated at the end of the century, led the way. Convinced that they exposed hapless participants to noxious influences, Morgan lambasted Wild West shows for their prurient sensationalism. "It is unwise for Indians to be allowed to appear before the public exhibiting their savage characteristics," he wrote in his 1892 annual report, because "it tends to create in their minds the idea that what the white man particularly admires is that which really is a mark of their degradation."[23] Morgan was, of course, absolutely correct about the public's taste; but because the Wild West depiction of Indians was so popular, officials were largely powerless to stop it. More than that, the public's appetite for dancing Indians and the easy availability of so-called Show Indians proved more than a match for reformers. Indeed, as Moses notes, even as Commissioner Morgan publicly thundered against such exhibitions, officials inevitably succumbed to requests for Show Indians, often on the grounds that it was a good way to get rid of troublemakers, as when the Indian Office authorized the hiring by Cody in 1891 of twenty-three Lakota Ghost Dancers.[24] In the end, the government's willingness to condone the Wild West shows and accommodate owners' requests meant that the shows so thoroughly trumped policy goals that dancing gained a new lease under the stewardship of Cody and his numerous imitators.

But limited success at controlling the shows did not deter officials from moving on other fronts, for if policymakers thought the Wild West worthy of close scrutiny, they also knew that they could neither stop it nor use it to suppress dances where they remained most troublesome — at home. Officials pressed the assault against what Commissioner of Indian Affairs Charles Burke (1921–1929) called "the vicious dance." As early as 1911, the Indian Office directed agents to provide specific information on dances in their annual reports, including the frequency with which they occurred, and, by 1920, the extent to which children and students were permitted to view them or to participate. Burke tackled dancing with the well-known 1921 Circular 1665 denouncing dances for their "acts of self-torture, immoral relations between the sexes, the sacrificial destruction of clothing or other useful articles, the reckless giving away of property, the use of injurious drugs or intoxicants, and frequent or prolonged periods of celebrations which bring the Indians together from remote points to the neglect of their crops, livestock, and home interest." Indeed, Burke was so appalled by dances that he opposed them on the grounds that they were a "disorderly . . . plainly excessive performance that promotes superstitious cruelty . . . [and] shiftless indifference."[25]

If commission circulars underscored the bureau's official position, they also revealed the problematic nature of the dance bans. Burke admitted in 1921, for example, that when it came to restricting Indians from attending fairs and engaging in dances, "The fact is, we do not have any real *authority.*" As a result, officials allowed dances as long as sponsors had formal permission, avoided explicitly religious rituals, and did not disrupt work. In a 1923 supplement to Circular 1665, Burke relaxed his position, stating that he would not too aggressively prevent those under the age of fifty from attending dances "if the occasion is properly controlled and unattended by immoral or degrading influence."[26] As Kiowa-Comanche-Apache agent and vociferous dance opponent C. V. Stinchecum put it in 1915, "I have no objection whatever to the Indians getting together and holding a picnic in a decent manner . . . but . . . dances of such nature as the ghost dance and give away dance must, if possible, be relegated to the dim past."[27]

Relegating dances to the dim past, however, required agency officials to control the context in which such gatherings and celebrations occurred. Previously frustrated by the Wild West shows, Commissioner Cato Sells (1913–1921) turned his attention to the Indian fairs and expositions that appeared on many reservations by the turn of the century. In them, he saw an opportunity to impose more stringent regulations in a way that he hoped Indians could not circumvent. As Moses notes, this made sense given the large numbers of fairs being held by the 1920s. "From just two in 1909," he writes, "by 1915, fifty-four reservations staged fairs, and eleven state fairs included Indian expositions." On the Southern Plains, the Muscogee Indian International Fair, the Craterville Fair, the American Indian Exposition, and many others attracted vast numbers of Indians. In addition to these all-Indian events, local county fairs invariably hosted large Indian encampments as well. To officials anxious for a solution to the problem of Indians who insisted on dancing, the Muskogee fair, which dated to 1874, seemed a harbinger of the possibilities and a model for emulation. Commenting on the first fair's success, the November 6, 1874, edition of the *Oklahoma Star* reported: "The fair is an advance step in the right direction, and it should be encouraged by everyone who desires the advancement of the Indian people. . . . The elevation of the race is in fostering industrial pursuits, the education of the people and the progress of moral teachings."[28]

Taking to heart the inculcation of industrial pursuits and moral teachings, the town of Duncan did its part by sponsoring an annual Peanut Carnival at which, Sidney Alonzo Bullard remembered, well-meaning Duncanites would "try to teach the Indians the many uses of the peanuts."[29] But if unraveling the mysteries of the peanut kept some Indians busy, the allure of the Peanut Carnival paled in comparison to other fairs, where it is safe to say that more exciting opportunities awaited participants and visitors alike. From the beginning, the Indian fairs featured traditional tribal entertainment, including dog and horse racing, gambling, and, of course, dancing. Envisioning the fairs as venues for promoting the agricultural and industrial programs that lay at the heart of assimilation, policymakers hoped to attract Indians to a combination of educational programs and wholesome entertainment, not to the dances that one agent described as gatherings "of the detrimental sort." But as officials soon learned, the task wasn't so much to ban dances as it was to regulate and manipulate them. Fairs meant dancing, and no amount of coercion seemed capable of preventing it. So, rather than enforce a total ban, Commissioner of Indian Affairs Robert Valentine (1909–1913) decided in 1909 that the best approach was to allow limited dancing and to use it as an inducement to get more Indians to attend the fairs, where after being wooed by other programs and activities, "some practical benefit must result." Armed with this dispensation and others during the years to come, however, it wasn't long before Indian fairs on the Southern Plains took on a decidedly pro-dance atmosphere. Meadows reports that a ledger book from a 1922 fair near Craterville Park, for example, depicts numerous military society dances and includes an entry reporting that "every tribe dances, Kiowas, Comanches, Cheyennes, etc." In 1929, a non-Indian promoter named Frank Rush sent reformers into paroxysms when he featured a Ghost Dance, of all things, at the Medicine Park Indian Fair.[30]

Of course, this was not quite what government officials had in mind. Most were willing to endure an occasional dance, but a Ghost Dance? What next, a Sun Dance? The best way to prevent such things, of course, was to control who was doing what. As early as 1888, the Indian Office cautioned agent E. E. White at the Kiowa-Comanche-Apache Reservation that delegations to the Muscogee Indian International Fair were to be "composed as nearly as may be, of the most progressive and industrious of your Indians." Four years later, the commissioner directed delegates to the same fair to reflect "the ways and customs of civilization usually represented by a well conducted agricultural fair among a progressive people."[31] In the context of the day, "progressive" referred generally to a cultural condition that reflected middle-class American values. Thus, Indians who wore white (or "citizen") clothing, sent their children to school, converted to Christianity, and became economically self-sufficient were deemed generally to be progressive. On the other hand, policymakers vilified the "traditionalists" or "conservatives" for their attachment to old ways, as in 1909 when the Pawnee agent disparaged the pro-dance crowd as the "uneducated full bloods." In the opinion of many agents, progressive Indians did not dance, a point that Kiowa-Comanche-Apache agent Stinchecum stressed in 1915 when he wrote that "proper dances were not Indian dances."[32]

In March 1914, Commissioner Sells turned his attention to the fairs and took a hard line, at least on paper. "If, *to the Indians,* the paramount features are to dance and wager on horse races," he wrote, "the quicker the fairs are terminated the better." Sells ordered agency superintendents to prohibit "the old-time dances during fair time," and insisted that "both the Indians and the public should be made to realize that these old customs retard the onward march of civilization." He imposed a three-day limit on "distinctively Indian fairs" and insisted that they promote decidedly civilized pursuits — slow mule races, for example, as opposed to the customary horse races.[33]

Sells issued circulars in 1914 and again in 1916, declaring that "Indian fairs should be as nearly as practicable a counterpoint of the white man's fair. Eliminate the Wild West features and the horse racing as much as possible." He elaborated his edicts, saying: "I want these fairs so conducted as to open to the Indians the vision of the industrial achievements to which they should aspire. Let . . . [the] fair mark the start of the Indian along the road [to] . . . self-improvement and independence — hereafter let your fair be a milestone fixing the stages of the Indian's progress toward that goal."[34] Above all, fairs should provide "helpful and constructive substitutes for the old-time practices." To that end, instead of the usual camp activities, Sells encouraged "athletic contests, feats of strength or skill, baseball games, footraces, etc." Aware that dances often took place after hours, the commissioner had an answer for that, too. He suggested, "If evening entertainment is thought advisable, stereopticon talks on suitable topics, band concerts, etc., might be arranged." Such gatherings, pointed out the commissioner, should limit the influence of "non-progressive Indians, who are not in sympathy with the purposes of the fair." But like Valentine, Sells also compromised his position, agreeing in 1916 to allow adults to hold "harmless dances" at the Standing Rock Fair.[35]

In 1913, several Oklahoma Indian superintendents proposed an "Indian State Fair of Oklahoma Indians" in the hope of providing the "opportunity to effect a big step in bringing the Indians and the State together. This is the big end of the Indian business of our service." Their proposal included a "pageant of the Old Life. . . . to amuse the old, [and] impress the young and the visitors with conditions in the Old Life alongside the New" and emphasized "models of farms, views of statistics, farm products of grain and stock, and the handiwork of women from beads to bread." Marching bands, athletic teams, and "Indian maids milking, buttermilking, cooking, [and] manufacturing delicious ice cream" would complete the presentation of "The Indian As He Is."[36] The plan was never realized, but in 1916 Stinchecum reported to Commissioner Sells that "the old time Indian Fairs . . . of course, have been relegated to the past at this jurisdiction." Indians at his agency no longer held a separate fair (he banned them), but participated in the Oklahoma State Fair, where, Stinchecum beamed, "our Indians mingle amongst the white people, [and] do business in the white man's way." This news delighted Sells, who believed that unlike county fairs, all-Indian fairs did not properly acknowledge the Indians' "community of interest with whites." Stinchecum permitted no old-time entertainments at the fair and countered complaints from the pro-dance crowd by sponsoring a "Better Babies Contest" with a cash prize. Satisfied that he had rebuffed the critics, Stinchecum assured the commissioner that the contest had been enormously popular and was far more meaningful than any dance. Having held the line at fairs, officials convinced themselves that modest cash prizes for the largest beets, the best loaf of white bread, "the fattest Indian, the largest Indian family . . . and the Indian coming the longest distance to the fair" had undone the deeper cultural complexities of Indian life.[37]

Agency officials also tried to control dances in reservation communities that hosted what the Indian Office euphemistically described as "picnics." Indeed, as long as Indians described their gatherings as picnics, the implicit understanding was that no unapproved dancing or rituals would occur. But when Indians redefined such semantic niceties to make room for all manner of dances, well, something had to be done. After gaining permission for picnics, many Indians then used the occasions to host dances according to tribal or societal dictates. Such was the case when a Kiowa family sponsored a "picnic" to celebrate Armistice Day in the early 1920s. Once assembled, however, the crowd quickly transformed the occasion into one that recognized and honored veterans according to Kiowa ways, including the recitation of war deeds and the naming of children. This was not what the Indian Office had in mind when it sanctioned such events.[38]

One of the most common tactics to prevent gatherings was to restrict or forbid travel. In 1882, for example, Pawnee agent E. H. Bowman warned Kiowa-Comanche-Apache agent P. B. Hunt that "an unauthorized party of vagrants" was headed from the Pawnee Agency to the Kiowa Agency "on a wandering and discredible expedition … for the purpose of giving dance exhibitions" and should be intercepted and returned immediately. Baptist missionary Lauretta Ballew contacted Captain Frank Baldwin at Fort Sill in 1895 with a similar concern, telling him "the Indians are planning a trip to the Cheyenne country to dance for ponys [*sic*]. Please use your power against it as it will counteract the good they have received."[39]

James Helms reported in 1893 that he believed the Poncas would let go of their dance traditions if he could somehow prevent the Winnebagos from visiting. When the Winnebagos proved uncooperative, Helms announced a ban on visits and authorized the county sheriff to arrest dancers and charge them with disorderly conduct. If the Poncas insisted on dancing, Helms promised to stop their annuity payments and withhold the money to be paid to scouts and soldiers.[40] Peeved at the agent's tactics, a Ponca man described by Helms as a "half breed agitator" sent a letter to Washington asking "have they the right to stop us if we disturb nobody?" Commissioner Morgan answered that as long as dances were for pleasure and did not interfere with regulations, he saw no harm. Mortified, Helms presumed to lecture the commissioner: "In the very nature of things, harm must result from the gatherings. Old traditions are revived . . . and civilization relegated for the time being to the past, and all the savagery in their nature [is] uppermost in their minds."[41]

Such accounts revealed that Southern Plains agents fought a never-ending battle in the war against dancing. The summation in Otoe agent J. P. Woolsey's 1894 report was typical: "The greatest evil we have had to contend with at Otoe, is the insatiable desire of nearly every member of the tribe for dancing." Although he had worked hard to suppress it, Woolsey conceded that he was "of the opinion that we can never stop the practice entirely." A decade later things hadn't improved much. In 1903, Commissioner William A. Jones's hopeful observation that "many of the brutal and bloody features of these dances have been eliminated" was leavened by the admission that official bans had failed to prevent every dance.[42]

Years later, Kiowa-Comanche-Apache agent Ernest Stecker wrote with palpable irritation to Commissioner Sells about the "dance crowd" and complained bitterly of "that class who . . . antagonize every effort made toward their uplift." In January and again in July 1917, his successor, Stinchecum, resorted to a blacklist containing the names of more than one hundred Indians known to have attended dances. To force their hand, Stinchecum froze their per capita payments — despite having no legal authority to do so — until they signed an affidavit pledging to desist. Of the 105 named in the July list, sixty-one, or nearly two-thirds, were under the age of forty, a fact that contradicted the agents' arguments that dance participants tended to be older and more conservative. And of that group, forty-six were Kiowas. By gender, the breakdown was seventy-one men and thirty-four women. By tribe, Kiowas led the way with seventy-nine, followed by the Comanches with twenty-one, and the Apaches with five.[43]

The blacklist approach, however, did not prevent gatherings. Consequently, agents often resorted to carefully orchestrated shows of influence and force. As early as 1877 the army dispatched troops to important rituals, ostensibly to keep the peace, but also to keep tabs on who was doing what and to curry favor with pliable tribesmen. When the Kiowas refused to give up the Sun Dance, authorities employed force, as in 1888 when W. D. Myers informed the tribes of Kiowa-Comanche-Apache Reservation that any attempt to hold the Sun Dance would compel him "to call on the military and cause the arrest of every Indian who expressed a determination to participate." One year later, Commissioner Morgan sanctioned the threat, ordering Myers "peremptorily to end the [Sun] dance" using "all proper means and precautions." Determined to destroy the Sun Dance once and for all on the Southern Plains, and especially among the Kiowas, Morgan added that he was "unwilling to modify in any degree the order. . . . It is my wish that the dance shall be prevented." It was; by the summer of 1890, military pressure ended the Kiowa Sun Dance forever.[44]

But generally speaking, agents refrained from using brute force, relying instead on less confrontational methods. In 1881, for example, E. L. Clark arrived at the Kiowa Sun Dance encampment to issue rations and annuity goods as inducements for the Indians to give up dancing. To deflect the authority of the head men, Clark reported that he would "try to disregard chiefs in issuing the beef," but admitted "if that method don't suit, I will have to come to their terms and let them kind of run the machine." The Kiowas proved more than a match for Clark, simultaneously ignoring his attempts to convert them even as they cheerfully took rations and annuities. Far from controlling the Kiowas, Clark was quickly reduced to a mere ration clerk. At week's end, the man who had intended to "disregard the chiefs," concluded his report by writing "the Lord knows when this will end."[45]

Officials eagerly welcomed the assistance of Indians who opposed dancing. In December 1890, for example, Kiowa-Comanche-Apache agent Charles

Adams heard from a Cheyenne man named James Deere who wanted assistance suppressing the Ghost Dance. Cheyennes were giving large numbers of livestock to the medicine man conducting the ceremonies, and Deere remarked "he is making our people very poor, they are going down hill very fast." In broken but understandable English, Deere went on to say that the Cheyennes "will have nothing pretty soon to live on when hard times come. Jesus is coming sure," but the Ghost Dance leader "tells our people do away with their cattle and hogs, they don't need them that the white people were treating them very bad. Everything He tells our people right contrary to civilization."[46]

If agents were encouraged by such accounts, they were even more enthusiastic when prominent leaders opposed dancing. In 1895 and 1896, Kiowa-Comanche-Apache agent Frank Baldwin heard from Big Tree, a Kiowa leader who had converted to Christianity and become a stalwart among Kiowa Baptists. Prior to taking the Jesus Road, Big Tree had been a notorious combatant, earning a death sentence for his part in a series of killings in 1871 called the Warren Wagon Train Massacre. His sentence was subsequently commuted, and Big Tree ultimately returned to his people. By 1895, he openly opposed the old ways associated with dancing. "I am not in favor of my people dancing," he wrote Baldwin, "neither is Lone Wolf," another notable Kiowa man. "I am trying to lead my people in a better road. It does not do any good for me to talk to them about dancing, so please use your strength to prevent it." One year later Big Tree sent Baldwin another letter, this time through Baptist missionary Marietta Reeside. "You are the father of these tribes," he began, "and so we ask you to help us when you see us going on the wrong road. . . . There are six Indian men who are trying to pull just the other way. . . . It makes me sad to see the young boys pulled back. I want you to talk to the leader of this dance, Sit-ah-pay-to (Afraid of Bear) and see if you can make him see the harm he is doing. . . . I ask you to talk to this leader to give up. If he will not, I ask you to punish him until he is compelled to submit, for you know he is on the wrong road. . . . Now the Ghost Dance has come. I am not strong enough to put it down, but you have the power and authority. I ask you to take it into your hands to put a stop to it once and for all. My friend agent, I know the right road, and you know it." Big Tree concluded by naming the six men leading the dance and signed the letter "Your Brother."[47]

Two years later, in 1896, Lucius Aitson, a Carlisle graduate and interpreter for the missionaries, informed the Kiowa Agency that some Indians were spreading tales about how Army officers and agency officials had encouraged dancing and approved the use of peyote at two Ghost Dances then in progress. "I do not believeth [the stories]," wrote Aitson, "because you are our agent [and] make these rules." Like Big Tree, Aitson named names, including Sit-ah-pay-to, Big Tree's nemesis. Aitson apologized for not being able to supply a complete list of names; he had had to cut short his investigations to attend church, but concluded on a hopeful note that "I do not find gambling and no horse racing."[48]

In 1904, a Kiowa named Odlepaugh joined a group of converts who intended to preach the gospel at a Ghost Dance camp. This event was made all the more remarkable because Odlepaugh was the son of Setainte, arguably the most famous Kiowa leader of the nineteenth century, and along with Big Tree, one of those condemned to death for his role in the 1871 Warren Wagon Train Massacre. Speaking to a childhood friend at the Ghost Dance he hoped to break up, Odlepaugh said, "I had a very bad temper and hurried up to get mad always. You see I am getting over it. I go to the Jesus House and I listen, and listen, and listen, and I try, and try, and try and it is Jesus and His Holy Spirit who are helping me." Odlepaugh's fellow Baptist Lone Wolf put it more succinctly when he said "the old people put us on the wrong road." [49] As far as he was concerned, it was the Jesus Road that Kiowas needed to follow, not the Dance Road.

On another occasion, agency officials actively enlisted a leading Kiowa man named Apeahtone (also spelled Apiatan, and pronounced Ah-pee-tone) to suppress the Ghost Dance. An outspoken foe of the Ghost Dance, Apeahtone denounced its promoters as frauds and denigrated the ceremony as just so much hocus pocus. Here was an Indian with whom agents could make common cause. In a dramatic public confrontation arranged in 1891 by officials from the Kiowa-Comanche-Apache and Cheyenne-Arapaho agencies, Apeahtone castigated Sitting Bull, an Arapaho who was leading the dance. Apeahtone's sister later recounted the event in an interview for the WPA narrative project. When agency officials sent Apeahtone on fact-finding trips to South Dakota and Nevada, she said he discovered "It was an easy matter to make believers of Indians, but A-peahtone soon saw that it was a hoax so he returned home and called a meeting at Anadarko for all tribes. They exposed Sitting Bull and forced the teacher to . . . leave the country, thus ending the Ghost Dance craze. A-peahtone did something that the Government officials could not do—ended this craze." As a reward for his assistance, government officials struck a special silver Peace Medal for Apeahtone with a likeness of President Harrison on one side and "figures emblematic of the Indian's progress in the ways of advancement and civilization" on the other. Commissioner of Indian Affairs Morgan proclaimed that the government "appreciates the valuable services he has rendered, and I hope it will be the means of inspiring him to renewed effort in the further enlightenment of his people." As L. G. Moses writes, it didn't take long for the government to make good on its gratitude: "Three years later, and with the commissioner's support, Apiatan became head chief of the Kiowas."[50]

If Indians requested permission for dances, agents bravely laid down the law.

When James Tonkeamah, a Kiowa, sought permission in 1917 to sponsor a July 4 dance at his allotment, for example, agent Stinchecum approved it as long as Tonkeamah agreed to abide by a set of strict rules. "If the Indians intend to have a one-day picnic, the same as white people, and have only the harmless social dances," Stinchecum wrote, "there will be no objection." But if Tonkeamah's guests crossed the line and engaged in either the Ghost Dance or a giveaway, the agent would "withhold at the next annuity payment the shares of those who participate therein, or who were in attendance." Stinchecum then ordered the agency's farmer to attend the dance and "ascertain the conduct of the Indians. If the matter resolves itself into a one-day picnic . . . all well and good. But if a give away dance is participated in or the ghost dance," Stinchecum warned, "I will want the names of all Indians participating in either one of those dances."[51]

Despite such restrictions, Stinchecum's directives rarely produced the intended results. In 1920 he admitted that the agency continued to be "cursed with a great number of Indian dances." Although he agreed that some dances were not of a "serious character," and that he did not oppose Indians "shaking their feet," Stinchecum despised dances because of "the opportunity for the spread of disease, immorality and vice and the great amount of time taken from . . . work." He insisted that "there is no doubt . . . the dances should be curtailed, and if possible altogether abandoned," but he also admitted that during the coming summer he expected a "continual string of dances from one end of the reservation to another."[52]

Resigned to the fact that holidays would inevitably be accompanied by large gatherings whose entertainment included dancing, officials attempted to manipulate such events just as they had the Indian fairs by promoting displays of patriotism and loyalty as worthy alternatives to old-time dances. In 1891 Commissioner Morgan encouraged elaborate festivities on Franchise Day, Washington's Birthday, and Arbor Day, among others, and directed agents to make "the exercises as . . . interesting as possible." Historical reenactments were encouraged, and often featured Indian students donning wigs and knee britches in their roles as colonial founders, or, in a striking role reversal, in black face as slaves from an earlier period of American history. Indian schools were especially crucial here. As Commissioner William A. Jones (1897–1905) observed in 1903, while "Indian schools recognize this love of dancing," they could "turn it from viciousness to harmlessness" by sponsoring "social entertainments . . . in a well-regulated dance" that would encourage habits of politeness and courteousness.[53]

When dancing did occur, it was to be a strictly secular, social occasion with agents closely monitoring the goings on. Controlling these events was especially important when circumstances encouraged the practice of old dances and the rituals that accompanied them. As had been the case during earlier July 4th celebrations that included Sun Dances and other rituals, during and following World War I many communities across the Southern Plains hosted numerous scalp dances, victory dances, and homecoming dances for returning Indian servicemen. To the unending discomfort of officials who hoped the war would be a catalyst for assimilation, it instead provided new opportunities to celebrate and revive old traditions associated with the martial ethos that many Plains tribes shared. In his 1919 annual report, Commissioner Sells included a section titled "War as a Civilizer," in which he observed that military service would introduce Indian soldiers to "the wondrously multiplied interests of trade, industry, education . . . professions, [and] statesmanship."[54] True enough, but the war also created a new generation of warriors, and Indian communities rushed to resurrect old society dances and rituals that now had renewed meaning.

As Meadows states, "The impact of the war and the traditional protocol necessitating the honoring of returning veterans was simply too much for even the agency to suppress." Thus tribes hosted dances at which they blessed departing soldiers according to old rituals, or gave returning veterans new names based on their wartime exploits. In addition to serving as occasions for the revival of warrior society practices, these dances sometimes featured the display of battlefield trophies, a practice that caused predictably high levels of exasperation among officials. A 1919 Cheyenne dance in Canton, Oklahoma, for example, reportedly featured the display of a German scalp. At other dances, participants displayed parts of enemy uniforms and weapons as in the old days and engaged in mock charges and battles against effigies in the form of the German kaiser. New songs made reference to modern enemies, extolled the valor of Indian doughboys, and accorded them the status of warriors. Indeed, all across the Southern Plains the war years breathed new life into old rituals, and dances once again became crucial conduits for the expression of venerated ideals.[55]

Predictably, the government's response was to blacklist dancers, withhold their annuities, and declare dances "acts of disloyalty and an attempt to subvert the will of the government." Commissioner Sells disparaged Indians for believing that "by reviving the native costume and some form of old war-dances they can best express complete approval of those who enlisted under the banner of American freedom." Even if dances eliminated what Sells called the "injurious and immoral features" that accompanied "the old form of dancing . . . [and] crude Indian music," such practices remained "objectionable." When a collection of Cheyennes and Arapahos attempted to hold a Sun Dance, the agent dismissed them with the comment, "We don't allow no Indian ceremony. In fact, no Indian doings during this war."[56]

For his part, Stinchecum ruefully admitted in 1919 that "it is almost impossible to prevent every dance, because the Indians are more and more realizing that they are citizens and that they have the right to do things which are not in violation of the State and Federal laws. . . . They realize that we have no hold on them whatever, and flagrantly violate the known wishes of this . . . Office." Indeed, in the wake of the flurry of post–World War I dances, Stinchecum admitted that "after more than four years hard work my entire influence was destroyed."[57] Disappointed but undeterred, Stinchecum countered with public parades and rallies. In April 1917, for example, he sent personal letters to influential Indians at the Kiowa-Comanche-Apache Reservation inviting them to participate in a "big monster celebration and loyalty meeting. . . . The Committee is anxious to have a large delegation of Indians present, and I am anxious also that our Indians stand out prominently as true, loyal, citizens of our country." As a further inducement, he planned a large parade and announced that "those having automobiles may participate in the automobile section, those riding ponies . . . and those driving teams in another section, also those on foot may participate in still another section."[58]

Better baby contests, stereopticon lectures, and loyalty parades — it all seemed so logical, so overpowering. As early as 1901, the Board of Indian Commissioners confidently asserted that dancing was under control: "These boys and girls who are allowed to go on with these dances do not believe in them."[59] Navajo agent David Shipley had said as much in 1892 when he reported that "the Navajos indulge in dancing, which has assumed the shape of harmless amusement." At the Cheyenne-Arapaho Reservation in Oklahoma, John Seger had been equally optimistic in 1893: "As an Indian expressed it, 'We have give up the ghost dance and joined the Sunday School.'" Two decades later the reports were even more sanguine. In 1920 the Mescalero superintendent reported that "a strict requirement for clean dances and good conduct is always exacted. . . . In my opinion a clean Indian dance does in no way retard the Indian's advancement and can have no bad effect on their morals." His colleague at the Pawnee Agency was sure that only mixed bloods (with "light hair and blue eyes") were interested in dancing, and was confident it did not appeal to the younger people.[60]

From Cantonment, Oklahoma, an agent reported in 1920, "I cannot see that they [dances] are offensive at all. . . . this custom of gathering and celebration should not be dealt with too drastically." From the Osage Agency came the revelation in the same year that dancing had no "evil effect . . . but, on the contrary, has a tendency to keep Indians more at home and from engaging in practices more harmful." His colleague at the Shawnee Agency confidently revealed in the same year that dances there were little more than "a social gathering," with little difference from the dances held by local whites.[61] Policymakers maintained the bans into the early 1930s, when John Collier ended them, but there was widespread agreement among many reformers that on the Southern Plains, at least, dancing had been reigned in, "relegated to the dim past" as C. V. Stinchecum had put it in 1915.

What does it matter for students of American Indian history that this debate raged a century ago? Several things are suggestive. First, dances were such an important target in the federal assimilation campaign that understanding the bans offers a revealing assessment of the implementation and limits of the era's policy. More importantly, the bans' limited success begs questions about the consequences of the failure. From the vantage point of the tribes, the government's failure to eradicate dancing was monumentally important. For as David Wooley and William T. Waters have observed, reformed and revived dances "offered salvation along with a message of moral integrity and identity with tradition. . . . that testify to the attempts of a people to come to terms with a new age." Moreover, as Lassiter writes, the result was a complicated cross-cultural encounter that forced both sides to the middle. These new forms, he notes, did not follow "an unchanging set of rules," but instead "evidenced the unique intersection of individual lives with tradition."[62]

In that sense, the bans did not suppress dance so much as they prompted accommodations that resisted the extremes of resistance or absorption. On the Southern Plains between 1880 and 1930, Indian people actively and deliberately reorganized dance culture to reflect new needs. In doing so they took advantage of permeable cultural boundaries, using symbols and actions that Loretta Fowler describes as "invented, discarded, and reinterpreted as they are adapted to new social realities." When the Shawnee superintendent announced in 1920, for example, that dances at his agency "are becoming modified . . . they are more of a social gathering than old Indian dances," he overlooked how and why Indian communities were deliberately manipulating the role of dance. When the Kiowas lost the Sun Dance, for example, the Tiah-Piah Society, which had previously policed the Sun Dance encampments, began to host an annual dance that coincided with the timing and purpose of the Sun Dance, and which incorporated many of its songs and practices into the new Gourd Dance. By transferring crucial ritual and spiritual actions from a dance that was banned to another that wasn't, the Kiowas created a dance that mediated the new social and cultural realities of the early twentieth century.[63]

In many cases, policymakers and reformers tended to be blind to a complicated set of accommodations being acted out on the Southern Plains. Dance culture was changing, to be sure, but it was not being reduced to insignificance. Whether as public show, private ritual, or tribal celebration, dance continued to constitute what Morris Foster calls "public gatherings . . . vital to community maintenance." Thus, even in the shadow of the regulations and bans between 1880 and 1930, such gatherings molded belief and identity. As evidence, we need look no further than the numerous dances across the Southern Plains in the wake of the World Wars and the evolution since the 1950s of the contemporary intertribal powwow. Equally persuasive are the tribally specific societal dances that survived the bans, including the Ponca Heluska, Kiowa O-ho-mah, Osage I'n-lon-schka, Apache Manatidie, and many others. Through those dances, Southern Plains people continued to celebrate the generosity, martial prowess, and ritual life that had historically sustained them.[64]

Policymakers doggedly banned dances, and white audiences clamored for "the Red Man as he was," but this did not prevent new forms of dance, or suppress the articulation of ideals and values based on those dances. Resistance, accommodation, and unevenly enforced federal policies produced a new Southern Plains dance culture that ultimately breathed life into another generation of adaptations. By the mid-1930s, when Commissioner of Indian Affairs John Collier overturned the bans, Southern Plains Indian people had already won much of the battle to maintain such practices. In the end, dance was more resilient than reformers, agents, and policymakers realized. Moreover, as Moses has noted in his work on Show Indians, Indians who maintained dance traditions "were spokespersons for the right of Indians to be themselves. They survived the contest. . . . they were never destroyed." Now, more than a century after the assault began, Southern Plains Indian people continue to maintain, adapt, and embrace the dance culture that their parents and grandparents gave to them. "These are *still* our traditional ways," says Ralph Kotay, a Kiowa. "Our people have been doing this all our lives."[65]

CHAPTER FOUR

"Five dollars a week to be 'regular' Indians"

Shows, Exhibitions, and the Economics of
Indian Dancing, 1880–1930

On November 18, 1890, seventy-nine Lakota Indians employed by Buffalo Bill Cody's Wild West Show met in Washington, D.C., to challenge Acting Commissioner of Indian Affairs Robert V. Belt's recently expressed opinion that shows featuring Indian dances were, among other things, "ruinous evils," and that Indians ought to "remain at home and engage in more civilizing avocations." The crux of the dispute was Belt's belief that earning a living by dancing in the shows was not only unseemly, it flatly contradicted federal Indian policy. Speaking for the troupe, a Lakota man named Black Heart reminded Belt that the Indians had been "raised on horseback." He explained, "That is the way we had to work. These men furnished us the same kind of work we were raised to do; that is the reason we want to work for these kind of men. . . . If [an] Indian wants to work at any place and earn money, he wants to do so; white man got privilege to do the same — any kind of work he wants." Echoing his fellow performer, Rocky Bear said if such employment "did not suit me, I would not remain any longer," and "if the great father wants me to stop, I would do it." There was no doubt that the Great Father wanted Indians to stop dancing. But in a comment that was cold comfort to federal officials who demanded that Indians become self-sufficient wage earners, Rocky Bear reminded them that he already was a wage earner; dancing in the Indian shows, he told them, "is the way I get money."[1]

Between 1880 and 1930, thousands of Indians joined dozens of shows, exhibitions, and fairs to earn a living by dancing, singing, and giving other performances. This work put money in their pockets, allowed them to escape the reservation, and rewarded them for portraying what they knew best — their traditional cultures. Yet, while scholars have shown interest in the changing contours and meanings of dance culture, few have taken notice of Rocky Bear's words and examined the economic side of dance shows and exhibitions, especially during the late nineteenth and early twentieth centuries when such shows were at their height.[2]

It is tempting to dismiss Show Indians as props in some inane native minstrel show tradition, hopping around for the benefit of white audiences, paid a pauper's wage to prostitute themselves. Indeed, contemporaries were often (and correctly) appalled by what they perceived to be the callous objectification of performers. Were some Indians forced into performing by the horrendous conditions on reservations? Yes, of this there can be little doubt. As Rocky Bear put it, on the reservation "I am getting poor." Did promoters and owners sometimes use performers crudely and insensitively? Again, there is no doubt that some did. As Michael Wallis notes, for example, the Miller Brothers 101 Ranch Real Wild West Show used Indian performers as "exotic lures to attract large crowds. . . . The Poncas would be put on display — just like prize livestock, award-winning pies and jams, and such freaks of nature as two-headed snakes and miniature ponies. The payoff was promising."[3] And was the payoff equitable? In most cases, no.

Yet, the cultural, political, and economic factors weighed by Indians as they contemplated joining the shows suggest that the decision to become a performer was complicated. Show dancing during that era was an economically significant venture for performers and promoters alike. If some shows were grossly exploitative, it is also true that dancing for pay was an attractive alternative to the chronic poverty and chaos that plagued many reservations. As Kills Enemy Alone, a Lakota who joined Cody's 1887 European tour, pointedly remarked, "I came over here to see if I can make some money." Sitting Bull — who in one biographer's opinion saw the shows as a way to "relieve the tedium of the reservation and to earn money" — knew that giving his earnings away according to Lakota values of generosity would affirm his status as a leader. And for a generation of students who know Nicholas Black Elk only as the ultra-traditional icon in John Neihardt's books, it might come as a surprise to learn that as a young man Black Elk "got disgusted with the wrong road that my people were doing . . . so I made up my mind I was going away from them to see the white man's ways. If the white man's ways were better, why I would like to see my people live that way." Black Elk seems to have had solidly practical motives, and as Moses has observed, "perhaps his enjoyment came . . . in the adventure of it all, in re-creating brave deeds, and in getting paid for it."[4]

Moreover, performers were not powerless. The Millers learned this lesson the hard way in 1914 when their refusal to pay wages for extra performances in England prompted a walkout by their dancers. Moreover, dancing for pay was hardly a fatal corruption of Indianness. As Joy Kasson notes, Indians exerted some control over the context and substance of their performances: Frank Fools Crow (Black Elk's nephew) remembered that "in our Wild West shows we Indians rode, sang, and danced. The dances were social performances, though, and never sacred ones." His uncle, however, reaped greater rewards from performing. Black Elk recounted that "as I traveled to competitions and toured with the Wild West shows, word of my healing and prophetic powers would spread. Then people who were doubters would ask me to prove what I could do by telling them my visions and performing my ceremonies for them."[5]

Indeed, Vine Deloria argues that the shows not only gave performers a measure of financial independence, they helped them make informed decisions about living in a world dominated by whites. "As a transitional educational device wherein Indians were able to observe American society and draw their own conclusions," he writes, "the Wild West was worth more than every school house built by the government on any of the reservations." Rita Napier observes that "Indians who toured with the Wild West could enjoy the best bitter in a London pub, mingle with royalty in a dignified and courteous fashion, and yet retain their own values as the basis for their 'vision' of life." Moses echoes these sentiments: "Ethnic identity need not be preserved through isolation, it may also be promoted through contact . . . [which] strengthened rather than weakened culture. . . . It would be wrong therefore to see the Show Indians as simply dupes, or pawns, or even victims. It would be better to approach them as persons who earned a fairly good living between the era of the Dawes Act and the Indian New Deal." Indeed, it is difficult to see them as dupes when, as Green has noted, show Indians did as much as they did to control the context in which they performed. Far from being put on display as automatons, many Indians who participated in the Wild West shows saw their experience as a form of cultural capital. "For Lakota headmen," she writes, "touring in the shows was a validation in the white world of their accomplishments as warriors." Moreover, returning Show Indians "infused Omaha dancing with renewed vigor, incorporating a showier and fancier manner which they had developed to entertain audiences."[6] Dancing for pay revealed that the relationship between victimization and agency rested on complex negotiations and mediations in which an either/or paradigm had little meaning.

That Indians danced at all — much less for money — had already prompted an intense debate by the 1880s. More than a decade before Belt's meeting with Cody's Indians, official alarm about dances and rituals perceived to be morally and spiritually objectionable spurred a fifty-year campaign to suppress dance culture, including theatrical performances. If performing with the shows provided some Indians with the means to become self-supporting, it also encouraged behavior that reformers deemed uncivilized and antithetical to the Indians' best interests. Official policy encouraged economic self-sufficiency based on a variety of pursuits, none of which included portraying what the Miller Brothers 101 Ranch Real Wild West Show publicized in 1912 as "pure blooded people of the wild old days . . . [who] remain strangers to work." In 1903, the Osage agent reinforced widely held negative opinions of Indians when he informed the government's director of Indian exhibits for the St. Louis World's Fair that if he wanted "an exhibit of great big fat juicy Indians in their native costumes doing nothing I can supply you with as many as you may want, or if you want a dancing party in native costume I can supply you with them. . . . but to supply the natives engaged in any constructive work will be an impossibility." In 1929, a writer lampooned one Ponca woman's work in a Wild West show by observing that because she weighed 450 pounds, "all she has to do is sit on a platform and let people gaze in admiration, mixed with awe."[7]

As these examples suggest, the debate was driven by more than the fact that some Indians made money from performing. Officials wanted Indians to earn their own keep, but a livelihood earned in the shows contradicted the government's assimilation agenda. As far as Secretary of the Interior Henry Teller was concerned, dancing wasn't work, it was an immoral waste of time that distracted Indians from an honest day's wages. "The Indian Question will never be settled," Teller insisted, "until you make the Indian blister his hands. No people ever emerged from barbarism that did not emerge through labor." And dancing, he thundered, was not labor, it was an indecent and barbaric spectacle that had to be destroyed. Indeed, officials and reformers never tired of extolling thrift, frugality, and self-sufficiency — virtues that they smugly insisted were conspicuous by their absence at dance shows and exhibitions. And as the Most Reverend John Ireland put it in 1902, thrift, frugality, and self-sufficiency were just around the corner, provided that the Indians followed a few simple lessons. "Teach the boys a trade of some kind," he wrote, "and teach them farming, which is, of course, the most important of all. Teach the girls the ordinary industries for which they are fitted. . . . Teach them cooking, teach them neatness, teach them responsibility. . . . do this and I tell you, you have solved the whole question of Indian civilization."[8] Any approach that did not rest squarely on this sort of work ethic was unacceptable.

Commissioner of Indian Affairs Cato Sells said much the same thing in 1914 when he observed that any activity that disrupted farming was "an economic and social crime." In 1922, Commissioner Charles Burke excoriated Indians who used dancing to "sacrifice real necessities to obtain money in the middle of a short growing season." Other officials decried dancing's corrosive effects on morals, as when Charles Shell declared in 1909 that dances at Oklahoma's Cheyenne and Arapaho Reservation were "accompanied by drunkenness, gambling, and other immoral practices." Audiences were thrilled by the Miller Brothers 101 Ranch Real Wild West Show, but most policymakers agreed with one man's assessment in 1932 of that show as "raw, unadulterated whore house entertainment" that deserved to be (and was by then) out of business. And it wasn't only traditional dancing that left policymakers fuming. When a representative of the 1919 Revue of Hitchy Koo recruited young Indian women as chorus line dancers at $35 a week plus transportation to and from New York City, the Cheyenne and Arapaho agent turned him down cold. There were no girls at his agency who met the requirements (16 to 18 years old, pretty, and with some knowledge of music), but even if there were, he was "not . . . willing that they should accept employment of this character."[9]

According to the mood of the day, it was unthinkable that dancing — either for Cody or the Revue of Hitchy Koo — would become a substitute for livelihoods in the officially mandated agricultural, mechanical, or domestic arts. John Whitewell tried to convince a group of Cheyennes and Arapahos who put on a dancing show in 1902 in Elk City, Oklahoma, that they "were being duped. That they were being used as an advertisement for the merchants, that the populace, not the merchants paid the money . . . and that what was received naturally went to the stores," not the Indians. Not much had changed two decades later when a Cheyenne man named Little Snake attempted to join a Wild West show in 1924, only to be reminded by an agency official named L. S. Bonnin that "it is the desire of the Department at Washington and this office that all able-bodied Indians support themselves by their own labor." Those who earned their living by show dancing, wrote Bonnin, were "hurting themselves and retarding their own progress, and assisting the white people in commercializing the Indians for profits. Personally, I would like to see every Indian refuse to act as a curiosity for people to look at and to earn money for someone else."[10]

Criticism of the shows also came from native people, as in 1914 when Chauncey Yellow Robe, a Sioux, published a scathing indictment titled "The Menace of the Wild West Show" in the *Quarterly Journal of the Society of American Indians*. Lamenting the "evil and degrading influence of commercializing the Indian," Yellow Robe, a Carlisle graduate, charged that the shows did little more than "depict lawlessness and hatred" and were "the greatest hindrance, injustice, and detriment to the present progress of the American Indian toward civilization." Show Indians had not merely been taken advantage of, he continued, they had been led to "the white man's poison cup and have become drunkards." Yellow Robe poured out a stream of invective against people who "think they cannot do without wild-west Indian shows, consequently certain citizens have the Indian show craze. . . . We can see from this state of affairs that the white man is persistently perpetuating . . . tribal habits and customs. We see that the showman is manufacturing the Indian plays intended to amuse and instruct young children, and is teaching them that the Indian is only a savage being." He asked, "How can we save the American Indian if the Indian Bureau is permitting special privileges in favor of the wild-west Indian shows, moving-picture concerns, and fair associations for commercializing the Indian?" What Indians needed, he concluded, were not more opportunities to earn a living by dancing in the shows, but "cleaner civilization," and, it is safe to say, jobs that did not include dancing for pay.[11]

In "The Effect of Wild Westing," an essay in the same journal issue as Yellow Robe's piece, E. H. Gohl (a white who claimed to be "an adopted clansman of the Onondaga") blasted "the morbid curiosity to see the red man as a savage in war-paint." In the Wild West shows, "managers compel the red man to act the white man's idea of a war dance. All is burlesque. The whole thing is deception." Gohl called for a "determined stand . . . to discourage and prevent whenever possible Indians making arrangements with wild-west shows, theatrical troups [sic], circuses, and most of the motion picture firms." In his judgment, "Touring the country with shows is demoralizing and a menace to the Indian. And all for a *'dollar a day and feed,'* with a good deal of the white man's 'rough house' thrown in. A wild-west show's contract is simply a sheet of 'guaranteed-to-catch fly-paper.'" Like Yellow Robe, Gohl believed that the Wild West shows destroyed the "pathway to self-help and progress," and he called on "all true friends of our American Indians" to support only those plays and pageants devoted to "historical or ethnological facts when under the auspices of colleges and historical societies."[12] The message was clear: Dancing was morally repugnant, and dance money was dirty money.

Yellow Robe and Gohl had a cadre of supporters at the Carlisle Indian School, where the student newspaper kept up a steady criticism of the Wild West shows and their dances. The newspaper first presented its position in an 1888 story that announced with a not-so-subtle hint of self-satisfaction that "the Wild West Show is at the Gentlemen's Driving Park, Phila. The Civilized East Show is at the Indian Training School, Carlisle." The August 6, 1897, edition of the *Indian Helper* reported that a group of Carlisle students had been allowed to see Buffalo Bill's show in the hope "that those who should witness the disgraceful exhibition of the so-called savagery of their kin, would have intelligence enough to see that the whole thing is only a bold scheme to get money out of portraying in an exaggerated and distorted manner the lowest and most degraded side of the Indian nature. . . . it is only the SAVAGE in the Indian that a certain ignorant, excitable element of society pays fifty cents and a dollar a seat to see. Carlisle tries to bury the SAVAGE that the MAN in the Indian may be seen."[13]

In the same year, the paper mocked Iron Tail, a Sioux performer with Cody's show who came to Carlisle to visit his son. Iron Tail was "a perfect picture of ignorance and superstition!" because "he was paid to dress that way. . . . Buffalo Bill pays him 20, 30, or possibly 50 dollars a month . . . to remain Indian. . . . He pays him to dance the wildest, most blood-thirsty savage dance known. He pays him…to rob stage coaches and to race on horseback around the track shouting the war-whoop, shooting and yelling till the peoples' hair stands on end." His participation in the show kept Iron Tail from recognizing the benefits of a civilized life, claimed the story, which went on to say, "He is not too old to learn. He could learn to speak English, read and write some and become a useful citizen if he were properly encouraged." Hope was on the horizon in 1911 when the paper approvingly noted that "the avowed intention of the American Indian Association to throw the weight of its influence against the luring away and employment of reservation Indians by the Wild West shows and circuses IS encouraging and should have the approval of right-thinking men."[14]

Federal Indian policy announcements about the dance question were wondrously unambiguous. Henry Teller's scathing remark that "the continuance of the old heathenish dances" was single-handedly responsible for much of the "debauchery, diabolism, and savagery of the worst state of the Indian race," for example, pretty much summed up an entire generation's opinion.[15] But ridding the Indian world of the dances that bureaucrats charged with causing debauchery, diabolism, and savagery proved a more daunting task than Teller and his legions of reformers had figured on. A decade later, the same outraged complaints typified official reports and begged questions about the effectiveness of the government's campaign, or for that matter, the government's adherence to policies. After visiting the government's Indian exhibit at Chicago's 1893 Columbian Exposition, for example, Superintendent of Indian Schools Daniel Dorchester declared it an affront to civilized values. Far from being an "educational" exhibit, he roared, the display was "a celebration of the most degraded phases of the old Indian life." Dorchester thought the entire exhibit appalling what with its display cases of stone-age weapons and tools, but it was a dance demonstration put on for an eager and appreciative crowd that completely mortified him. It was a "disgraceful affair," he said, fueled by whiskey, arranged by avaricious whites of questionable tastes, and performed by Indians who with their "paint, feathers, buckskin, bells, breechclout, and other toggery, revive and exhibit the quondam degradation of the tribes."[16]

Such displays, wrote Dorchester, were "diametrically opposed to all efforts to [Indians'] education and true elevation, . . . disinclines them to settle down to labor, and dooms them to the life of vagabonds." That white people paid to see the dance was a sin only slightly less serious than the dance itself, for Dorchester reminded readers that there was more at stake than the nickels and dimes given by ignorant spectators to the Indians. The fare was not only detrimental to Indians, he observed, it corrupted whites as well. Women were reported to have fainted at the sight of the "Indian torture dance," at which others — gasp — had applauded. It was bad enough that Buffalo Bill had set up shop right next door to the fair with his daily shows featuring all manner of wild Indians, but Dorchester had seen an officially sanctioned government exhibit that was no better, in his opinion, than Cody's blood and thunder. What sort of message, he pleaded, was all of this sending? Dances carefully staged "within proper limitations could be reasonably tolerated . . . in the interest of historical and ethnological inquiries," Dorchester wrote, but "naked, painted, bedecked Indians in scalp and war dances" were too much. "And this at the end of the nineteenth Christian century," he thundered, "in a Christian America, in a Christian city, with a full corps of strong policemen, as an entertainment at our great Columbian Exposition, for 5,000 at least nominally Christian people . . . was not the city of Chicago able to prevent so diabolical a spectacle? . . . Was not the management of the World's Fair able to prevent such an infamy?"[17]

How did things get to the point where official policy could be more or less ignored, crowds would pay good money to see dancing, and some Indians could make a living by being, well, Indians? One of the most important factors was the ambivalence of official policy. On the one hand, policymakers insisted ad nauseam that Indians must earn their living by the sweat of their brow — preferably as agriculturists. On the other hand, the same officials regularly permitted dances for scientific or ethnologic purposes, or for what they hoped were sanitized, meaningless social events. Moreover, because the dance bans were never enacted as federal or state laws, officials lacked statutory authority to prevent Indians from hiring themselves out as performers. As a result, officials routinely allowed dances and approved employment in shows and exhibitions, as long as promoters agreed to take care of their employees and participants promised to forswear torture, sexually explicit behavior, and the wanton giving away of property.

Policymakers sent mixed messages, moreover, when they solicited shows and displays for official exhibits. In 1876, for example, Commissioner of Indian Affairs Edward P. Smith requested displays for the nation's centennial celebration that would illustrate "the native condition and habits, recent or past, of the American Aborigines." It was the "intention of the Government to have everything peculiarly American represented," he wrote, adding "a marked deficiency would exist were the characteristic features in the life, habits, and history of the North American Indian omitted." In 1893, the dancing Indians at the Columbian Exposition that had sent Daniel Dorchester into paroxysms were part of the government's own "educational" exhibit. Five years later, an official memo for the Omaha Exposition stipulated, "it is desirable, of course, that the primitive habits and customs of the tribes should be faithfully and fully portrayed." And in 1905, Theodore Roosevelt's inauguration committee invited the Comanche Quanah Parker to ride in the inaugural parade, but only if he came "fully equipped with Indian clothing as gorgeous as possible in its make-up and complete in its representation of the old Indian dress."[18]

By supplying Indian performers to these exhibits, government officials were helping to whet the public's appetite for a particular image of Indians. The perceived primitivism of Indians was especially provocative, and never more so than when they donned dance clothes. In a 1905 letter to the Kiowa and Comanche agency, a man named H. A. Hall from Comanche, Indian Territory, requested a group of dancers for that town's annual carnival because they would be "the best drawing card we have." Of course, promoters like Cody had already seen the promise of showcasing Indian performers, and had aggressively capitalized on it. The appeal of Plains imagery was especially strong, and promoters paid top dollar to performers who could act the part of the Western Indians who were synonymous with the nation's frontier history. An early 1880s handbill for a show calling itself "Great Extra Attractions," for example, promised "forty wild Indians dressed in buckskin suits, with war paint and feathers just as they are seen on the Western Plains, under a strong military guard." The show featured a lacrosse game "almost as exciting as a battle: the frantic leap, the whoop, the agile bound, the savage assault, the screaming of the squaws, the blows, the painted and bleeding players, and the wild, desperate and savage fight for the ball is a scene that savage life alone can furnish. These Indians (40 in all including Squaws and Papooses) are genuine Western Indians." In a letter to the Quapaw agent seeking permission to hire Indians from that agency, the show's proprietor wrote, "I can get all of the Indians I want in Canada but I had rather have them from the *West*."[19]

And it wasn't only shows and exhibitions that were whetting the public's appetite; in the United States, the growing interest in Indians was apparent in everything from National Park programs to the Boy Scouts to mass culture. Park officials at Yosemite, for example, created "Indian Field Days" in 1916 ostensibly to "revive and maintain [the] interest of Indians in their own games and industries." In reality, it was a carefully choreographed tourist show that Mark David Spence says "often degenerated into little more than an excuse for tourists and park officials to pose in buckskin and feathered headdress." In a rare reversal of standards, women were better paid than men ($2.50 for women, $1.00 for men per show), and there were $25 prizes for the "Best Indian Warrior Costume" and "Best Indian Squaw Costume." At Mesa Verde, visitors in the

1920s flocked to exhibitions of Navajos who sang and danced, while Glacier and Yellowstone eagerly hired "some good type Indians. . . . [who] have good costumes, put on a good show, and live in peace and harmony." And in an enterprise worthy of Cody himself, the Eastern Band of the Cherokees and the Great Smokie Mountains National Park collaborated in the early 1930s on a short-lived show called "Spirit of the Great Smokies."[20]

An especially exoticized version of Indians, complete with dance pageants and an appeal to primitivist values, appeared in 1915 when two Boy Scout leaders from Philadelphia created the Order of the Arrow as an honor society to recognize outstanding service by youth and adult Scouts. Within a decade it had spread across the country; by 1936 sixty "lodges" were introducing young boys to highly stylized and exoticized Indian imagery through a program "built around Indian symbolism in the Lenape tongue."[21] The Order of the Arrow continues to flourish today, with rituals rooted in the romantic appeal of Indians as its stock-in-trade. Tellingly, "authentic" Indian dances remain one of its most cherished traditions, and Scouting groups like the Koshare Indian Dancers of Pueblo, Colorado, spread Scouting's version of the gospel to groups across the country every year.

Professional anthropologists and ethnologists, of course, were as interested as the general public in Indian culture and were willing to pay for the same dramatic displays that thrilled audiences. Indian agents thought the arrangement ridiculous. A case in point occurred in 1903 when John Seger, a long-time employee of the Cheyenne-Arapaho Agency, pilloried George Dorsey, the curator of anthropology at Chicago's Field-Columbian Museum, and James Mooney, of the Bureau of American Ethnology, for paying Cheyennes in Oklahoma to perform a Sun Dance complete with the "torture" that simultaneously titillated and appalled audiences. Seger, an ardent opponent of dancing, reported that he encountered Dorsey, Mooney, and a photographer at a Cheyenne encampment where they were busily photographing dancers engaged in old-time rituals. A man named Red Leggings obliged them, but Seger condemned the Indian for play-acting, derided the scientists as fools, and declared "it was very plain to me that the torture had been paid for." Seger, who had attended Cheyenne Sun Dances two decades earlier and thought himself something of an expert on the matter, claimed, "There is as much difference then and now . . . as between day and night. The old way . . . was the real thing. The torture I saw was a fake . . . and I think on the whole he had well earned his fifteen dollars that was reported to have been paid."[22] But if respectable scientists paid Indians to dance, why shouldn't audiences do the same?

As Black Elk, Kills Enemy Alone, Rocky Bear, and Black Heart affirmed, making a living by dancing seemed a legitimate enterprise to them and to their appreciative audiences as well. If it contradicted the government's notion of proper living, it nonetheless provided gainful employment and experience in the wider world, something that reformers, entrepreneurs, and Indians alike valued. Moreover, as most observers knew, the government's reservation-based assimilation program was collapsing. Hard-pressed and cash-starved, Indians like those at the Cheyenne and Arapaho Reservation in western Oklahoma, who bitterly reminded William Freer in 1912 that their lease monies had not been paid in months, believed dancing for money made complete sense. Young Bear told Freer, "I come like a person carrying two crying babies. It is six months since I have had money. . . . We understand that the Government wants us to follow the white man's way. We must have money to work with." A man named Hail observed that "we try to do what the Commissioner wants us to do in the direction of farming, and we ought to have our money." Another man named Ute tersely noted, "A man without a horse cannot plow."[23]

John W. Troutman's work reveals that similar conditions and responses prevailed across the Plains. Charges that dancing interrupted farm work were met with derision at the Crow Agency in 1923, where a group of twenty-three Indians sent a stinging rebuke to Commissioner of Indian Affairs Charles Burke. Noting that grasshoppers had destroyed their crops, that they lacked irrigation systems, that wheat and oats were unprofitable, and that government bureaucrats "did not give us intelligent help," the group suggested that in light of the government's failure to adequately fund or competently administer its own programs, it "would be better to have no land at all."[24] It is difficult to imagine that similar complaints by whites would not have prompted action from government authorities. And surely, whites were never banned from having square dances and the like at harvest festivals, county fairs, and church bazaars.

Economic opportunities for Indians steadily eroded after the 1890s, when federal officials closed schools, scaled back treaty-mandated annuities, and repeatedly amended the 1887 Dawes Act, leaving a majority of Indians landless. The results were catastrophic. In 1928, the Meriam Report revealed that per capita annual income of Indians was $100–$200, compared to a national average of nearly $1,350. With fewer and fewer alternatives, it is not surprising that some Indians regarded the shows as a way out of their dilemma. "Some may have been attracted by the decent wages Buffalo Bill paid that could be sent home or used to purchase luxuries—even necessities—no reservation Indian could afford," points out Napier. At Wisconsin's Grand Rapids Agency, the agent reported in 1924 that Indians "were making more money dancing for whites in local Pow-wows than they possibly could in farming and stock raising because of the low price of farm commodities; nevertheless he vowed to continue to pressure the Indians to stay at home, tending fields that brought virtually no returns." Moreover, as Moses notes, once the Bureau of Indian Affairs required contracts, bonds, and "fair and reasonable" wages, dancers in the larger shows could command salaries of between $25 and $90 a month; those at the top end of the pay scale earned about two-thirds of an agent's salary. "Few Indians who took out allotments and farmed the land or ran livestock," writes Moses, "could boast of comparable incomes."[25] Reformers routinely denounced Show Indians as being of the lowest sort; but was being scorned really worse than sitting out another South Dakota winter eating spoiled beef?

For their part, promoters claimed that they could simultaneously make money, entertain the public, and, they solemnly promised, expose Indians to a new way of life as assimilated citizens. In 1907, for example, J. B. Dickinson, wrote agitatedly to the Pawnee agent who had refused to sanction a dance exhibition that Dickinson insisted would introduce Indians to the wonders of modern life. If Dickinson made a little money in the bargain, well, so much the better, but he assured the agent that he was motivated by a higher purpose. "It is quite possible that you do not fully understand the nature and intent of the grand celebration," he wrote. "We are simply trying to have an ideal Indian meeting, which will no doubt result in bringing together an immense crowd of friendly fullbloods in order that they smoke the pipe of peace and discuss ways and means of more fully taking up the 'white man's burden,' or in other words become better able to cope with modern civilization and begin the process of real progress and development." And if that wasn't good enough, Dickinson took the high ground: "To be frank with you . . . it is our aim to collect a goodly number of Indians for the week . . . for the benefit of several thousand visitors . . . and by this means dispel eroneous [sic] ideas they may entertain about the Indians of this country." Dickinson's philanthropic musings notwithstanding, the agent remained unpersuaded.[26]

In the most famous example of the argument that employment with the shows was the most effective brand of assimilation, Cody assured government officials that Indians in his shows were well treated, fairly paid, and were learning all the ins and outs of civilized life. During their stay in New York City in the winter of 1886–1887, for example, he informed federal authorities that his Indian employees attended church twice each Sunday for two months, had visited city hall, a newspaper office, Central Park, Bellevue Hospital, and "all the principle places of legitimate public entertainment in New York. . . . I know from personal knowledge that these Indians are acquiring benefits in their Eastern life." And as Cody liked to remind his detractors, Indians with his show were earning good money, paying their own way, and learning to live like whites. To critics who charged that Indian performers were being duped by whites who shortchanged them, Nate Salisbury (Cody's right-hand man) pointedly noted in

1891 that in his estimation performers with the Wild West Show knew "the value of a dollar quite as well as a white man."[27]

At the local level, and especially in the small fairs and town celebrations where most of the performers found their work, dancing for pay might not bring exposure to "Eastern life" (an altogether good thing, in some peoples' opinion), but it did bring wages, however modest, the chance to travel, an opportunity to escape the strictures of reservation life, and the opportunity to present their cultures in ways that Indians found satisfying. Typical of the promoters was a man named C. Thornburg who recruited Kiowas, Comanches, and Apaches in 1894 for a show that would tour the "smaller places and public in general [that] have not had the opportunity of studying the Red Man as he was." Thornburg promised happy results for Indians and audiences alike; performers would get a taste of life outside the reservations, and whites "would be both interested and instructed." Tellingly, Thornburg added, "Of course we don't claim to be impelled wholly by motives of philanthropy actuated by a desire to perpetuate the history of the West. . . . We expect to make money."[28]

The payoff for working in many of the shows and government-sponsored exhibits was a combination of room, board, and expenses, something that appealed to many performers given the chronically unreliable distribution of annuities and rations at the nation's Indian agencies. A typical offer reached the Cheyenne and Arapaho Reservation in 1905 from the Cedar Point Pleasure Resort Company of Sandusky, Ohio. Seeking Cheyennes and Comanches as "an educational exhibit," their letter made no mention of pay, but the Ohioans promised "excellent quarters for the Indians . . . the best of care . . . expenses to and from their home . . . and board and lodging." The agent turned them down on the grounds that there were "no Indians who could be spared without detriment to their interests." Two years later, showman Zack Mulhall offered expense money and transportation to Comanches willing to join a bizarre combination of automobile races and Wild West shows (horses and autos to be supplied at no extra cost to the performers!).[29]

Some communities planned ahead, as when W. B. Garnett informed the Kiowa and Comanche agent in 1901 that Tonkawa's citizens had "subscribed . . . quite a little fund" to sponsor an all-Indian "entertainment." Hoping for "quite a company of the Apache Indians," the town's Fair Association promised "to care for them, to feed them well, and furnish pasture for their ponies." Moreover, Garnett's colleague, G. C. Brewer, assured agency officials "the Indians are to receive the gate receipts that will be divided between those that take part." Other communities and promoters wrote to ascertain the going rates, as when M. F. Wren inquired in 1905 as to the chances of hiring Cheyenne and Arapaho dancers for his town's fair: "What it would cost us if they can come? We are willing to do the best we can by them." A 1910 request from Thomas, Oklahoma, promised a "high moreal [*sic*] tone" complete with plans to "advertise this extensively and make it a paying proposition to both the Indians and ourselves." In the same year, the Weatherford Commercial Club guaranteed $750 for expenses and premiums for Indian performers at the town's fair, "it being understood that the agent will take proceeds of the sale of tickets to Indians." Moreover, in return for a "free Indian moon dance in front of the Grandstand . . . with camp fires," the dancers could charge and keep an admission fee of fifteen cents for all other dance demonstrations.[30]

Government exhibits typically did not include outright payment on the grounds that dancing for wages sent the wrong kind of message. Instead, policymakers believed that expenses and the chance to see the world were ample rewards. When Commissioner of Indian Affairs William A. Jones recruited performers in 1898 for the Trans-Mississippi and International Exposition in Omaha, for example, he declined to offer wages, and pointed out that in addition to the thrill of being "a most interesting part" of the government's exhibit, performers would be "well cared for" by virtue of having their transportation and living costs covered. Samuel McCowan made the same argument when he solicited artisans, craft workers, and performers for the government exhibit at the 1904 St. Louis World's Fair. Strapped for expenses himself, McCowan confidently predicted to one correspondent that "after I bring them here [Chilocco School in north-central Oklahoma], pay their expenses, take them to St. Louis and return them, it ought to be compensation enough." Not everyone agreed with that sentiment, and at least one group negotiated for wages as well as expenses. Writing from Florida, the Reverend Henry Gibbs informed McCowan that while it might be "a grand thing" for a group of Seminoles to join the exhibit, "nothing but large financial inducements would get them to go so far as St. Louis. And whether their part of the attraction would be a paying one . . . is hard for me to tell." McCowan stood his ground, agreeing to pay only travel expenses plus room and board for sixty days. Interestingly, he paid cash wages to Indian carpenters, who "have families . . . and derive their support largely from their trade." Could the same not be said of the dancers?[31]

While they sanctioned participation in all kinds of shows and exhibits, authorities tried to be mindful of what they deemed inappropriate demonstrations, and on occasion they drew the line. It was one thing to let Cody or the Millers hire Indians, but it was another thing altogether to give every would-be performer or promoter free reign. When one Cheyenne man produced a contract for five hundred Indians to perform at a 1923 July 4 show in Ft. Reno, Oklahoma, for example, officials refused to sanction the deal despite promises by the townspeople of "a good feed and half the gate receipts, providing they give a dance in their native costume." The agent's reply was brief and to the point: "Nothing doing."[32]

Yet, as every agent knew, because the federal dance bans lacked statutory authority, officials could not always prevent Indians from dancing for money. As long as they did not break the law, Indians could not be stopped from dancing. This is not to say that agents could not, or did not, forcibly prevent dances. They could, and did, withhold rations and annuities from dancers, hold sponsors on one charge or another, and impose arbitrary ground rules that they hoped would make dancing more trouble than it was worth. When the Comanche County Fair Association entered into negotiations with a group of Arapaho performers in 1909, agent Charles Shell expressed his disappointment that "dissolute Indians will persist in attending the gatherings . . . and that white people of questionable character will encourage them to do those things which retard their advancement and ruins them physically." But he also admitted that because they were "free and independent citizens, they cannot be prevented from going if they so desire," a fact underscored by the 1879 Standing Bear decision that left Indians free from "the arbitrary control of the Indian Bureau and allowed all the rights and immunities of a free man." And as Cody reminded government officials in 1887, "I claim that these Indians, as Americans, have a perfect right to hire their services where they please. They earn a good salary here."[33]

A less problematic way to discourage dancing for pay was to provide attractive substitutes. This was a typical tactic at the annual agency fairs that were designed to introduce Indians to commerce, industry, and individualism, and to discourage dancing and other traditional pursuits. Because he believed "Indians and the public should be made to realize that these old customs retard the onward march of civilization," Commissioner Cato Sells in 1914 prohibited "old-time dances" at the fairs.[34] Yet even as officials made such pronouncements, they also permitted some dancing as long as participants observed restrictions on when dances could be held, what dances could be performed, and who could attend. How federal authorities could realistically hope to end dancing by embracing contradictory positions is unclear.

Officials also discouraged dancing by making sure that it didn't pay as well as other fair events. At the 1900 Cheyenne and Arapaho fair, for example, premiums for horse races, foot races, and athletic games ($558), band concert expenses ($244.57), and contests ($843.75, which included prizes for the fattest baby, best behaved baby, and fattest baby under one year of age) came to $1,088.32. The premiums paid to Indians who put on dances came to $68. Of the fair's total disbursements of $3,834.04, money for dancing constituted only 1.75 percent. A decade later, premiums at the same fair showed a similar trend against traditional crafts and dances. First place in the tug-of-war brought $20, and the winner of the mule race pocketed $10. The best pen of ducks was worth $3, the winning pound of country lard was good for $1, and the best loaf cake earned a coffee pot. The oldest Indian woman took home a $5 gold piece, and the prettiest baby received an "Indian robe" valued at $6.00. Meanwhile, the best pair of moccasins brought $1, the best pipe $2.[35]

The lure of a payoff for the best jelly and tastiest light bread notwithstanding, dancing remained as popular as ever, and white audiences flocked to see the shows. In 1902, a Wichita *Eagle* story about a dance performance by two hundred Cheyennes ran under a headline announcing "White Men Participated: Indian War Dance at Elk City Was a New Feature." Agency officials subsequently denounced the event as an advertising scheme concocted by local merchants, but readers no doubt agreed that "a war dance wherein the white man steps the light fantastic is a new one. A large crowd paid their two-bits admission and were well entertained. . . . The performance closed with a dance in which the white man had the privilege of dancing with a squaw by paying a dime. Several tried the game."[36] Daniel Dorchester would have been mortified; in 1893 at Chicago, the audience had merely observed the dances, but now they were actually participating, and paying for the privilege to boot.

It also didn't help matters that well-known Indians joined shows and became a public relations and advertising bonanza that promoters eagerly exploited. As Cody confided to William F. "Doc" Carver in 1883, "I am going to try hard to get old 'Sitting Bull' . . . if we can manage to get him our ever lasting fortune is made." One year later an agent wrote to a friend that where Sitting Bull's show career was concerned, "there is money to be made from this if properly managed." In fact, Sitting Bull signed on with Cody in June 1885 and quickly became one of the show's most notable attractions, and one of its best paid Indian performers. Joy Kasson notes that Sitting Bull was guaranteed a salary of $50 a week with two weeks' wages in advance, a $125 bonus, and free transportation to and from the show. He demanded a retinue of five men at $25 a month, three women at $15 a month, and an interpreter of his choosing at $60 a month. Sitting Bull also amassed a considerable pile of cash by controlling the rights to his autograph and photo, mementos which Robert Utley reports he was selling for $1.50–$2.00 each by 1883. In all, Sitting Bull did remarkably well. "Within only four months," writes Kasson, "Sitting Bull would earn nearly half the annual salary of an Indian agent and two-thirds the annual salary of an agency physician."[37]

Other notables followed suit, including Geronimo, who informed his agent that he would be happy to go to the St. Louis World's Fair in 1903 as part of the government's Indian exhibition, but not at the $15 per month that Samuel McCowan was offering. "He was paid $45.00 per month at the Buffalo Exposition (Pan American)," wrote his representative, and expected to receive at least that much to go to St. Louis.[38] Hoping to capitalize on an association with America's best-known warrior, the United States Fidelity and Guaranty Company of Baltimore, Maryland, also offered to sponsor Geronimo's appearances at St. Louis. The firm's representative in Lawton, Oklahoma Territory, commented somewhat breathlessly that the Apache had "between eighty-five and one hundred white scalps to the credit of his savagery; also a vest made of the hair of the whites whom he has killed." This claim was absolute nonsense, of course, but who wouldn't pay to see Geronimo? The firm also made a pitch to sponsor the Comanche Quanah Parker as well, calling him "unquestionably the finest specimen of the red men in the great Southwest . . . [he] embodies all that we saw pictured in the history read in our school days."[39]

Promoters knew a good thing when they saw it, and Geronimo was in high demand for even the most absurd spectacles. In 1905, for example, the Miller brothers offered $1,000 in cash to anyone willing to be scalped by Geronimo as part of "The Buffalo Chase," a gala celebration on the 101 Ranch grounds which the Millers hoped would draw several thousand spectators. Rumor had it that one man agreed to try it, but he was nowhere in sight at the appointed moment. Geronimo's opinion of the stunt (and his compensation) went unrecorded.[40]

The most lucrative opportunities came from the larger shows that flourished between 1880 and the First World War. With nearly one hundred shows on the road every year, the opportunities for employment were generally good, and shows had little trouble filling their needs. The giants of the business (Cody and the Millers, for example) held auditions on reservations that attracted large numbers of aspiring performers in search of a contract and cash bonuses for the best dancers with the fanciest outfits. Sarah Blackstone writes that "the pay was reasonable for famous chiefs (up to $75 a month plus picture and autograph sales), but most of the others received less than the average national wage of $20 a week. A common wage was $25 a month."[41]

As Blackstone suggests, pay for performers varied widely even after the Bureau of Indian Affairs required individual contracts, scrutinized pay scales, and demanded that show owners post a cash bond when they hired Indians. On the lower end of the pay scale were promoters like W. A. Husted, who offered $12.50 a month plus room and board in 1896 for Kiowas and Comanches willing to join a "regular series of dancing and ball playing." Generally speaking, full-time adult employees could expect to earn roughly a dollar a day, plus food, lodging, and rudimentary medical care. In 1903, D. Bigman reported that Indian performers with the Kennedy Brothers Indian Congress, Wild West, and Hippodrome Show were earning $5 a week. Bigman received $7 dollars a week as interpreter, and he approvingly reported that the show's owners "give us anything we need." In 1906, salaries for Indians with the 101 ranged from $5 a week for men to $4 a week for women. Three years later, the rates went from $1 a week for children to $7 a week for grown men. In 1924, the 101's yearly round-up advertised that one thousand Indians would put on sports and native ceremonies. Admission was one dollar, and the Ponca agent reported that "the Indians who participated in the 101 Rodeo were paid about $3.00 a day for thirty minutes of work and also had their rations furnished them."[42]

Federal regulations obliged owners to cover travel, food, and medical costs, but most shows required dancers to provide their own show clothes. During most of its history, for example, the 101 required performers to provide "one set of Indian clothes, head dress, moccasins, etc." And in 1910, Joe Miller specified that Indian men were to be "as nearly as possible long-haired or have good wigs and good costumes." Those who could meet the requirements, he promised, would earn "five dollars a week as 'regular Indians.' " In some cases the pay was prorated according to the work schedule. In 1914, for example, the proprietors of the Days of '49 Wild West Show had a sliding pay scale: $2 a day while the show was being organized, and $5 a day plus transportation and meals when the show was in production.[43]

Comments from Indians working in the shows suggest a wide variety of experiences, many of them positive, some glowing. Luther Standing Bear wrote that Cody's show provided him, his wife, and newborn daughter with a standard of living that they could never have earned at home on the reservation. Standing Bear, a Carlisle graduate, later remembered that the decision to put his newborn daughter on display during a 1902 tour in England "was a great drawing card for the show. . . . The work was very light for my wife, and as for the baby, before she was twenty-four hours old she was making more money than my wife and I together." Others expressed similar appreciation for the chance to work in the shows. "I know if I was at home I would not do anything," admitted Bigman in 1903, "because there is no work for me to do." He deemed life with the Kennedy Brothers Indian Congress, Wild West, and Hippodrome ("the most reliable combination on earth," boasted its letterhead) was just fine. They were dancing twice a day and "doing well and making money." Julia Roy, a Ponca working for the 101 in 1914, wrote that "everything is . . . as pleasant as it needs to be or can be. Only the climate is a little bit colder than in Okla. [She was in New York City], but at the same time it is very nice to get out and travel a little bit and see something of the world."[44]

Richard Davis, a Cheyenne (and Carlisle graduate) who also worked for the 101, wrote Joe Miller in 1911 to tell him, "I have 8 farms, a good city home, and money in [the] Bank and we care for no one else only yourself and the other Miller boys and we would like to patronize your show this summer just for pleasure." Confessing that he and his friend Walter Battice, another long-time 101 employee, were anxious to get back into the shows, Davis informed Miller, "If you want two of your old boys that will stay with you write at once." Miller hired them right away but, as Moses notes, reduced their pay from forty to thirty dollars a month because the two were so overweight they couldn't sit their ponies very well. James Pulliam, an Oglala with the 101, informed Pine Ridge agent Ernest Jermark in 1929 that "I like it fine here" (he was in Ogdensburg, New York). "If I had to pay for what I have seen so far, I would be broke for the rest of my life." Along with four associates from Pine Ridge, Pulliam saved enough money from the show to buy a new Model A Ford, which they drove home to South Dakota once the tour ended.[45]

Elmer Sugar Brown, an Oto-Missouria who danced as a young child with the 101 Ranch Wild West Show and the Ringling Brothers, Barnum and Bailey Circus in the 1930s, as well as with his family's "Sugar Brown Dance Troupe," recalled that life in the shows had its ups and downs. "Everytime we needed money, we'd go over to the 101 and break broncs. Pay was $2 or $3 dollars a horse — depended on how bad the horse was. But when some of our guys got hurt, we asked for more money. And we made more money dancing anyway — $100 a week sometimes." Sugar Brown parlayed his circus experience into minor roles in a number of Hollywood films, including *Drums along the Mohawk,* with Boris Karloff, and *Distant Drums,* with Gary Cooper, and told me that films paid better than almost any other kind of employment. Where wages were concerned, the 101 Ranch Wild West Show was "okay, but we did even better in front of the movie cameras — they'd pay you a whole lot for that."[46]

When he was working for the Ringling Brothers and other circuses, Sugar Brown and his siblings performed in the circus acts during the day (where he picked up some of the flips and acrobatic moves for which he would later gain renown on the powwow circuit); in the evening, the family's dance troupe performed shows in the center ring under the circus big top. Like other Show Indians, he fondly recalled traveling across the United States, and had especially strong memories of traveling abroad. "We went to all of the big American towns," he said, and also to Cuba and England, where as a ten-year-old he once gave a solo dance performance for the queen. "One of the guards came and got me and said 'the queen wants you to dance for her.' Boy those people really liked it. There would be signs up all over that said 'Come out and see the Wild Indians.' We'd do the circus stuff and then race horses in the hippodromes (and they just *loved* me because I'd really go fast), and then we'd give dance shows with round dances, two-steps, fast war dancing — all of the things you see on the powwow trail today. It was really a lot of fun."[47]

While the money was better than what many of them could have earned leasing land or farming, it was much less than what the show's non-Indian performers received. While regular arena performers, including some of the more experienced Indians, typically earned between $35 and $50 a month, non-Indian headliners like Buck Taylor could expect to get as much as $200 a month. Superstars could count on much more, as when prize fighter and Great White Hope Jess Willard signed with the Miller brothers in 1915 to put on five months of boxing shows for a staggering $100,000. (The deal also included a private railcar, chauffeur, automobile, chef, and porter.) If white cowboys didn't do as well as Willard, they nonetheless earned better wages than their Indian counterparts. When Indian dancers were taking home $5 a week in 1915, experienced horsemen were earning $7.50 a day breaking horses. The gap between pay for men and women was also striking. Writing of Cody's show, Moses says that well into the 1890s Indian women "received the same considerations for medical care, food, and clothing as their husbands," but on average earned "ten, and occasionally fifteen, dollars a month (a little less than half the pay of an arena performer)." Wages did not rise significantly during the three or four decades in which the shows were popular. Indeed, one recruiter was paying wages in 1906 that Cody had offered in the 1880s.[48]

It was also true that government regulations could not always protect performers from the predatory actions of promoters like W. H. Barten, a self-styled talent agent for Wild West shows with a penchant for self-reward that was boundless. Between 1906 and 1908, Barten secured dancers for the Miller brothers with contracts that required Indians to surrender most of their pay to him as a crude rebate. One man signed on for $5 a week, for example, but by the terms of his contract had to return $4 to Barten. The performer's wife received $2.50 a week, but had to return $1.50. Moreover, Barten demanded payment for his services before the shows paid the Indians, a tactic that led owners to garnish ten percent of their Indian performers' wages as a service charge to settle their agreement with Barten. Partly to protect his employees from the likes of people like Barten, after 1885 Cody enforced a provision known as the "hold back" whereby his performers were paid as much as a third of their wages after they returned home. The practice also muted criticisms that performers were wasting their money and ignoring their relatives' needs.[49]

Sometimes performers and their families also suffered unanticipated financial setbacks, as when the Millers pressed a claim for expenses associated with the death of one of their Indian employees (a young boy) during a 1907 tour. "We had his body embalmed and paid his expressage back to the Agency . . . which was $180. As he no doubt leaves an estate I presume this amount can be reimbursed to us." Not all show owners were that callous. When one of Cody's Indian performers died of tetanus in 1891, the showman promptly sent the widow $500 plus the deceased man's back wages of $120, and agreed to pay the woman $25 a month for the rest of her life.[50] It is interesting to note that the 101's 1909 show profits were $47,000; by 1915 they were $200,000. In 1910, Gordon "Pawnee Bill" Lillie's show did so well that he spent $75,000 building and another $100,000 furnishing a home on his ranch in Oklahoma. Anxious to establish his reputation as a philanthropist (and not a money-grubbing entertainer), he also spent $55,000 to build a schoolhouse. Cody took in one million dollars in 1885, and he once told his brother that the show was making so much money that he was running with the likes of the Rothschilds.[51]

Just how high a standard of living the dancers enjoyed is difficult to assess. One enthusiastic writer reported in 1929 that performers with the 101 "are just like ball players in spring training. Sleeps and eats are to be had for light work. No pay until they play the schedule. But if admission is charged they split the gate. . . . at a recent rehearsal the gate provided 26 performers with $5 each and left $20." Other accounts suggest that it was hardly "light work," and that the money wasn't always as good as $5 a day. Some performers lived hand-to-mouth on wages that kept them barely afloat. In 1907, a performer named High Chief implored Charles Shell at the Cheyenne and Arapaho Reservation to forward lease payments as soon as possible. "I get $8 per week," he noted, "my wife $3 and children $2 to $1 per week . . . ," but it wasn't enough to provide for his family's needs. Lillard High Chief, a performer with the 101 on tour in Suffolk, Virginia, during 1914 (apparently not the same High Chief mentioned above), pleaded for assistance on the grounds that "I am sick awful bad and I would like to get my mother's leace [sic] money so that I could go back their [sic] right away. The wild horse throw me of [sic] and [I] got hurt bad and [the show] didn't pay me for it, please send me the money, I need it bad." The agent wired $50 immediately. Others were not so lucky. In 1915, officials at the Cheyenne and Arapaho Reservation refused a request for lease funds because they did not believe that the couple requesting the payment actually needed it. "He is getting $25 a month . . . and his wife $12.50 and all their expenses," went the explanation from the agency farmer, "so I see no reason why he should need this money and I think it would be a good idea . . . to save this twenty dollars a month until he comes home as he would probably spend it all if it was sent to him."[52]

And all too often performers were abandoned without pay. A group of fifteen was stranded in San Antonio in 1910 when their show's proprietor "left the whole bunch of us Indians here. . . . If we had [a] little money it would not be so bad, but the trouble of it is he still owes us for more than a month's wages." In an urgent appeal to the Cheyenne and Arapaho agent, the writer pleaded that "the majority of these . . . are women folks, that is what makes it impossible to work our way home." Despite a letter from a San Antonian describing the group as "destitute," the agent replied that because more than half of the group had been given the privilege of managing their affairs some years prior, they "should go to work and earn sufficient money to bring themselves home." Apparently San Antonio was a poor place indeed for performers to visit. Thirteen years later to the month and day, the city's International Fair Association informed the same agency that it had "sixteen Indians left on our hands . . . what will be done with them?"[53]

Between 1880 and 1930, show dancing was an economically significant enterprise for many Indian people. However, working as a performer was complicated by the tensions that arose between dancers who took pay as performers and audiences who thought of shows as merely entertainment to be purchased; working as a performer was not simply good or bad, not entirely enjoyable or entirely distasteful. Obviously, life as a Show Indian was not always what aspiring performers had hoped for. They were racially marginalized, the overwhelming majority of the dancers were paid less than their non-Indian coworkers, and as with the groups abandoned in San Antonio, they followed an avocation in which the gap between security and desperation was often narrow indeed. Their wages stagnated over time, and as Anne M. Butler and L. G. Moses observe, twentieth century capitalism did not do much to broaden their economic opportunities. Still, many of them earned a living in which they took pride and by which they could achieve a measure of financial gain, often by the only avenue open to them — as entertainers.[54]

The shows put money in the performers' pockets when the alternatives were limited and the chances of making it on their own at the reservations were stark. This is not to minimize the risks and the problems, only to suggest that we should seek to understand both the economic incentives and drawbacks of show dancing as complicated negotiations and decisions in which Indians and whites alike played pivotal roles. As Blackstone notes, there were many reasons to join a show, and many Indians "continued to tour principally because they could make a better living performing in the Wild West than they could on the reservation." Guy Dull Knife, Jr., recalled that his grandfather's decision to join the Wild West meant "a hard life in many ways . . . but at least it gave him something to do at a time when there wasn't a lot of options. It gave him something to do and it brought in some money that helped his family survive until things got better."[55] The Wild West, it seemed, touched dance culture on a number of levels.

In the end, we are left with owners like the Millers, who pinched an Indian family for burial expenses, and Cody, who promised to do as well by his Indian performers as he could, and did so in at least one case by providing for the needs of a widow. The hand-to-mouth life of Lillard High Chief, the young man whose injuries from being thrown off a horse forced him to plead for $50 of his mother's lease money, was set against the bounty that Richard David reaped as a Wild West performer. And Indians who went on strike because they objected to manual labor were joined by those like Henry Pahocscut, who wrote to tell the Kiowa and Comanche agent in 1906, "we are getting along very nicely with this show," and added that with the exception of three Comanches who left because the owner barred them from visiting the saloons, "we been having a good time."[56]

47TH ANNUAL TULSA POW WOW

AT TULSA'S MOHAWK PARK
JUNE 25, 26, 27, & 28, 1998

DANCE COMPETITION IN ALL CATEGORIES • DRUM CONTEST

 $25,000.00 PRIZE MONEY

HOST DRUMS		EMCEES	
STAR BLANKET	GRAYHORSE	SAMMY "TONEKEI" WHITE	BEULAH SUNRISE
Regina, Saskachewan, Can.	Tulsa, Oklahoma	Kiowa • Oklahoma	Pueblo/Navaho • Albq., N.M.

HEAD DANCERS		ARENA DIRECTORS	

HEAD DANCERS

Northern

CRAZY HORSE BISON	LISA EWOK/CLEVELAND
Cheyenne/Dakota	Cree
Regina, Saskatchewan, Can.	Whitebear, Saskatchewan, Can.

Southern

RALPH HAYMOND	JANESE LASLEY
Otoe	Sac & Fox/Osage
Pawnee, Oklahoma	Grayhorse, OK

Special Fancy Shawl Contest • $1,000.00 • Winner Take All
sponsored by outgoing Princess **LILA OSCEOLA**

ARENA DIRECTORS

REDCLOUD ANQUOE	CECIL NETOOSE
Kiowa • Tulsa, OK	Cree • Hobbema Alberta, Can.

1998 Princess
SKYLEEN CLASHIN • OSAGE & NAVAHO

HONORING KIOWA WWII VETERANS
GUS, GEORGE, DIXON, AND (KIA) LYNDRYTH PALMER

SPECIAL GUESTS
KIOWA GOURD CLAN • KIOWA BLACKLEGGINGS SOCIETY

FEATURED GUEST DANCERS
MESCALERO APACHE FIRE DANCERS

PLENTY OF GOOD CAMPING SPACES AVAILABLE, SECURITY ON GROUNDS AT ALL
TIMES. HOST HOTEL: RADISSON INN TULSA AIRPORT • 2201 NORTH 77th EAST AVE.

USE OF DRUGS, ALCOHOL, FIREARMS PROHIBITED AND STRICTLY ENFORCED. POW WOW AND PARK NOT RESPONSIBLE FOR ACCIDENTS.
PUBLIC INVITED • EVERYONE WELCOME!

SILVER HORN, FRANK RUSH, AND TSAITOKEY.

Frank Rush with Silver Horn and Tsaitokey, two Kiowa men who were frequent visitors to the Craterville powwow. No date, but from the late 1920s or early 1930s. (Denver Public Library, Western History Collection, photographer unknown, x-32436)

Horse racing at the 1926 Craterville Park powwow. (Oklahoma Historical Society)

Fancy war dancing contest, Craterville Park. Based on the long bustle trailers, and the use of extensive body coverings, this is probably from the early 1920s. (Denver Public Library. Western History Collection, photographer unknown, x-3261)

Kiowas in the parade, 1941 American Indian Exposition, Anadarko, Oklahoma. The women left to right are Augustine Campbell, Caroline Tsoodle, and Eva Lou Ware. (Tartoue Collection, Oklahoma Historical Society)

Kiowa War Mother's Dance, May 1947, Carnegie, Oklahoma. Note the singers sitting on benches, and women in the left foreground wearing War Mother's shawls. (Tartoue Collection, Oklahoma Historical Society)

Generations brought together by the sound of the drum at the Wichita Tribal Powwow, Anadarko, Oklahoma, 1995. (C. R. Cowen Collection, Oklahoma Historical Society)

Round dancing at the 1947 American Indian Exposition, Anadarko, Oklahoma. (C. R. Anthony Collection, Oklahoma Historical Society)

Three female dancers at a small dance in the early 1950s. (Courtesy of Shalah Rowlen)

1950 Memorial Day Powwow, Shawnee, Oklahoma. Tartoue Collection, Oklahoma Historical Society)

1950 Memorial Day Powwow, Shawnee, Oklahoma. (Tartoue Collection, Oklahoma Historical Society)

Fancy dance contest at the 1941 American Indian Exposition. Note the dancer in the middle with his legs kicked out and one arm extended to the ground. This is the sort of athleticism that came to characterize fancy dancing by mid-century. (Oklahoma Historical Society)

Friday Night Program

BAND CONCERT (Short)

SONG—Purple and Gold.

GIRLS' DRILLS

BOYS' DRILLS

Band—STAR SPANGLED BANNER.

Old Indian Dances

Dancing Contest Exhibition—The Eagle Dance will be presented by members of the Pottawatomie tribe from Mayetta, Kansas. This is considered the most beautiful of all Indian dances and is interpretative of the flight and rythm of action in the movements of the American eagle.

A Patriotic Soldier Dance will be presented by Indians. A large number of Osage women have been invited to appear in this dance. Other tribes will be invited to appear in interpretative dances which cannot be announced as this program goes to press.

No entertainment or program planned especially for Indians would be complete without some form of Indian Dancing Contest. As the Haskell Homecoming program has been formulated throughout with the sole intent of pleasing and entertaining our many Indian friends who are with us we too have included in a small way this Dancing Contest.

Dancing Contest

1, War Dancing Contest.

2. Old Man's Dance, (limited to Indians fifty years and over.)
   N. B.—The above two dances will be judged by chiefs of visiting tribes.

3. Fancy Dancing Contest.
   N.B.—The winner will be determined by applause received from the audience.

Song—AMERICA.

Advertisement that appeared in the Haskell Indian Leader *student newspaper announcing the famous 1926 Haskell Powwow where Gus McDonald won the world's championship in fancy dancing. (Courtesy of Sandy Rhoades)*

CHAPTER FIVE

"This is the first powwow circuit in the United States."

The Powwow Comes into View

As the experiences of Indians who danced with Wild West shows and in community dances, exhibitions, picnics, and fairs suggest, dancing survived despite repeated attempts to suppress it between the 1880s and the 1930s. There were losses, to be sure, and the price paid could be steep. But the fact of the matter is that the Kiowa O-ho-mah song that encouraged adherents to dance and be arrested rather than submit to government bans was emblematic of a larger movement across the region that kept dance alive and meaningful. As the twentieth century began, dancing not only survived, it flourished. As the century matured, new adaptations and revivals pointed the way toward the powwow as a cultural form that would come into its own by the 1930s and 1940s.

There were several strands of influence at work. As chapter one noted, the warrior society revivals and revitalizations that occurred in the late nineteenth and early twentieth centuries made dancing meaningful once again, or reinforced its continuing influence. The Kiowas, for example, held on to their O-ho-mah Society with remarkable energy, just as the Poncas maintained the Heluska. As Howard notes, moreover, when the Heluska shifted to a more religiously oriented occasion marked not by the retelling of war stories but by prayer, this adaptation was accepted as one that kept the dance rooted in old values. Other tribes revived dances, as in 1919 when a delegation of Poncas assisted the Comanches. William Collins, Sr., a Ponca who took part, recalled that his people "were invited to the Commanche [*sic*] tribe in 1919 to reorganize them as they had forgotten the ways of this dance. They had one song that I remember. The old chiefs and a few of us younger fellows showed them how it was done and they watched us perform this dance. We had our Ponca singers and we left four slow songs, four moderate songs, and two give-away songs. Four of our old men danced the taking-of-the-food after the dance. Long ago they reached into the hot food and took a hot, steaming meat from the pot. But in modern way they just touched the food with the tip of their fingers at the end of the song."[1]

Lassiter, Meadows, Foster, Kracht, Kavanagh, Young, and Green provide informed and complex discussions of various society-based revivals, revitalizations, and accommodations in the late nineteenth and early twentieth centuries. Collectively, they confirm the continuing vitality of societies and their dances and offer compelling evidence of the degree to which such gatherings were changing. Green, for example, notes that at Fourth of July celebrations, Lakotas often managed to "subvert colonial rules. Manipulating the presentation of certain events at the Fourth of July, for instance, by using the colonizer's rhetoric of performance as a folkloric display of heritage and as entertainment, the Lakota were able to deflect attention from the current social, and in many cases ceremonial, significance of events, particularly as they related to the collective maintenance of distinctly Lakota identities."[2]

It is that change with which I am concerned in this discussion, for it takes us in the direction of the powwow. As these scholars suggest, revivals and revitalizations were notable in their own right, for they confirmed the continuing relevance for many Southern Plains people of the martial, ritual, and historically rich role dancing played in communities across the region. Meadows writes that the dances and rituals used to welcome home veterans of the world wars "preserved older forms of dances and songs. More importantly, veterans were honored according to traditional cultural forms."[3] Indeed, as chapters one and three confirm, armistice celebrations, victory dances, and homecoming dances often turned into occasions for the expression of old-time, traditional values. Frances Densmore reported that when the Pawnees welcomed home their World War I veterans with dances, for example, "one man had composed words which mentioned airplanes and submarines, these words being sung to an old tune."[4]

The Osage tribal council went the Pawnees one better in the 1920s when it used the war as inspiration for an entirely new dance practice, albeit one firmly planted in an earlier warrior society ethic. After receiving a certificate in 1924 from President Calvin Coolidge expressing his personal gratitude for the tribe's "unswerving Loyalty and Patriotism, the splendid Service rendered, the willing sacrifices made, and the Bravery of their Sons, in the Military and Naval services," the tribal council created the Osage Soldier Peace Dance and passed a resolution ordering that it be held twice a year in one of the three Osage districts. "Said dance shall correspond in Custom with the old Osage Dance," went the resolution, "in which both men and women participated, and shall be the principal feature of these occasions." Josephine Walker, an Osage, recalled in a 1968 interview that the dance was well received and proved to be very popular. "Back in '22, '23, '24, we were all dancing Soldier Dance," she said. "Everybody . . . took [an] interest in it, you know. . . . everybody dances as usual."[5]

These events were obviously important for the role they played in maintaining connections to earlier practices and values that Indian people deemed psychologically and culturally meaningful. Yet, as Meadows notes, such occasions also had their limits and over time were not what sustained dancing on the Southern Plains. In the case of returning Kiowa veterans from World War I, for example, he asserts, "There is no indication that any direct association with the older men's societies continued beyond this short-lived period." However, the connections strengthened again after World War II, when far greater numbers of Indians entered military service and then returned home to communities where dancing was no longer officially suppressed and in which warrior societies were coming into vogue again. But by then other changes were already apparent, not the least of which was that during the immediate post–World War I years "newer forms of social dances were rapidly becoming the primary dance and social events in community gatherings, especially for younger generations."[6]

Lassiter points out that as these societies and their dances gained a renewed sense of importance, they were simultaneously revitalizing and reshaping dance culture in a wider way. A sort of parallel development was occurring in which older forms of society-based dance enjoyed a new relevance *and*, at the same time, inspired a different set of forms, functions, and needs. So, while the older societies continued to dance, and indeed to flourish as expressions of "traditional" ways, they were also helping to create something altogether new: an increasingly secularized, intertribal, performative, public dance culture that by the 1930s was beginning to be called the powwow.

In addition to the revival or revitalization of old dances, agency officials were forced to negotiate how and when dances would be held. As chapter three reveals, agents across the region were only too aware of these developments, and they complained regularly to their superiors, who just as regularly ordered them to redouble their efforts. Agency officials dutifully attempted to suppress dance gatherings, but generally failed to stop the dancing for any length of time or to any appreciable degree. In fact, they soon found themselves surrounded by a dance culture that was revitalizing and reforming itself before their very eyes, eluding many attempts to suppress it, and creating imaginative responses to opposition. One of the consequences was a burgeoning and unstoppable powwow culture.

Blacklists and threats of jail notwithstanding, most agents learned that they could push only so far, and in the end they often resorted to cooperation and negotiation. By the early twentieth century, moreover, their ability and willingness to inspire fear in Indians had eroded. Unlike an earlier era, Indian people began to act with greater levels of confidence and simply rejected the bullying on which agents had typically relied. Consequently, agents increasingly tended to downplay efforts to ban dances. Correspondence files from the Southern Plains agencies clearly reveal that by the 1910s many agents believed that the headaches associated with trying to stop dancing were hardly worth the effort. In a 1909 letter to the Commissioner of Indian Affairs, for example, Pawnee agent George W. Nellis admitted that while he personally considered dances harmful to the tribe's progress, he believed that "there is nothing connected with the dances that savors of obscenity or immorality," and he conceded that "some of our most truthful, honorable, sober, moral people are ardent devotees of the dance. I do not consider . . . that the dances render them less amenable to discipline." Nellis's superiors were unconvinced by his logic; but they also failed to understand the difficulties confronting agents across the region. Aware that negotiating a middle ground was his only alternative, Gloria Young writes that Nellis concluded that his best option was to take a "position of cautious acceptance of dance as a necessary part of Pawnee life" until such time as the dances simply ended on their own. Nellis was not alone in his viewpoint. In 1912, the Kiowa Agency's annual report admitted that as far as dancing was concerned, "a point blank refusal would create . . . dissatisfaction and result in secret dancing without supervision."[7] Other agents quickly came to see the wisdom in following the same path.

For their part, dance advocates became increasingly unwilling to toe the line, a fact that prompted agents at the Kiowa-Comanche-Apache Agency to complain regularly of their inability to force the Indians to comply with rules. In the summer of 1913, for example, Agent Ernest Stecker dejectedly reported that "a cheap class of lawyers" had emboldened the "dance crowd." He resorted to threats of withholding annuity payments from dancers, whom he described as "that class who seize upon every effort made toward their uplift," but failed to scare them into abandoning their pursuit. When C. V. Stinchecum replaced Stecker in April 1915, it didn't take long for him to note that the Indians openly flaunted his edicts. "They can with impunity actually disobey instructions," he fumed, bitterly adding that "during the past twenty-five years . . . no punishment has ever been inflicted."[8]

Indeed, punishment could not be inflicted in many cases because agents lacked statutory authority to impose sanctions that went much beyond withholding rations and annuity payments. This they did, of course, but in time the practice yielded fewer and fewer results and became rare after the 1920s. In the meantime, the dance crowd upped the ante. The impasse at the Kiowa-Comanche-Apache Agency reached a breaking point in 1915 when a Kiowa man named Red Buffalo sought advice from local attorney J. S. Rhinefort on challenging the dance bans. Rhinefort infuriated Stinchecum by telling Red Buffalo that the agent had no real power to ban dances, including the Ghost Dance that

Red Buffalo intended to host at Carnegie on July 4, 1915. Authorities could not interfere with dances, Rhinefort informed Red Buffalo, as long as property was not given away. "You have the same rights of citizenship as any white person," wrote Rhinefort, "and are permitted to worship as you see fit." The agent might try to "bluff you out," he concluded, but "nothing will come from it." Red Buffalo went ahead with his plans, and along with another 104 Kiowas, Comanches, and Apaches ended up on a blacklist. Stinchecum, who was one of the last hardliners when it came to dancing, also withheld annuities, threatened to jail dancers, and generally made life miserable for the dance crowd. An anonymous Department of Interior memo that appeared in the days following Stinchecum's actions explicitly supported the agent's decisions: "We are justified in going a long ways," he wrote, "and probably stretching our authority if thereby we may put a stop to celebrations of this sort."[9]

Stinchecum might have felt justifed to stretch his authority, but as the Pawnees proved in 1917, Indians increasingly had the law on their side when it came to dancing. Weary of their agent's harassment, a collection of Pawnee chiefs asked fellow tribesman and ethnologist James Murie in 1914 to query the tribe's attorneys as to their knowledge of "any law declaring that Indian dances are a crime, and if the Indian Dept. can legally interfere with these religious dances and dances that are gotten up for pleasure." After heated exchanges between the Pawnees, their lawyers, and government officials, the Pawnee agent in Oklahoma grudgingly admitted in 1917 that there was "no way in which such dance[s] could be prevented upon land not upon Governmental jurisdiction."[10]

When other tribes showed a similar determination to demand their legal rights, agency officials did what they could to dissuade Indians who resisted official policy, but by the 1920s the sort of bluster that Stinchecum had used was less prevalent. At the Sac and Fox Agency, for example, officials expressed alarm in 1923 when a Kickapoo dance went on for nine days, but they moved cautiously. In a letter describing the affair, J. L. Suffecool expressed the usual moral outrage, charged that Indians were being duped by whites, and then came to his main point: "I am also informed that the Indians are holding this dance for the purpose of obtaining funds with which to defray the expenses of delegates whom they wish to send to Mexico and to Washington for the purpose of looking into titles of lands and other tribal affairs." He was anxious to derail their plans, but Suffecool was unsure as to the limits of his power and asked what steps he could legitimately take to stop the dance and "what authority I may use" to deny them permission to travel.[11]

As these cases suggest, some Indians didn't hesitate to call the bluff of agents if they tried to play it. One of the more notable examples of this occurred in 1917 when the Cheyenne-Arapaho agent refused to allow a Sun Dance to pray for the well-being of Cheyenne and Arapaho soldiers, and to raise money for them. "No Indian doings during this war," he declared. Tribal leaders took their case to Oklahoma's congressional delegation, its United States senators, the Commissioner of Indian Affairs, the Secretary of the Interior, and finally to President Woodrow Wilson. Turned down at every step, Jess Rowlodge, an Arapaho (and graduate of Haskell Indian School), hit on the novel idea of enlisting support from another corner: the Red Cross. Rowlodge drove to the Western Union office in nearby Concho, Oklahoma, and promptly made his case in a telegram to Red Cross National Headquarters in Washington, D.C. "I wrote a telegram . . . [with details] of what we were trying to do . . . raise money for the boys that's already drafted in the army — that was conscripted. . . . And those that volunteered in the first World War." At about 1 P.M. that afternoon, Rowlodge received a reply stating, "Your request for an Arapaho Sun Dance is hereby approved by the National Red Cross, to start on the 10th of August to the 25th." Armed with this authorization, Rowlodge mobilized ceremonial leaders (including those among the neighboring Cheyennes who "got turned down, too, like that, you know"), and one day later began preparations for the dance. "My statement in that telegram," he recalled in 1969, "was that the purpose of this old time Arapaho Sun Dance was to donate money by different social organizations. . . . to send to the National Red Cross for the boys of the Cheyenne-Arapaho tribe for their cigarettes and all those things. And we raised three hundred and forty-four dollars during that Sun Dance. So I run over the President of the United States that time!"[12]

Other officials fared about as badly; not even the Commissioner of Indian Affairs inspired the fear that officials had come to rely on. A good example of this turn of events occurred in 1921 when Commissioner Charles Burke issued the notorious Circular 1665 in which he instructed agents to prevent "dances . . . celebrations, powwows and gatherings of any kind that take the time of the Indians for many days." In that circular, and in subsequent announcements and letters, Burke derided the "evil or foolish things" that occurred at dances and reiterated his belief that such gatherings kept Indians from their crops, encouraged them to give away their property, and caused some of them to engage in self-torture and the handling of poisonous snakes. But when Burke's instructions were presented to Indians, they were not particularly impressed by the circular's language. The Pawnee agent reported, for example, that Burke's sentiments were "duly communicated to the Indians," all of whom listened politely before a large contingent headed off to "a ceremonial feast, dancing, etc."[13]

John W. Troutman reports that when Burke's edict was presented to a group of Wichitas, Delawares, Wacos, Keechies, and Tawakonies in Oklahoma, the commissioner got more than he bargained for. One observer wrote that the

Indians "were in a good humor all the way through the reading of the letter" and "smiled a little" at Burke's charges and allegations, but were generally unconvinced by the commissioner's arguments. Unwilling to be the passive targets of yet another lecture by a pompous bureaucrat, the tribes fired back a letter of their own in which they defended their practices and lampooned Burke's presumptions by asking him to answer several questions:

1. Please explain the meaning of "Pow-wow."
2. What is a "Snake Dance?"
3. When have the Wichitas or Delawares neglected their crops, gardens, and homes?
4. When and where did these tribes give public shows of their customs?
5. Tell us more about handling poisonous snakes.

Their reply pointedly implied that not only was Burke barking up the wrong tree, he was hardly in a position to criticize Indian dances. Writing that "perhaps some few [Indians] have taken on the evil ways of the white folks. . . . most of them do not," the Indians retorted that "the jazz-dance is offensive to us . . . we would be very glad to have the Board of Health of Reviews or Censors to contrast our manner of dancing with those of the white-folks and from the stand-point of saneness and morality and healthfulness show which of the Dances are more in keeping with standards as set out." In a final, dismissive blast, the letter concluded that Indians would never allow their children to "degrade themselves to go to one of such dances as the white folk put on if we could help ourselves. . . . We are willing to go on trial . . . to prove to the world that our manners and customs are much superior in many points of virtue over our boasted white brethren."[14]

It is not difficult to imagine Burke's reaction; but the fact was that from the beginning, the federal government's power to stop dances had always been limited by the failure to give policy directives the power of law. Once Indians realized that they had legal options, the government's ability to coerce them eroded steadily as the years passed. Indeed, in an ironic twist, the government's decision to extend citizenship to Indians seriously hampered its ability to prohibit dancing. Beginning in 1887 with the Dawes Act, and concluding in 1924 when Congress mandated citizenship for all Indians, federal authorities insisted that citizenship would end the dependence of Indians on the government, and dissolve a sprawling and inefficient bureaucracy.

The irony, of course, was that citizenship did not put an end to ethnic identity; it potentially protected it by extending equal protection — especially under the First Amendment — to Indians.[15] And when that was combined with the fact that many Indians lived on fee-patented lands that lay outside the jurisdiction of the Bureau of Indian Affairs, dance advocates could increasingly ignore attempts to ban dances and ceremonies. As a result, threats from the agents became increasingly ineffective; the government's own policies had seen to it. When Ponca agent George Hoyo's superiors charged him in 1924 with failing to use his influence to prevent dances, for example, Hoyo responded that "a good many of the Ponca Indian[s] have a patent in fee status and I know of no way to keep them from dancing so long as they conduct their dances in an orderly manner and do not carry them to excess. I know of no way to keep them from going over there [to visit the Osages and dance] other than to tell them that it is in their best interests to stay at home. . . . If there is a way of preventing the Indians from attending or taking part in these Rodeos I should like very much to know how this can be done." Even Commissioner Burke recognized that his hands were tied. While he could still terrorize Indians on reservations, he admitted, "it is a different question where you have Indians residing in different localities, a portion of them citizens to the fullest extent." As Troutman observes, "Citizenship, for so long a goal of the assimilationists, endowed the Indians with a right to perform the activities that the agents had for so long tried to control and suppress."[16]

When authorities tried to transform the dance question into a debate about the limits of Indian citizenship, they sometimes found themselves in an uphill battle against not only the Indians, but against their own agents as well. By the late 1910s and early 1920s, agents across the Southern Plains were increasingly ambivalent about the supposed evils of dancing and were less inclined than an earlier generation to spend limited time and dwindling resources combating something that no longer seemed all that bad. In fact, their perception of dancing had changed so dramatically that Young believes "most of the agents in Oklahoma appear from their correspondence to have been ready by the mid-1920s to ignore or defend Indian dancing." In case after case, agents admitted that nothing would dissuade Indians from dancing, and also reported that dancing posed few economic, social, religious, or political threats. In 1921, for example, the Pawnee agent informed Commissioner Burke that he had "seen nothing that could be considered dangerous or contaminating" concerning dancing, and added that while he appreciated the "desire of the Office to use its influence for more progressive assemblies, and to discourage in all possible ways activities that may be detrimental, I do not hold to the belief that everything that is Indian is necessarily bad because it is Indian, or good because it originates among whites."[17]

A measure of just how far things had gone occurred on June 18, 1928, when the Oklahoma City *Daily Oklahoman* ran a story under the headline "Ponca Indians Will Conduct Big Dance." The story related details supplied by Ponca agent A. R. Snyder about the much anticipated dedication of a new dance hall on private property near the old agency grounds at White Eagle. The event was to include contest dancing and other assorted entertainments, and Indian delegations from all over the region were planning to attend. Not surprisingly, the commissioner of Indian affairs demanded an explanation. By way of reply, Snyder reported matter-of-factly that the dance hall had been built because the Poncas spent "about half of their time attending dances on the Osage reservation." They reasoned if they had their own dance hall, Snyder wrote, they "would stay at home more."[18]

It surely rankled officials in Washington to learn that their man in the field had adopted such a casual attitude, but we can only imagine the gnashing of teeth caused by Snyder's comment that not only did he support the hall's construction, he'd signed on to the plan for financing construction as well: "It was agreed we should build the hall and then later make an effort to pay for it." The agent's choice of words is revealing, for it is difficult to imagine that federal officials ever thought of themselves and Indians as "we"; Snyder's account amounted to the admission that he was cooperating with the Poncas, a notion that must have left his superiors astonished. (In contrast, C. V. Stinchecum routinely referred to the Kiowas and Comanches as "our Indians.") As it turned out, the July 4 dedicatory dance was a splendid success that raised nearly $200 for the building fund. A large and orderly crowd took in the dancing contests and a baseball game between rival Ponca and Pawnee teams. Except for one young man being arrested on a liquor charge, things went off without a hitch. One year later, the commissioner ordered agency officials to prevent a second such powwow, but it too was held on private property, the organizers simply ignoring both the agent and the telegram from Washington ordering them to stop the dance.[19]

This attitude became increasingly typical across the region. As Young suggests, after World War I agents were not especially powerful, and usually they were not to be feared. Young notes that "men and women of all ages participated [in dance], and many appeared to wish to continue whatever the consequences. The withholding of per capita annuity shares had little effect on the state of Gift dancing as a whole in Oklahoma during the second decade of the twentieth century. The giving of gifts was a custom too important to intertribal friendship to be abandoned because of the insistence of a few agents."[20]

Attitudes weren't the only things changing. Dance styles were also taking on new forms, one of the most important of which was the appearance by the 1920s of a new and faster style of men's dance called "war dancing" (also called "fancy dancing" and "feather dancing"). Many tribes claim to have originated the style, but it is difficult to say with certainty where and when the trend really began. Most observers agree that the Wild West shows played an important role by encouraging and rewarding increasingly faster and more exciting dancing. A generation of Ponca dancers led by Gus McDonald is invariably given credit for inventing and popularizing fancy dancing during the 1920s. One widely told story is that they were inspired by the bobbing head, pawing hooves, and quick turns of a spirited horse — movements that soon came to characterize the new dance style. The faster and more complicated dance steps that McDonald and his contemporaries favored soon became crowd favorites. In addition to the Wild West shows, the powwow circuit that appeared in the 1920s also popularized the style and helped to spread its influence on an intertribal basis. As Elmer Sugar Brown, an Oto-Missouria, told me, "We went everywhere and learned all kinds of dance steps. People would say, 'That guy Elmer Sugar Brown used nine or ten different kinds of tribes and steps in his dancing.' I learned a lot watching those other boys — McDonald, Lefthand, Mopope, Snake — all them guys could really get after it. But I watched them. That's how I got to be World Champion."[21]

By the 1930s a cadre of increasingly well-known fancy dancers including McDonald, Brown, Chester Lefthand (Southern Arapaho), Steve Mopope (Kiowa), Dennis Rough Face (Ponca), Henry Snake (Ponca), and George "Woogie" Watchetaker (Comanche) were appearing at dances all across the Southern Plains, and as we'll see, were creating a contest circuit through which they vied with one another for top honors. With their large feather head-crests, circular feather bustles on the arms, back, and neck (and occasionally on wrists and ankles as well), long strands of bells running down each leg, beaded suspenders around the neck and down the chest, and body coverings fashioned from dyed union suits and leotards, fancy dancers stood out as the marquee performers. Dancers fashioned their outfits from new materials, including skull caps covered with sequins and fringe and bustles decorated with dyed rooster hackles. Reginald Laubin recalled seeing a fancy dancer in Oklahoma whose back bustle was spread with a 1934 Ford V-8 hubcap! (Some contemporary fancy dancers have kept up that spirit of innovation by using CDs and DVDs to spread their arm bustles.) In addition to the bustles and other accoutrements, faster and increasingly complicated steps featuring splits and flips became the new style's hallmarks. Elmer Sugar Brown, for example, electrified audiences in the 1940s when he began turning backflips timed to land on the last beat of a song. "Took me a long time to learn it," he recalled, but when he perfected it, "I got world famous doing that." Gus McDonald added cartwheels and splits to his dance routine, and his sister recalled that as a young man in the 1920s and 1930s, he could pick up a $100 bill from the ground by leaning over so low that he could get it with his teeth and never touch the ground with his hands.

Such was McDonald's prowess that one account described him as "the athlete with a warrior's presence who introduced fancy wardancing [*sic*] to the circuit." Indeed, this new dance style was so radically different from its predecessors that some Poncas are said to have described it with the Ponca word for "drunk," which they translated into English as "crazy dance."[22]

Today, McDonald is remembered as one of the first great innovators on the powwow circuit. The Osage poet Carter Revard paid homage to McDonald in his 1980 poem "Ponca War Dancers," which recounts the memorial feast held at McDonald's funeral:

> He was the greatest of Ponca dancers
>   yet when he came to see
> some of my white uncles
>   and they went off to drink
> how come I never understood
>   he was a champion
>   but saw a heavy-bellied man
>   that kids swarmed round,
>   full of jokes and laughter,
>   never seemed to brawl or argue —
> till at the Osage dances one June when he
>   was sixty-something
>   I saw him dance for the first time
>   and everyone got quiet
>   except to whisper "the champion" —
> and here came Uncle Gus
>   potbellied but quick-footed went
>   twirling and drifting,
>   stomping with the
>   hawk wing a-hover then
>   leaping
>   spinning light as
>   a leaf in a whirlwind
>   the anklebells shrilling, dancing
>   the Spirit's dance. . . .
> I've set down this winter-count for a kind
>   of memorial song
>   to Shongeh-ska, one
>   of the greatest of Ponca dancers,
>   to dance once more. . . .

> For those who saw him dance
> and learned from him the way,
>   he is dancing still.
> Come to White Eagle in the summer time,
>   Indians dance in summer time —
> he is back with his people now.[23]

Gus McDonald, Chester Lefthand, Steve Mopope, and others were the shape of things to come, and it didn't take them long to shape dance culture according to new forms and ideas. As Meadows notes, for example, society dances declined all across the Southern Plains after an initial post–World War I spurt, but dance gatherings of other kinds increased in frequency. Meadows believes the "extremely high frequency [of dances] suggests the growth of social War Dancing in the form of the burgeoning 'War Dance' or 'powwow.' Multiple consultants indicated that dances during the 1920s and 1930s were focused primarily on War Dancing and various forms of social dances." Importantly, in a cycle of events repeated in other communities, the popularity of warrior society dances was declining to the point that by the mid-1920s "the older dance forms ceased to be performed" in many communities, but "social dance forms" including the fancy war dance increased in popularity.[24] And in most cases, that meant that a younger crowd was coming to the fore. Foster comments that by the late 1930s, "the last members of the prereservation military society generation had passed on, and the character of and participants in the dances had begun to change. Both peyote and powwow gatherings were drawing new, younger members from church memberships."[25]

One of the most momentous innovations was the introduction of the fancy war dancing that McDonald and others were popularizing. In Apache communities, for example, Meadows notes that encampments featuring war dancing between 1890 and 1920 "may have functioned as a surrogate for earlier tribal-level communal gatherings with the decline of the other Apache men's societies in the late nineteenth century." Moreover, there is no doubt that by the 1920s, fancy war dance choreography and dress styles had begun "to supplant the earlier style of dance and dress." Meadows' oldest Apache consultant remembered seeing bustled dancers for the first time in 1922 and "attribut[ed] the spread of the Fancy Dance and new dance styles to Chester Lefthand (Southern Arapaho) and Steve Mopope (Kiowa) who had introduced the style in the local area by 1917."[26]

The new dance culture emerged similarly in Comanche communities. Foster's Comanche consultants told him that annual summer encampments began in the first decade of the twentieth century (the first was reported in 1906) that were initially "focused around traditional dances." Tennyson Echawaudah remembered, "They'd camp different places. Mostly just the elders took part [that is danced]." Leonard Riddles recalled that in the post-allotment era of the early nineteenth century "each community began having its annual thing. Maybe two, three, four powwows a year, only summer." But change was in the air, and by then new influences and practices were already becoming apparent. Field matrons' reports from 1913, for example, indicated "unusual wanderings of the Indians . . . as picnics and dances took them from one place to another." Furthermore, that summer produced the first report of the so-called gift dance with a giveaway and dancing.[27]

Meadows and Foster suggest that one of the most important characteristics of such gatherings was the youth movement that eventually dominated them. Whereas Tennyson Echawaudah told Foster that "mostly, just the elders took part" in the early encampment dances, Meadows notes that "the rise of social War Dancing through the diffusion of the Plains Grass (War or Omaha) Dance became an alluring element which attracted many younger individuals away from the older society dances." Meadows and Foster both point out that because some elderly Comanches were reluctant to pass on the knowledge needed to sustain society practices, alternative forms of dance were more readily accepted by a younger generation anxious to dance. One elder told Meadows that "the old people said, Why celebrate, you're done whipped. Why celebrate your defeat . . . why celebrate your own end." Leonard Riddles told Foster that the prevailing sentiment in some quarters was "they wouldn't let those young people come in, just those [older] people that were involved and their close relatives." Sylvester Warrior, a Ponca, revealed during a 1968 interview that "some of these dances were abolished by the government and some were considered so sacred that they did not pass the dance to the next generation, for the simple reason that they were considered sacred and the people that would know anything about it eventually . . . died out." Born around 1908, Warrior commented that as a young man he did not learn some of his tribe's traditional dances: "I never did witness them because they were danced before my time." Otis Russell, an Osage who was in his late eighties when he was interviewed in 1969, noted that some Osage dances had not been carried forward from the old days because "I think they were no good. Went, by and by. Something go wrong with it."[28] For younger Indians who wanted to dance, war dancing became the best alternative.

Fancy war dancing was introduced in Kiowa country in 1917; the first contests appeared a year later. Importantly, the conduit for war dancing was the O-ho-mah Society, which continued to meet regularly. That fancy war dancing was introduced and practiced in the context of the O-ho-mah helped to confer some legitimacy on the new dance, for it could claim association with a venerated and traditional encampment that enjoyed status and prestige. Moreover, between 1910 and 1925, July 4 O-ho-mah encampments were the scene of intertribal gatherings that included Cheyennes, Arapahos, Poncas, Otoes, Osages, Pawnees, Comanches, Apaches, and Taos Pueblos — tribes that were playing central roles in the emergence of the powwow. These intertribal visits were occasions to share new dance traditions, a pattern that had already been set in the Wild West shows, fairs, and exhibitions where, as Young notes, "Indian performers had a chance to exchange ideas, songs, and dances with members of other tribes and to bring home to their tribes new ideas and activities." Allotment, citizenship, and the government's incapacity to stop dances, she surmises, "must have resulted in a new opening of channels of communication and a new sharing of ideas," a process that had already begun with the spread of the Grass Dance.[29]

It is worth noting, however, that several O-ho-mah members insisted in conversations with me in the summer of 2002 that their society dances never became a powwow and that they have kept the O-ho-mah separate from the influence of such events. As one of them put it, "We don't go in for that powwow stuff." Another member, however, lamented the fact that "today, at O-ho-mah, they don't even wear the right clothes. When you go out there in the afternoon, you're supposed to have those O-ho-mah dance clothes on, not powwow clothes. That's why I don't go or take my boys yet. Until we get their clothes all set, we won't go." In truth, the O-ho-mah is not a typical powwow; even at its evening sessions emphasis is clearly on singing family and individual songs associated with O-ho-mah members, not intertribal powwow songs.[30]

Importantly, the youth movement that emerged in tandem with this intertribal dance culture was pushing dance gatherings in new directions. "As was occurring in neighboring tribes," writes Meadows, "participation in the older traditional [Kiowa] tribal dances such as military society dances was limited primarily to middle-aged or elderly men, while younger generations were attracted to and participated in newer, more social forms of dancing." Earlier scholars had reached the same conclusion, as when Alice Marriott reported that society dances occurred at a 1937 Gourd Dance near Carnegie attended by Kiowas, Otoes, Pawnees, Poncas, and Osages. But she also commented on the generational division that characterized the dance sessions: "The afternoon dances were primarily for the older people, few of the young ones taking part. . . . The dances in the evening were largely for the younger people. . . . Most of the dancers were men."[31] Young Indian people, especially men who had never had access to war honors and their accompanying prestige, found the new styles of dress and dance suited to their tastes and needs. One Pawnee man suggested to me that the status associated with contest winners, for example, had become a kind of contemporary replacement for the war honors and status that had characterized another era. "It's still Indian," he commented. "*We* decided who deserved the glory; *Indians* were recognizing them young men as models to follow. And people looked up to those singers and dancers back then, just like people had looked up to their grandpas way back there."[32]

One of the most popular of the new dances, and one that appealed particularly to younger powwowers, was the Forty-nine. Based on old song and dance practices previously used to honor war parties (Kiowas called them "war journey songs," for example), by the 1920s the genre had been transformed into a social occasion dominated by young people. There are numerous accounts, but no clear consensus, of how the dance came to be called Forty-nine. One tradition holds that the name refers to a group of fifty warriors who went to battle but only forty-nine returned. In a variation of that story, one man told me that the name came from the fact that only one warrior returned and forty-nine died. Other explanations hold that the name refers to a group of Indians who got caught up in the gold rush of 1849, or to a collection of honky-tonk dancers who were featured in a carnival sideshow titled "The Girls of '49." Leonard Cozad, Sr., a highly respected Kiowa singer with more than eight decades of powwow experience, told Sandy Rhoades and Scott Swearingen that "in the 1920s, I think it was, somebody called it 'forty-nine.' I don't know what that means. And then the younger men began singing them old songs and they kind of pepped it up, made it a little more rapid."[33]

Then as now, Forty-nine dances were popular with young people who used them to meet their friends, and — in the opinion of the dance's many critics — indulge in all manner of things that usually revolved around drinking and carousing. Not surprisingly, agency officials harshly discouraged Forty-nine dances and denounced them as pernicious and lust-filled drunken spectacles. Some powwow associations, including the Craterville Fair board of directors, also opposed them and offered assurances that they would not condone or allow Forty-nines. If the dance's presumed excesses were (and are) often exaggerated by outsiders, Forty-nines nonetheless became a way for young Indian people to carve out their own sphere in the powwow world and to stamp at least part of the goings-on with their own brand of adaptation. Song texts, for example, were changed to include English lyrics reflecting the timeworn themes of lost love and youthful suffering:

> Oh my dearest,
> Uncle Sam is calling me.
> I must go.
> Will you wait for me dear?
> Don't you worry, don't you cry.

Or, as the song sometimes called "Mae West" puts it:

> To hell with your old man,
> Come up and see me sometime.

Or on a somewhat loftier note:

> Take me back,
> I'm on my knees, I beg you please,
> Don't ever leave me.
> 'Cause you know I love you so.

In time, some songs also referred to the powwow circuit on which many young people were meeting one another:

> Last year at Taos, we had a good time with each other.
> Now, you're back in Dodge
> And you don't know me.
> Guess its over.

As William L. Kennan and L. Brooks Hill note in one of the few studies of Forty-nining, the dance has served from its beginning as "a rite of passage in which young men grow, develop singing and dancing skills, and meet young women en route to manhood; as such forty-nining entails traditional qualities and contemporary adaptation."[34] Such dances brought together young people from different groups, and in time played a crucial role in the powwow's appeal.

The level of intertribal visiting and sharing was on the increase as tribes took advantage of relaxed regulations and a less restrictive environment, and an increasingly public aspect was coming to characterize many dances. In a 1968 interview, Sylvester Warrior, a Ponca, recalled that by the 1930s and 1940s, the powwows he attended were already very different from the society dances he'd seen as a young man. "In this day and time, all the different tribes in the state of Oklahoma are more or less intertribal in their dances and celebrations and doings . . . we have modern transportation, the automobile. . . . It's nothing for one to get in his car and drive a hundred miles to another tribe's tribal doings. It wasn't so forty, fifty, sixty years back because the Indian couldn't afford a car at that time. . . . So, back there in them days . . . they retained a lot of their own traditional dances. And a good many of the tribes did not know what this War Dance was until here recently . . . they saw the War Dance and they adopted it and copied it, made up their own songs and called it War Dance. But it wasn't so thirty years in back."[35]

By the 1920s, the intertribal, performative quality of such dances was gathering momentum and starting to drive the development of powwows toward their familiar form. Dancing in public, of course, was already an established practice. The Wild West shows, small-time medicine shows, local fairs, and town celebrations had all combined to attract growing numbers of dance participants and spectators alike. As things turned out, it was a short step from those exhibitions to the powwow. Young notes that such events "provided opportunities to dance the new war dance" for appreciative audiences, and Meadows suggests that these events were crucial to the development and survival of war dancing and contests. "County fairs and exhibitions run by local Anglo entrepreneurs profiting from tourism encouraged Indian 'contest' dancing," he writes, "and became the medium through which War Dancing survived" during the first three decades of the twentieth century.[36] Moreover, because such events were clearly secular and intertribal, officials couldn't complain that they were religiously immoral. Across Oklahoma, writes Young, these "secular intertribal events were continuing to attract the attention of residents of the state. These events were called homecomings, picnics, celebrations, and finally, after 1925, powwows. They were just as popular with non-Indian audiences as had been exhibition dances and ceremonies such as the Sun Dance and Green Corn Feast."[37]

Indeed, by World War I the powwow was becoming part of the vernacular in the most unlikely places and with the most unlikely audiences. A case in point occurred in 1918, when the Metropolitan Opera staged a performance of *Shanewis,* an opera in one act by Charles Wakefield Cadman and Nelle Richmond Eberhart that told the story of an ill-fated romance between an Indian maiden and her white lover. Cadman's use of an Oklahoma powwow in part two of the opera is an interesting bit of staging, one that suggests the degree to which powwows were becoming something of a set piece in the portrayal of Indian culture by Indians and non-Indians alike. Cadman's description of the scene went like this:

> Approaching sunset. The closing scenes of a modern summer encampment or powwow of an Oklahoma tribe of Indians are in progress. The camp is on a level stretch of ground but in the distance is seen a rolling farming country. . . . The powwow is held in an enclosure of canvas fence stretched on tall slender poles beyond which are tepee tops and improvised canvas shelters for the campers. The ceremonial dancers in full regalia stand against this fence awaiting their turns. The crowd consists of full-blood Indians and half-breeds in ceremonial, mongrel, or modern dress and white spectators in holiday attire. Booths decorated in red, white, and blue bunting occupy

the middle stage. Several Ford automobiles stand about. An Indian pony hitched to a red and green wagon filled with Indian children is tied to a tree. Ice-cream and lemonade vendors are crying their wares. Balloon sellers add noise and color.

At one point, a chorus of spectators sings "powwows are picturesque and quite grand" and a group of four old Indians sings an Osage ceremonial song, "by permission of the U.S. Bureau of American Ethnology," Cadman assures his audience.[38]

Audiences at the Met may have been swept away by Cadman's romanticized vision of life on the Oklahoma prairie, but by the 1920s, it was increasingly Indians, not whites, who created and controlled both the venues at which dancing occurred and the context in which they were presented. ("*We* decided who deserved the glory; *Indians* were recognizing them young men as models to follow.") This shift in agency is important, for it heralded a decisive turn in the battle to protect, promote, and maintain dance culture. As Foster notes, for the generation of Comanches who matured after World War I, and who began to dominate dances by the 1930s, dances satisfied the need to establish their own sense of identity. "Powwows provided these younger Comanches with their first opportunity to participate actively in a Comanche-derived, rather than an Anglo-derived, form of gathering. Consequently, they marked off the focused activity of the gathering — dancing — from the surrounding social occasion. . . . The reservation-era generation had not needed to make explicit their claim to traditional authority. The generation that had grown up with allotments, though, emphasized the ritual of gatherings as a way of claiming a tradition from which they had largely been excluded."[39] Indeed, many Indians showed a determination to dance regardless of what whites thought or did. How deeply devoted some people could be to this pursuit was revealed in 1927 during the fourth annual Convention of Oklahoma Indians. When asked "What class of work is desired by a good many of your Indians?" members of the Ponca delegation replied "to sing and dance for the Osage Indians."[40]

In the years immediately following World War I, then, official ambivalence and dance advocates who refused to kowtow prompted a reappraisal of the situation on the Southern Plains. These influences began to come together in a discernable way by the 1920s, when observers and participants alike began to describe dance gatherings as powwows. Young believes that the word was used for the first time, at least in an official context, in the 1920 Kaw Agency annual report when the agent commented (inaccurately, it would seem) that "Indian Pow Wows do not appeal very strongly to many of the younger people." One year later, Commissioner Burke used it in Circular 1665 when he referred to "dances . . . celebrations, [and] powwows."[41] Other phrases, though, were probably more common at the time, including picnic, fair, exhibition, and dance contest.

Regardless of the terminology — and it wouldn't be long before "powwow" trumped all the others — it was clear that dance culture was moving into a new era in terms of organization and purpose. Several different kinds of gatherings led the way. First, as chapters one and three discussed, the Indian fairs sponsored by agency officials quickly became the scene for dance demonstrations, shows, and occasional contests. The Indian International Fair at Weatherford began in 1910 and was shortly joined by others. The Cheyenne and Arapaho Fair was revived in 1925 with a much enlarged program devoted to dancing exhibitions and contests. In 1929, organizers added an "Indian maiden" contest, something that shortly became standard fare at every large powwow. The Sac and Fox Fair appeared in 1926, as did similar gatherings among the Poncas, Otoes, and Pawnees.[42] By the 1910s and 1920s, moreover, the prominence of dancing at these events began to increase.

One notable example began in the 1920s when the Osages began holding "Osage Day" in late September to celebrate what its founders described as the blessings of the wealth that the Osages had derived from their considerable gas and oil holdings. Francis Claremont undertook the task of convincing others to hold the event, and as Leonard Maker recounted, Claremont "explained it in kinda a odd way. . . . He said that the white man, they had a day set aside — Fourth of July, and we should set aside one day to where kind of a giving of thanks to the Almighty and the Great Spirit for showering all these blessings on the Osage Tribe and that. . . . he couldn't rest until they more less ban together and have a dance. . . . And it was decided that they should." A committee was formed, the dance was organized, and it flourished until the 1960s when, according to Maker, the committee began to have "a little trouble gathering all of the people together." The date of the dance was changed to accommodate people who had moved away, as well as young Osages who were in school or at work in places distant to the Osage homeland.[43]

As the Osage example suggests, tribes began to gain the upper hand in managing and directing dances. By the late 1920s, writes Young, "Indians had taken their cue from white businessmen and launched an era of Indian-sponsored commercial dances. The Shawnee Agency Annual Report for that year stated: 'A few of the younger ones . . . will put on an Indian dance somewhere and invite the white people from towns to come out and witness some great War Dance and charge admission and raise a little money this way.'" Other tribes were already following suit, and by the late 1920s, a number of them were sponsoring annual powwows that attracted large numbers of participants and spectators.

By 1928, according to Young, the Pawnee, Quapaw, Osage, and Ponca powwows "were becoming institutions." According to a story in the *American Indian* magazine, the 1928 Quapaw Powwow included band music, baseball, foot races, war dances, and "contest dancing between different Indian tribes." The 1928 Pawnee powwow was such a success that it was held over for an extra day. Three thousand Indians crowded onto the grounds, joined by throngs of spectators who took in baseball games, a terrapin derby, war dancing, and a solo dancing contest that the *American Indian* magazine had promised would "draw the best dancers in the Southwest, who upon doing their 'Kickapooing' will pull small eagle feathers with their teeth from the wooden platform."[44]

Indeed, the *American Indian* coverage of the Pawnee Powwow included a description that in many ways became the blueprint for the powwow culture being created on the Plains:

> Indians from the Pawnee, Kaw, Otoe, Osage, Ponca, Euche, Iowa, Kiowa, Sac and Fox, Pottawattomie, Comanche, Creek, Cheyenne, Arapahoe, and other tribes were present. The manner in which the Pawnee Indian Junior Council conducted the affair was commendable. The best of order was preserved. The program prepared in advance was carried through each evening. A variety of dances and other forms of entertainment was presented. The committee made preparations to care for the crowd. The visiting Indians went away satisfied and the white spectators were pleased. There appears to be sentiment among the citizens of Pawnee that these affairs should be staged each year just as this one was held, under the auspices of the Pawnee Indian Junior Council or some other organization. The people of Pawnee seem to feel that by proper advertising such affairs will attract a large number of people from Tulsa, Oklahoma City, Enid, Arkansas City, and even states east of the Mississippi.[45]

A firsthand account by an Indian school teacher named Will Spindler of a 1929 Armistice Day powwow on the Pine Ridge Reservation in South Dakota offers more insights into the changing contours of Plains dance culture. While Spindler described a Northern Plains dance, he nonetheless witnessed an event that had close ties to the powwows then emerging on the Southern Plains, and because of that, his account merits a lengthy passage:

> The big log dance hall was crowded when we entered, the women and girls on one side and the men and boys on the other. In each of the four corners stood an old wood-burning heating stove, two of them made from fifty-gallon oil barrels, with a roaring fire in each. One end of the hall was deco-

rated with white sheets, U.S. flags, red and white bunting, and a few brightly colored home-made quilt tops for Armistice Day.

Two Coleman gas lamps and several old fashioned kerosene lanterns furnished plenty of light. In one corner on benches and stools was grouped the "orchestra" for the big dance or "pow wow" — seven or eight men gathered in a circle about the big tom tom (drum) each with a padded stick with which to beat the tom tom.

Quite a number of the Indian men and women, as well as a few boys and girls, were decked out in their gaily colored, glittering ceremonial regalia — bright rodeo shirts or brightly dyed winter underwear, beaded moccasins, eagle feathers, long strings of little bells, beadwork, painted faces, elk tooth decorations, a few bear claws, necklaces, and some war bonnets for the men and boys; brilliant shawls, painted faces (mostly red and yellow), beaded moccasins, some beaded buckskin dresses and vests trimmed in gleaming elk teeth and other polished bone decorations, and a few necklaces and head bands for the women and girls. . . .

How shall I describe this, our first Indian pow wow ever witnessed inside a real Indian dance hall? To say the least, it was a perfect riot of color, glitter, and noise, especially when the old time Indian "Omaha" dance was going on. . . . The "Omaha" dance is chiefly the old folks' dance, although a few younger men and girls, as well as some small boys and girls, usually participate in it. It is the dance the Indians put on at rodeos, fairs, and other celebrations. . . . In it, the men really "go to town" in rapid, rhythmic action. . . . The "Rabbit" dance is more for the younger folks, although Indians of all ages danced it. It is danced with partners . . . [who] face the same direction, each has his or her arm about the waist of the other and they proceed in a big circle about the dance hall, one couple behind the other. . . . The Indian young folks love it and often jokingly term it the "bunny hop." Lulu, Clara, and I were soon doing it along with the rest of the . . . crowd, and enjoying it, too! [Some readers will recognize this as the Northern Plains version of the Oklahoma Two Step.]

The "give-away" — some persons giving as a gift to others anything from a horse, fancy quilt tops, to articles of beadwork, etc. — and the speeches of acceptance, thanks, and much praise for the givers following. Donations of money [are placed in] the tin cup sitting on a tiny shelf . . . this money going to a sort of revolving fund for the sick and needy, helping the aged and crippled, etc.

Speeches of thanks and praise to the giver [are made by] by the "teller," the elderly man in the role of a sort of toastmaster. Auctioning off the various donated articles by the "seller," the money received to end up in that magic tin cup on the tiny shelf. . . .

The time element is a very minor factor at your Indian pow wow. Very few time pieces are found among the full-blood Indians, and time seems to stand still as these various ceremonies listed above stretch out endlessly hour after hour. When things get too tiresome and boring to the young folks, they drift outside to seek recreation there in any way they can. When at long last they hear the old tom tom beating out the rhythm of the Rabbit dance once more, back inside they file to get partners for this, the only part of the pow wow most of them really enjoy. Just a little of that other stuff goes a long way with the young and romantic.

The big supper was naturally the crowning event of the pow wow. . . . Suddenly, as if by magic, from nowhere, aluminum, tin and granite plates, small pans, and cups appeared in the hands of everyone . . . and all were seated in a big circle on the benches. . . . Sometime after midnight we left the dance hall and climbed up the winding trail out of the badlands canyon.[46]

At dances like the 1928 Pawnee Powwow, it was all there: fancy war dancing, contests and cash prizes, intertribal visiting, hometown boosterism, and a good time. All that remained was for this burgeoning powwow culture to become the dominant form of dancing on the Plains. As things turned out, it didn't take long before Indian people were traveling the beginnings of a powwow circuit in Kansas, Oklahoma, Texas, and New Mexico. Charles Chibitty, a Comanche, recalled that "way back in the late 1920s. . . . dad would always bring the stuff [dance clothes] and then we'd go to Dallas or Fort Worth. They were dancing over there. I don't know how much they paid daddy, but we always danced all our lives." By then dances were springing up all over the region, so many in fact that in 1930 the Pawnee agent reported that "the modern Pow-wow has broken up the old dance religion."[47] Thanks to several key events on the Southern Plains, powwowing was taking on a life of its own.

One of the turning points occurred in Lawrence, Kansas, in 1926 when the Haskell Indian School dedicated its new football stadium prior to a game against Bucknell. Envisioned as both a celebration of football and an affirmation of the role of sports in exposing Indian students to American culture, the three-day dedication was laden with meaning for those who saw the stadium and football as metaphors for battle in the culture wars of the Indian schools. According to John Bloom, football was "a game that would come to symbolize progress . . . like no other." Paraphrasing a 1912 speech by Superintendent of Indian Education H. B. Peairs, Bloom contends that Peairs "reflected ideas about sports consistent with those of reformers during the Progressive era. He suggested that physical recreation would improve not only physical health but also moral character, and that it would promote the ideals of delayed gratification, hard work, and individual responsibility."[48] According to Peairs, sport was the blueprint for life.

But if football was the Holy Grail for whites, something altogether different galvanized the Indians who attended the festivities (held, ironically enough, during Halloween). Anxious to give visitors a little exotic entertainment before getting down to the morally serious task of beating their opponents' brains out on the grid iron, school officials organized an Indian pageant complete with a tipi village, parade, dance contests, and a rendition of *Hiawatha*. The point of the exercise was to juxtapose savagery against progress in such a way as to leave visitors confident that places like Haskell were doing their part to bring Indians into the orbit of civilized pursuits. Students could take pride in their cultural heritage before trading their loin cloths, Indian princess crowns, and war dance songs for raccoon coats, flapper skirts, and the doggerel of "two bits, four bits, six bits a dollar, all for Haskell stand up and holler." Organizers thought of the pageant as a fond remembrance of old times long gone, a domesticated Wild West show about to be overrun by the technological grandeur of the stadium and the cultural juggernaut of football. As a statement about the perceived cultural superiority of white America, the pageant sought to confirm the logical unfolding of events that relegated Indianness to museum cases and dime novels, where educators and federal officials thought it belonged.

Not surprisingly, the event that got the most attention was the large contest powwow that attracted participants from more than seventy tribes. "Framed as a kind of picturesque relic of the past," writes Bloom, the powwow was supposed to be an exotic but ultimately empty charade that would "demonstrate the evolutionary ideology that guided federal Indian policy . . . [and made] . . . traditions meaningless."[49] All of this must have resonated deeply with those in the crowd who had grown up under the spell of Frederick Jackson Turner's Frontier Thesis and its celebratory notions of inexorable progress and triumph.

But a funny thing happened on the way to assimilation via the forward pass. The pageant and dances scheduled as mere amusements quickly became the centerpieces of a cultural tour de force that participants used to make a bold statement about their culture and identity. One newspaper account reported that "a caravan of Oklahoma cars . . . took hundreds of Indians to Lawrence," where they joined tribes from as far away as Santa Clara Pueblo in a powwow that was not exactly a simple tableaux of natives reenacting a colorful but dead past. As it turned out, the past was still very much alive. Various tribal contingents gave dance demonstrations during the afternoon hours; evening sessions featured dance competitions, including world championships in war dance, fancy dance, and "old man's dance." The intertribal dance sessions brought out several hundred enthusiastic participants wearing the latest powwow dance fashions.[50]

The Indian Leader, Haskell's school paper, ran predictably saccharine stories extolling progress and transformation (if ever editorial freedom was hamstrung, surely it was in an Indian school newspaper office). Its October 15 edition announced "a big war dance for the Indian dancing championship of the world," but also went on to note in the same passage that visitors could also take in "a buffalo barbecue, the [stadium] dedication program, the principal speech to be made by United States Senator Curtis . . . , a gigantic parade showing the advancement of Indian education, and last but not least the football game between Haskell and Bucknell." The powwow was only one of many activities slated for the weekend, and as far as the paper was concerned, it was the football game ("probably the greatest intersectional rivalry clash this far south in the Missouri Valley," it intoned) that really mattered. One week later, *The Indian Leader* promised, "In the dancing contest competition will be sharp. Many of the best Indian dancers will be present," and told readers, "If you enjoy rhythm in action, gracefulness, and poise, you have to be present Friday evening, October 29." Several pages later, however, the same edition reported on a visit by Secretary of the Interior Hubert Work to the Indian camp by lampooning those with whom he spoke as semiliterate "big chiefs" and "old squaws" who grunted their way through conversations. Football was the road to the future, and in its October 29 issue the paper's editors noted that while ten thousand spectators had taken in the dancing, it had all been little more than one final hurrah: "Probably never again will so many tribes be brought together to present their fancy dances." Haskell's football victory, on the other hand, was nothing less than "the eloquent expression of thanks on the part of the school to the older Indians who built the stadium."[51]

Other press accounts hinted that what was going on at the Haskell powwow was not the transformation of Indians into models of white, middle-class civility, but rather the continuation of dances and rituals that, to quote Bloom, "seemed to resist the very values and behavioral norms with which progress had become associated." With the papers' prurient interest in sexual imagery and savagism aside (an October 30 *Kansas City Times* story on the powwow was headlined "Like Birds and Beasts," and informed readers that "There is madness in the air. . . . it was diabolism."), few readers could have concluded that the powwow was a genteel or benign display of colorful native ways.[52] Even in their rush to burlesque the dancing and ceremonies — and readers could not have learned much from stories loaded with breathless musings about heathen spectacles, dancing savages, and modern-day "Indian invasions" — no one could deny that things just weren't turning out the way administrators had intended.

Haskell won the football game 36-0, but the powwow opened a Pandora's box. Fancy dance bustles trumped raccoon coats that weekend (and have ever since).[53] By the time it was over, the powwow had sparked such a positive reaction from participants that Young believes it was *the* crucial turning point in twentieth century Indian dancing. "The modern powwow era in Oklahoma began in 1926," she writes, "at Haskell Indian School."[54] In fact, the Haskell powwow led to a series of developments that had decisive effects on powwow culture across the Southern Plains. Among them was the rise to prominence of Gus McDonald, the Ponca fancy war dancer often credited with beginning that style of dance and clothing, and with him the world championship fancy dance contest held at the annual Ponca Powwow held near White Eagle, Oklahoma, every August. Both trace their roots to the Haskell powwow, which, as it turns out, was used to settle differences between McDonald and others, including Chester Lefthand, a Southern Arapaho, and Steve Mopope, a Kiowa, as to who was the acknowledged fancy dance world champion. The Haskell powwow was used to settle the score. Frank Turley recalled that "in the days when fancy dancing was a comparatively new style, several tribes claimed to have had the best dancers. To pacify complaints, an intertribal fancy dance contest was held in Lawrence, Kansas. It was then stipulated that the winner's tribe was to sponsor all future championship contests at an annual dance. Since a Ponca named August 'Gus' McDonald was named winner, the Poncas have made the contest a traditional feature of their powwow."[55]

Together, the new fancy dance world championship contest and the lure of McDonald and other leading fancy dancers made Ponca Powwow one of the leading dances in northern Oklahoma by the 1930s. The August 26, 1938, edition of the Ponca City *News,* for example, reported that the opening days of the annual Ponca Powwow had gone swimmingly. A princess was named and crowned, a visiting delegation of Lakota dancers from Pine Ridge, South Dakota, had arrived, and the story cheerfully noted that there were "tom-toms beating in perfect rhythm as the annual pow-wow of the Ponca Indians got underway before a more than capacity crowd." Two days later, a reporter wrote approvingly of the "age-old songs and dances of the Ponca Indians, brought through many generations, featured in the nightly festivities of the Ponca Indian pow-wow," and mentioned something that would shortly become a commonplace facet of powwow life: a large group of Ponca dancers had just hurriedly returned from yet another powwow in Mulvane, Kansas, to participate in the festivities at home.[56] By 1940, Ponca Powwow was a five-day event hosting some four thousand people. "Patriotic Dances Mark Opening of Poncas' Big Five Day Pow-wow

Event," announced the headline in the August 23, 1940, edition of the Ponca City *News;* opening night was "American Legion Night" (legion members from Buffalo Post #38— an all-Indian American Legion Post formed in 1918 in Ponca City and named in memory of Bob Buffalohead, a Ponca killed in World War I — were judges for the princess contest). The story described how "the old and new is represented at the reservation as numerous Indians drive up in cars, go to their tepees . . . and cook over an open campfire with the aid of electric lights."[57]

At about the same time, a number of other intertribal powwows were either starting or coming into their own as permanent, annual events. The Otoe Powwow, for example, outside of Perry, Oklahoma, was large enough by 1930 to gain the attention of the local press. That year the nearby Ponca City *News* carried a brief notice of the dance, calling attention to the good attendance (contingents from ten tribes were there) and commenting that "dances, games, and contests will feature the day and night program of the Indians." In southwest Oklahoma, the Dogpatch Powwow, Dietrich's Lake Powwow, the Craterville Indian Fair, and the American Indian Exposition became fixtures on the powwow circuit during the 1920s and 1930s. Alfred Chalepah, an Apache, recalled attending dances at Dietrich's Lake and at a site called Capitan's during the 1910s and 1920s. "Diedrick's Lake [*sic*] . . . they had a big dance over there. This Diedrick, he's supposed to be some Comanche. . . . Put on a big dance for all different tribes. They come there and take part in the program. So I danced."[58]

Chalepah's memories of the Capitan Powwow during the late 1910s and into the 1920s were more expansive: "They have big dance[s] there. And they get together and kinda organize. They pledge beeves a year ahead [to feed the camp]. . . . We lived right there, [with] my grandparents. Pretty soon the camp start coming in, in wagons. Boy, I tell you, it was a big place there. When all the campers come in, you could see their horses out in the pasture. There was eighty acres. . . . Then when they get started, in the morning, before that Brush Dance [a component of the old Sun Dance adapted to the new powwow] — they have a parade on horseback. Boy, everybody got on horses. . . . . [I was] eight years old. It was 1918 when they first started. Right there. They made Flag Song. . . . They had a dance here at Fort Cobb at Apache Jay's. . . . And they had another one here at Apache Jim's. And they had another one at Bitsidi's. . . . Boy, they come in early. Sometimes people come there about two weeks [early], . . . big camp. They camp here about two weeks, I guess, before the pow-wow starts." When the interviewer asked "did they call it a 'pow-wow' back then?" he answered "yeah."[59]

Dogpatch and Dietrich's Lake were typical of 1920s and 1930s powwows in southwest Oklahoma. Dogpatch, for example, was held east of Clinton, Oklahoma, on an allotment owned by the Heap of Birds family, who began sponsoring the dance sometime in the 1920s. No one seems to know where, exactly, the name comes from, but Mary Belle Curtis Lonebear, a Cheyenne, laughed when she said "probably 'cause there was a lotta' dogs there. It was kinda like a little community, you know, like the funny papers, and it just got the nickname and it just stuck. Everyone knew where Dogpatch was." The dance ran through the early 1940s, was popular with locals, and is fondly remembered today. Lonebear (who was born in 1928) danced at Dogpatch as a young girl. "I remember the first powwow I went to was at Dogpatch. That was the first time I got to wear my buckskin dress, 'cause I never did get to go anywhere else. I must've been about 12 or 13, and it got in my blood. I danced after that, you know, danced all the time after that."[60]

Another powwow that got its start early in the twentieth century was the Murrow dance, an annual gathering that has been held every summer southwest of Carnegie, Oklahoma, for eighty-five years. Because the Murrow Powwow did not begin as a social powwow, and has never lost its connection to the tribally specific dances that typified its earliest events, its history reveals how dance culture has changed over time to accommodate new needs and practices. The dance's origins lay with a Ghost Dance held around 1909 that Madeline Hamilton's mother, who was born in 1900, remembered witnessing as a child. Acting on a vision to establish a dance ground for the Caddoes, Madeline's great-grandfather cleared land and erected a Ghost Dance pole. As Madeline recounted, her great-grandfather said that "the message came from the Lord. This pole and the dance ground were sacred and good for us." In the decades that followed, Caddo people continued to gather for the Ghost Dance, and for Caddo social dances as well. But by the 1920s, those social dances began to take precedence over the Ghost Dance, and the purpose of the gathering began to shift away from its religious roots. In the 1940s, members of the Kiowa O-ho-mah Lodge began to visit in larger and larger numbers, often conducting their own Brush dances in the morning as they moved into their camps, and looking on as the Caddoes performed their tribal dances. "Before long, they were helping us put on the dance," said Madeline. "They'd come and sing for us, that's why we have such a long association with those O-ho-mah families. It's good that our Indian people can learn from one another and help one another like that."[61]

The theft of the old Ghost Dance pole in 1957 threatened to stall the dance, but the family decided to carry on the tradition, all the while maintaining hope that they would eventually recover the pole. (In fact, it was found in a nearby museum and there are plans to repatriate it to Madeline's family in the spring of 2003. It will be received, fittingly enough, as part of a dance gathering.) Even after the O-ho-mah Lodge began co-hosting the dance, it remained true to its Caddo roots. To this day, the Murrow Powwow features traditional Caddo dances each afternoon that must be completed before sundown. After a dinner break, intertribal dancing begins and lasts through the evening. But the dance committee does not sponsor contests ("contests can really cause a lot of problems — they can bring out the wrong bunch," Madeline observed), and it does not appoint head dancers, singers, or other head staff. In this respect, it has managed to distance itself from the powwow culture that dominates the dance scene in southwest Oklahoma. And that suits its supporters just fine. As one long-time singer for the dance described it to me, "Murrow's reminds me of those small dances way back there when people got together for a good time. It's very relaxed out there, people come to see their friends, hear good music, and just enjoy themselves." For Madeline Hamilton, the dance remains an important link to her family's history. "Before she passed away, my mother told us to carry on the dance just as long as you can," she said. "I've tried to do that, I've tried to keep it the way they wanted it."[62]

The Murrow Powwow was not a fair, and it did not revolve around ball games, craft contests, or other activities designed to attract a crowd. It was, above all, a community event that drew families and friends together. "They *danced* at those early powwows like Dogpatch and Murrow's," said Jim Anquoe. "They got after it. If you wanted to do those 'Indian Fair' things — the rides and carnivals, you know — the 'white' things, so to speak, well, you went to Craterville and Anadarko Fair. But at some of those other dances, well, you'd better come ready to get down to business. And the camps — man, you just wouldn't believe how many people would come in the week of the dance and set up. Tipis, arbors — it was a sight." Lonebear alluded to this as well, saying that Dogpatch was "a three-day powwow, and it was Indian-owned, Indian-run . . . just a good powwow, clean powwow. We camped. . . . my dad would stay there all week. We'd all go home on Sunday night and he'd stay on and visit his brothers, camp there — and people camped there year 'round. My dad would visit around 'til almost Wednesday and then move home. But it was just something just real enjoyable." Anquoe, who began dancing in 1943 when he was four years old, recalled that "when I was just a little guy, I mean *little*, on Friday night we'd get on the wagon and hitch the team and go to whatever dance was nearby. Mom and Dad were Catholic, so they'd go to Mass first. Sunday night we'd be coming home, it'd take all night from Anadarko. So, we'd get home, brush up a little bit, Mom would feed us, and we'd go on to school. We *never* missed school on account of powwowing. We've been singing and dancing all of our lives." Dietrich's Lake, Dogpatch, Bitsidi's, Murrow's, Apache Jay's, Apache Jim's, Capitan's, Pawnee, White Eagle, and Stroud were coming to represent the new order of things. "Remember this," Jim Anquoe told me with a discernable measure of pride, "this is the first powwow circuit in the United States. We've been at it since way back there at Dietrich's and Murrow's. Poncas had the best war dancing in the country up to the 1960s. To me they still do."[63]

Many powwows remained small affairs comprised of kin and community members, especially in the 1930s and 1940s. The Osage Day dances, for example, were organized by a handful of families in Hominy led by Francis Claremore. Murrow's Powwow followed the same pattern when a group of prominent powwow people, including Chester Lefthand (Southern Arapaho), Jack Hokeah (Kiowa), Steve Mopope (Kiowa), and George Watchetaker (Comanche), helped to popularize the dance. Jim Anquoe said that in Southwest Oklahoma "the people who danced were people, I thought, who kept up their traditions. To me, the people around Red Stone, Mt. Scott, Stecker, Ft. Cobb, Anadarko, and Washita [in the old Kiowa-Comanche-Apache Reservation] — these were the ones that did it. We all knew each other. Uncle Jack [Hokeah] — he was all the time coming over to get us to go to the dances." Interestingly, Anquoe's father, a Kiowa who began singing in 1912 and became a renowned head singer in Oklahoma, was a good example of the emerging intertribal context of the powwow. He spent considerable time in Ponca country, where he was given a song by Ponca friends. "Dad's song, it's in the Heluska. When Dad got that song, probably around 1909, well, his family gave away a horse in thanks." Anquoe chuckled as he finished the story: "Dad really hated that song because they gave his best horse away!"[64]

Many of these early dances were modest by today's standards. For every Diedrich, Dogpatch, and Capitan, there just as many smaller dances, especially in the 1930s and early 1940s. "It was hard times, you know — the Depression was on, and then of course the war," remembered Anquoe. "All the dances I went to when I was small, they were just tiny. There were just a very few of them that were large gatherings. There weren't that many dances, and I'll tell you this — singers were hard to find. Now there were plenty of guys who would just hit the drum you know, but *real* singers — they were hard to come by." Contest prizes were similarly modest, but an ethic of feeding people and taking care of their needs emerged that was clearly reminiscent of the older society dances. "They didn't have much prize money — ten bucks, five bucks — back then," according to Anquoe. "What they did, though, was feed you well. Gave you food, gave you a little gas money. Even now, ten bucks will get you across the state, so back then two or three bucks would do it. And when they had giveaways they'd give fruit — hard to get a hold of, almost unheard of. This one Ponca man, he wanted this old lady to have this fruit he'd gotten. She was *really* honored. Food, he's giving her food, best thing he could do. First thing she does is get a rag and cover it carefully to take it home."[65]

Yet if many dances were (and remain) small and localized, there were grander experiments on the horizon by the 1920s and 1930s. Ponca Powwow, for example, was bringing in thousands of participants and visitors by the 1930s, as were the Pawnee and Otoe powwows. And there were promoters who hoped to capitalize on this burgeoning movement. Taking their cue from the old reservation fairs that authorities had once hailed as the blueprints for transforming Indians into farmers and stockmen, the promoters began to propose annual fairs at which dancing and traditional activities were the central attractions. Like the powwows then beginning to appear all over the region, these all-Indian fairs featured contest dancing and exhibitions, were intertribal, and, of course, were planned with the public in mind. Seen as moneymakers and marketing tools for tribes and communities alike, the momentum for these fairs began to build during the 1920s.

Not every proposal made it past the drawing board. When several promoters (including a U.S. congressman from Oklahoma) made a pitch to Kiowa-Comanche-Apache agent C. V. Stinchecum in 1921 for permission to build a campground and exhibition building near Ft. Sill expressly for the purpose of staging dance shows, the agent turned the request down on both ethical and practical grounds. As the self-appointed guardian of local codes of morality, he sourly called dances "a nest of iniquity of the worst sort" that encouraged immoral practices and produced "a goodly number" of illegitimate children. Moreover, Stinchecum was indignant that such enterprises might be financially motivated: "I cannot help but feel that Mr. Banks has in mind the possibility of commercializing the attractions which the Indian dances offer to the white public." Noting that the proposed site was near the well-known resort at Medicine Park, Stinchecum surmised that he could "readily see how an Indian camp and Indian dances would be an added attraction to the people visiting this resort . . . but I do not believe that our Indians should be thus commercialized. I can see absolutely no good to be accomplished on behalf of our Indians and can foresee much sorrow and degradation, to say nothing of the results upon the industrial activities of our Indian population." The day was coming, he added, when "they will be expected to take their positions in the community alongside the white man and it has always been my idea that nothing should be sanctioned that would encourage the Indian in the feeling that he was a race separate and distinct from the white man."[66]

Stinchecum derailed this attempt, but the victory was both lonely and short-lived. Three years later, the July 24, 1924, edition of the Lawton *Constitution* carried a front-page story under the headline "Comanches Hold Stomp Dances." If the paper got the name of the dance wrong (stomp dances are from the Five Civilized tribes), it conveyed the details in a way that suggested the shape of things to come. "The big Indian picnic and dance being held this week at John

Whitewolf's farm is attracting wide attention, Indians from all over the country being in attendance," went the story's opening lines. "About thirty Indian 'braves' dressed in the most gorgeous and elaborate costumes seen among the tribes in many days received hearty applause for their dancing. . . . It is estimated that 1500 attended the dancing last evening. The Whitewolf farm is located two miles north of Carter's store on the main Medicine Park road."[67] The Whitewolf dance was huge by the standards of the day, played to an appreciative audience, and managed to get publicity that included not only a celebratory description of the goings on, but directions to the site as well.

And it wasn't the only game in town that summer. Three weeks before Whitewolf's dance, the same newspaper had run another front-page story about a white promoter named D. E. Oswalt who was putting on a combination rodeo and exhibition of "real Indian dances" at nearby Medicine Park July 4–6. "Indians in their native costumes will dance each night," said the story, and the public could expect "a good show for their money."[68] One year later, twenty-five hundred Indians from all over the region crowded into Medicine Park again for what the Lawton *Constitution* billed as "the annual picnic which is held for the purpose of getting the Red Men together for cementing the friendship of various tribes." Under the headline "War Dance Tonight Will Be Feature of Today's Program," the paper's July 31 edition informed readers that "some of the best dancers in the state are at the park."[69]

Two days later came news of yet another large contest powwow: "Indian Dance At Buffalo Pasture is Declared One Of Best Held in State, Seventy-Five Bucks From Five Different Tribes Compete Friday Night." While not as large as the Medicine Park dance, the Buffalo Pasture Powwow staked a claim to quality. "Dancing of every known fashion was displayed," reported the story, "with two of the most important dancers of the state — Steve Mopope and James White Buffalo, both Kiowas, being present. . . . These two boys have danced practically over the entire state of Oklahoma taking off prizes at the contest held this spring at Ponca City when the meeting of the State Society of Oklahoma Indians was held."[70]

It is apparent that the powwow, to paraphrase Gloria Young, was coming of age, with a regular circuit, significant prize monies, a collection of stars, and an appreciative audience.[71] Communities, tribes, and families were sponsoring a variety of dances on a regular basis, and it was clear that the government's assimilationist agenda was no longer going to impede their efforts. Yet, there was more to come, especially when dances moved into large public arenas during the 1920s and 1930s. Beginning with Craterville Park in 1924, and the American Indian Exposition in 1935, powwow culture was about to become much larger and more widespread than anyone could have imagined.

CHAPTER SIX

"Enormous crowds attracted by the war dances"
Craterville Park and the American Indian Exposition

In 1924, a new order of things appeared when a white man named Frank Rush and a coalition of Indians from the Kiowa, Comanche, and Apache tribes created the Craterville Indian Fair at Rush's private amusement park west of Lawton and Ft. Sill. Rush had purchased the Craterville Park west of Lawton in 1923 when he retired after a career of twenty-six years with the ranger force at the Wichita National Forest and Game Preserve. He was well known to local Indians, knew a winner when he saw one, and figured that an all-Indian fair would be a lucrative investment. Seizing on the momentum that such events were generating, Rush and the Indian men signed an agreement on May 25, 1924 to create an annual all-Indian fair at the park. The agreement (Rush called it a "covenant") read like this:

> Whereas it has become necessary for the American Indians to take steps for the advancement and uplift of their people, especially to teach their children the values of building character and becoming self-supporting, this covenant is entered into as a means to that end. . . . The object of the fair will be to create self confidence and to encourage leadership by the Indian for his people, a belief in the capacity of the Indian to better his position and to take his place on terms of equality with all other races in the competitive pursuits of everyday life. . . . All Officers, Directors, Judges, and Exhibitors . . . must be Indians and . . . must be elected by the Indians themselves.[1]

An intertribal board of directors was chaired by Big Bow, a Kiowa. Vice-President Tommy Martinez, a Comanche, Secretary-Treasurer Herman Asenap, a Comanche, and Director Ned Brace, a Kiowa, assumed responsibility for planning and running the event, but Rush was never far from the center of the action. For their part, Big Bow and Herman Asenap enthusiastically applauded Rush's plan (especially his decision to admit Indians free of charge to the fair) and publicly acknowledged Rush's commitment in the August 15, 1924, edition of the Lawton *Constitution*. "He has undertaken to do something for the Indian that no other

white man has ever tried to do, and we should take pride in giving him every assistance," went their letter. "Frank Rush has promised a square deal for everybody, and all of our people should do all they can to make this Indian fair a
success. No so-called 49 dance, no gambling, and no intoxicants will be permitted. The Craterville Indian Fair will be what the Indians make it."[2]

In its early years, Rush's vision of the event as equal parts county fair, agricultural exposition, dance show, and rodeo clashed with the powwow's somewhat sharper emphasis on celebrating Indian culture and traditions. One week
before the first fair opened, for example, the Lawton *Constitution* ran a front-
page story describing it in glowing terms as "one of the biggest affairs and at
the same time the most original and unique entertainments, both instructive
and entertaining, that has ever been held in this county." The three-day extravaganza opened with a parade that included the "greatest number of Indians
ever seen in buckskin costumes at one time." Day two featured "interesting old
Indian plays . . . among them being an Indian stage coach robbery," while day
three — "a most interesting day" — included Kiowa and Comanche girls playing "a fast game of basketball." At the end of the story there was a brief mention of the "Indian war dances" that were the featured entertainment each
evening, but on balance, dancing got short shrift. Indeed, the story reported
that "this is really a fair, and the entertainment is second to the real good and
encouragement which the Indian farmer will get out of the fair." Whites and
Indians alike crowded the park, and by the time it closed, the fair had been a
resounding success. A headline in the August 17 edition of the Lawton *Constitution* announced "2500 Indians Participate in First Agricultural Fair," and the
paper reported on the "enormous crowds attracted by the war dances and three
Indian nations," as well as by a cavalcade of pony races, games, and exhibits.
With evident satisfaction, the story went on to note that "such an array of gorgeous Indian raiment has never before been seen in this section."[3]

The fair's second installment in 1925 relied on the same line-up as its prede-
cessor. If anything, it did even more to emphasize and exoticize Indian culture
by resorting to the worst stereotypes. Headlines in the August 23 edition of the
Lawton *Constitution* somewhat breathlessly announced "Old Stage Coach Rob-
beries, Attacks on Whites Features Annual Indian Celebration," and a front-page
story promised a dramatic "Indian play" featuring the "sneaking and creeping
of the warriors." Three days later, the same paper assured readers that the stage
robbery had been the most exciting event of the entire fair and was "not only . . .
interesting to witness, but also very educational." Once again, dancing got relatively little play in the papers, certainly not as much as the thirty-piece band,
horse races, roping contests, and parades that Rush had planned.[4]

By the 1927 fair, however, a shift was apparent; dancing got more attention, promoters assured spectators that prominent powwow dancers would attend, and the press began to cover the contests in greater detail. In 1927, for example, the fair's premium booklet announced that Steve Mopope, one of the most accomplished and well-known fancy dancers on the Southern Plains, would take charge of the war dancing. (Mopope was still at it in 1930, when the Lawton *Constitution* announced that he would again direct the dancing.) Coverage of contest dancing, which was quickly becoming the most popular event at the fair, also expanded to receive nearly equal billing with the pony races and tipi villages. By then, moreover, it was apparent that having big names from the powwow world mattered, and that the fair was becoming a big player on the powwow circuit. Indeed, in a surprising show of civic boosterism that would have been unimaginable only a decade earlier, the Oklahoma state legislature appropriated $1,000 for fair premiums in 1929 to promote the Craterville Fair against its larger and better known rivals in New Mexico, the Gallup Ceremonial and the Santa Fe Southwest Indian Fair. (It is helpful to recall that Charles Burke had issued Circular 1665 banning all dancing only nine years earlier.) The state legislature further endorsed the fair in 1931 by passing a resolution changing the name of the event to the "Oklahoma State Indian Fair" (but most people continued to call it Craterville Fair) and funding a silver Governor's Cup for the best agricultural exhibits.[5]

In 1931, the Lawton *Constitution* covered the "age-old" dances on no fewer than three days and proudly announced in its August 31 edition that the fair had just hosted the world's fancy dance championship. The Poncas probably had a thing or two to say about that claim, but the *Constitution* left little room for doubt as far as the Craterville crowd was concerned: "Comanche Youth is Proclaimed Best Dancer in Colorful Contest at Craterville State Indian Fair." The paper reported that the final rounds (held the previous evening before thousands of appreciative patrons) had yielded a champion truly worthy of the title. The contest, moreover, had pitted two of the giants in fancy dancing against one another in a spectacle of motion and physicality so fantastic that the reporter could adequately express it only by appealing to images plucked from industrial modernity:

Joe Atocknie was declared the champion Indian dancer of the world. . . . Chester Lefthand . . . won second place. Atocknie made a colorful and striking figure as his graceful young body kept perfect time . . . exhibiting splendid footwork and showing almost perfect rhythm as he imitated steam engines, airplanes and other late methods of transportation. The young

Indian also displayed his ability in imitating in contrast birds, eagles, and animals.[6]

In 1932, delegations from fourteen tribes attended the ninth annual fair, and luminaries in the crowd included humorist Will Rogers, described by one reporter as a "close friend of Mr. Rush." The governor was a regular visitor by then, as were various and sundry political figures, civic leaders, and, ironically enough, officials from the Bureau of Indian Affairs. Buoyed by claims the previous year as host of the world's champion contests, announcements for the 1932 fair invited the public to see the "world's champion Indian war dance" again. The contests, however, were paired with a new and different kind of dance show — "a series of exhibitions of . . . dances Sunday night, including practically every dance staged during the fair." When I asked a Kiowa man who attended these dances as a young man what he thought the significance of this program was, he replied, "Well, Craterville was sort of, you know, getting a regular program together that became one way to do a powwow. You know, grand entry, then some round dancing, contests, intertribals, then a princess contest, then visiting tribes' dances and shows, hoop dance, visitors being asked to come on down and dance, all like that. You know, just like what you see these days."[7]

But the end was near for the Craterville Fair. The 1933 event — the tenth — was the last. Coverage in the Lawton paper that year was sparse; the celebratory tone that had typified stories on previous fairs was missing. Indeed, the paper ran a lone story on the fair, reporting that hundreds (but not the customary thousands) of Indians were gathering "to turn back the pages of history," and that the pony races, "Indian games," and exhibits would be "unusually good."[8] There were no other accounts of the 1933 fair in the Lawton paper, a curious thing in light of the broad coverage it had previously received. It was an astonishingly quick end. Only one year earlier, Will Rogers, one of the most famous personalities in the country, had found time to attend. Thousands of Indians from more than a dozen tribes in Oklahoma crowded into the park year after year for the week-long fair, putting up a fantastic array of tipis and camps and giving demonstrations of everything from dancing to arrow making. Newsreels captured the spectacle for a curious audience. The best contest dancers on the Southern Plains competed for one of the region's most coveted titles, and the grandstands were filled to capacity night after night and year after year. How could all of that so suddenly end?

While popular opinion soon came to hold that the new American Indian Exposition in nearby Anadarko had spelled Craterville's demise, the reasons were more complicated. The crucial factor was the death on April 7, 1933, of Frank Rush from a paralytic stroke at the age of 68. Funeral announcements invariably noted his connection to the fair and stressed his pioneer roots. The April 7 Lawton *Constitution* (which appeared only hours after Rush's death) hailed him in a front-page headline as a "pioneer state resident," while the April 8 Oklahoma City *Daily Oklahoman* noted that "Frank Rush, Indian's Best Friend, Dead." Two days later, the *Daily Oklahoman* carried another front-page story headlined "State Indians Laud Life of White Friend . . . Tribal Leaders Point to Colorful Figure as Their 'Brother.'" Closer to home, the April 10 Lawton *Constitution* called Rush "Comanche County's first citizen and the greatest friend Indians of Southwest Oklahoma have ever known."[9]

The Craterville Fair got its fair share of attention in the stories, as when the April 8 *Daily Oklahoman* noted that "one of the outstanding achievements of Rush's career and of which he was most proud was his sponsorship of the all-Indian agricultural fair held each year at Craterville Park. . . . The Indians believed the fair ground at Craterville Park was a hallowed spot — a place designated by the Great Spirit for them to gather once each year and turn back the pages of history by staging their dances and donning their tribal costumes. Because of his great interest in their welfare, Rush was considered by the Indians as one of their best friends among the white men. They considered him a wise and trustworthy counselor and went to him many times to settle their differences and decide matters of utmost importance." The Lawton *Constitution* proudly reminded readers that "Rush originated and sponsored the only all-Indian agricultural fair in the world, at his home, Craterville Park."[10]

Indians were prominent at the services (as were Boy Scouts and Masons), and the family asked Hunting Horse (Kiowa), Guy Quoetone (Kiowa), George Wallace (Comanche), and Herman Asenap (Comanche), all of whom were on the Craterville Fair board, to serve as honorary pall bearers. Several Indians gave emotional speeches during the services, including a Comanche named Millet who said the tribes were there to "pay respect to the man who has been the best friend to the Indians." The April 10 Lawton *Constitution* reported that "Indian speakers and ministers characterize him as an advisor, director, and leader among the tribes . . . one who has done his part in serving humanity. The stoic faces of Indian friends broke under the strain of sadness and sorrow. Many Indians shed tears as they viewed the remains of their dearest friend for the last time." Herman Asenap added that "we lose a great friend in this man, Mr. Rush. We loved him because of what he had done for Indians"; while the venerable Hunting Horse (who was also the one-time chair of the Craterville Fair board) noted that "we loved him with all our hearts. We thank you white people for coming and paying respects to him."[11] Even in death, Rush's legacy was prominently tied to the Craterville Fair, and many Indians mourned his passing as the loss of a true friend.

Rush's death aside, other serious problems were already on the horizon. First, as the Depression deepened, it must have been increasingly difficult for Rush to maintain his budgets. By the late 1920s and early 1930s the nation's economic crisis was at its worst, but the fair was still quite large, and Rush continued to extend an enormous level of generosity, including rations for the camps and free admission for Indians. All of this probably began to take a bite out of his wallet that he couldn't replace. And when he couldn't pay performers and contestants as much as they asked, or as much as other venues promised, dancers went elsewhere. Moreover, getting the best dancers grew more difficult with each year as other powwows, fairs, and shows emerged. By the early 1930s, Rush faced competition from events that were as good as his, including the Ponca Powwow (whose dates often conflicted with Craterville's), numerous county fairs, community powwows, and most notably from the nearby Anadarko American Indian Exposition.

One man whose father had been a regular at the fair told me that "Rush did favors for Indians, sure, but you know a lot of people thought he was really catering to whites, not to Indians, and after nine or ten years of being told what to do, Daddy and them they just up and went over to Anadarko, where Indians were in charge. Took the whole family. So did a lot of others. Old Man Rush, he was plenty mad to hear my daddy tell it, but what was he going to do? Personally, I think some people got tired of the dog and pony show at Craterville — too much shoot 'em up and 'wild Indians,' so to speak. And at Anadarko you had Indians in charge." Another long-time Anadarko resident put it this way: "Well, after about the early 1930s, the Expo was just the place to be. Craterville — it was a good time while it lasted, but you know, people move on. Better money in town [Anadarko], closer to home. Pretty soon, that's where all the Indians went."[12]

Indeed, the sentiment among many Indians was that Craterville had outlived its usefulness. Jethro Gaede has written that the matter at hand was "a significant desire for self representation and cultural expression," and that the Craterville Park fair had been "the most compelling agent of discontent."[13] In an unpublished essay written sometime in the late 1980s or early 1990s, Parker McKenzie, a Kiowa who helped start the American Indian Exposition, recalled that "during the early 1930s, talk amongst various Indian individuals of the Anadarko area began to circulate about starting strictly an Indian-managed fair. There was at the time considerable dissatisfaction amongst Indians who seasonally attended the Craterville Fair near Cache, Okla., over the fact that the promoter there was plainly 'using' the Indians for his own financial benefit, and allowing but a trickle to them." In a l993 letter to Richard Tartsah, then the newly elected president of the Exposition, McKenzie sought to dispel the often repeated story that "the Exposition had its start at Craterville and then 'moved' to Anadarko for its first event there in 1932." He wrote, "The Exposition had nothing to do with the Craterville event, which was run by Frank Rush, a white man who owned the land where the fair was held. . . . He was sole boss of everything, his Indian 'board of directors' was just a figurehead; most spoke no English. In fact, the Craterville event was still a going event each season the first three years of the Exposition. The latter caused its demise." In a 1989 newspaper story, McKenzie had been more emphatic: "I wish to emphasize . . . that this Indian event sprouted at Anadarko and was [in] no way associated with the then on-going Craterville Fair near Cache, as some persons believe."[14]

McKenzie and others also pointed out the Caddo County Fair in Anadarko wasn't doing much better than Craterville at attracting the best dancers and Indian exhibitors, and he later insisted that their cumulative shortcomings prompted the creation of the American Indian Exposition. Held every August in Anadarko at the county fair grounds, the Caddo County Fair — like the agricultural fairs held in every neighboring county — had long featured Indian encampments, native arts and crafts, pony races, and show dancing.

When the Caddo fair began to cut back on its Indian program in the early 1930s, however, trouble began to brew. "The matter definitely came to a head in early 1932," explained McKenzie, "when the Caddo County fair board trimmed its operating budget . . . on account of the depression that then was rearing its ugly head. Naturally the first whack fell on exhibits of Indian arts and crafts." When the fair ended all premiums for Indian exhibits, Anadarko Agency superintendent John Buntin and field matron Susie Peters convinced the Bureau of Indian Affairs to provide $75 in premiums for Indian exhibits at the fair.[15]

Buntin then suggested to Jasper Saunkeah, a Kiowa, that "the funding might be the beginning of the long-dreamed-of fair" that Saunkeah and a dozen or so others had been mulling over for several years. As McKenzie remembered it, "Saunkeah came immediately to my desk at the BIA office where I then was employed." After discussing the idea of an all-Indian fair, "We at once decided, 'why not?' " Saunkeah became the first president, and McKenzie signed on as vice president. In order to make it all "seem more businesslike," McKenzie named the organization the Southwestern Indian Fair Association, and under its auspices secured booths at the Caddo County Fair for Indian exhibits. Fair officials also gave control of the Friday evening show over to the new association, which promptly scheduled a dance program. The proceeds went to the

Indians, and McKenzie later recalled that "it was their only income, and it was quite negligible." Indeed, the whole escapade ran on a wing and a prayer. "Money was scarce in the so-called Great Depression," McKenzie recalled. "We Indians were bold — maybe foolish — to start an enterprise at that time."[16]

Yet if the beginning was inauspicious, it wasn't long before McKenzie, Saunkeah, Lewis Ware, and Maurice Bedoka took control of the new association and launched an event that many associate with the powwow's golden era on the Southern Plains. The issue of control became a matter of public record on September 21, 1932, when the Anadarko *Tribune* ran a story on the new association under the headline "Permanent Indian Fair Association Being Organized" and reported that members were hopeful "that plans will be worked out whereby the Indian fair may be operated by Indians themselves as a separate unit." The story went on to reveal that a twelve-member board was in place with Lewis Ware as president and McKenzie as secretary, and with representatives from the Kiowa, Comanche, Apache, Cheyenne, Arapaho, Caddo, Wichita, and Delaware tribes. The paper also reprinted a resolution authored by McKenzie and Ware, and adopted the previous week at a meeting in Anadarko, calling attention to the new order of things.

> Whereas we, the members of western Oklahoma Indians, consisting of Kiowa, Comanche, Apache, Cheyenne, Arapaho, Wichita, Caddo, Delaware, and other affiliated tribes, realize the necessity of depending upon ourselves in any line of endeavor in our contact with the white people to be successful and fully enjoy the benefits resulting therefrom; that we further realize the necessity of co-operating with the white people and relying upon them to some extent for assistance in order to fully accomplish our objects, and that we are forever mindful of all past co-operation and assistance obtained from this source,
>
> Whereas, there has been held in the state of Oklahoma, various events for the past several years designated as 'Indian Fair,' 'Indian Pow-wow,' etc., which are not strictly Indian in their management although Indians participate. That it is the belief of this body that such events are merely money making ventures on the part of individuals or of groups, that the advancement of the Indian in his industrial pursuits is not the paramount object of those responsible for these events, and that it is the belief of this body that in order for the Indian to fully receive all benefits of such affairs, it must be his duty to participate in all phases of such an event — from the managing body on down.
>
> Resolved, therefore, That this body authorizes the president to appoint a committee to present this resolution to the Honorable William H. Murray,

Governor of Oklahoma, and request that any future appropriation made by the State of Oklahoma for an Indian fair or some similar event in any part of the state should be made after a careful investigation, in order that the object of the state in making the appropriation shall be fully observed and carried out.

Resolved, That this committee shall ask the Honorable Governor of the state of Oklahoma to give the fair board for the western Oklahoma Indians a fair and impartial consideration when any appropriations are made for this purpose, in order that it may receive some of the financial assistance that may be forthcoming in this respect."[17]

The resolution was remarkable for several reasons, the most dramatic of which was the determination of Indian people to claim overt control of such events. When seen in the context of the explosion of dancing that occurred in the 1920s and 1930s, the resolution was a definitive moment in the history of Southern Plains powwow culture. Here, for all to read, was an unambiguous call for recognition and control that no one could fail to understand.

The resolution's intent was revealing for other reasons as well. Notice, for example, the complaint that previous fairs had emphasized dancing and old-time entertainment to the neglect of "industrial pursuits." Craterville's stage-coach attack with its "creeping" and "sneaking" warriors, and its camps full of Indians "prepared to turn back the pages of history" seemed out of place and offensive to McKenzie and his associates. In their opinion, if Indians were to compete favorably with whites, then the fairs ought to do for Indians what they did for whites: promote, encourage, and reward hard work. Implicit here was a critique of the dancing and other exhibitions that became centerpieces of fairs. In light of what the fair would soon come to represent, there is some irony in the fact that the aims expressed by McKenzie and Ware were less about celebrating dancing than encouraging models of self-sufficiency based on avowedly white models.

An Anadarko *Tribune* story on the 1932 Caddo fair, for example, featured three photos of old-time culture complete with tipis and travois over a cutline that read, "The best Indian amusements have been provided for the entertainment of the public. The colorful blending of the old with the new. Good horse racing each day — Indian horses, Indian riders."[18] Amusements, entertainments, and colorful blending might capture the fancy of white audiences, but it seemed lowbrow to the Southwestern Indian Fair Association's founders. The remedy, they argued, was to place control of Indian fairs in the hands of educated, progressive Indians who would provide the tribes with suitable environments for fair goers. It is worth remembering, moreover, that one of McKenzie's criticisms of Frank Rush was that his board of directors "was just a figurehead; most spoke no English." Conversely, the Southwestern Indian Fair Association's directors were what we might generally concede to be "progressive" Indians: fluent in English, boarding-school educated, and prominent in local circles as business figures, ranchers, and civic leaders.

And yet, as events proved, it is too simple to say that the Southwestern Indian Fair Association was in the hands of assimilationists who intended to do away with dancing or other traditional elements of the program. The board's members were hardly toadies to the local Indian superintendent. McKenzie, for example, might have extolled the virtues of hard work and success, but he was also a renowned linguist whose work on the Kiowa language was published by the Smithsonian Institution and became a landmark in the maintenance of native ways and beliefs. Herman Asenap was a stalwart in the Comanche community and a deacon at the Post Oak Mennonite Church, where a deeply meaningful and thoroughly Comanche spirituality had blossomed. Ned Brace, a Kiowa, had attended Carlisle, but came home to become a prominent figure in the Native American Church and an outspoken supporter of the right of Indians to use peyote in their religious ceremonies. Jess Rowlodge, as we have seen, was very active in Cheyenne and Arapaho traditional ceremonies and had led the way to the 1917 Sun Dance in which he triumphed over hard-core assimilationists in the Indian bureau.

The Southwestern Indian Fair was held in conjunction with the Caddo County Fair for two years, 1932 and 1933. On August 31, 1932, the Anadarko *Tribune* explained in a story headlined "Indian Department at Caddo County Free Fair" that the "all-Indian fair" under the direction of the Indian Fair Board of the Kiowa Agency would be conducted "along the same general lines as that of the Caddo County Free Fair." The Kiowa Agency had provided $500 for premiums, and the fair announcement promised that "Friday night the Indians will have complete charge of an entertainment in front of the grandstand. Indian dances will be the principal attraction, and prizes will be offered for best dancer, best costumed man and best costumed woman."[19]

By 1933, however, it was apparent that the Indian fair's future lay with a separate event. Following the 1933 fair, McKenzie and the other directors informed the county fair association of their decision to set a separate date for 1934, one month ahead of the county fair. Whites dismissed the move as suicidal, and the president and secretary of the Caddo county fair association were "much amused" when Lewis Ware pointedly told them, "You know, men, one of these days the Indian fair is going to kill the county fair." Writing in the late 1980s, McKenzie remarked, "Today, no one will deny that the Indian fair has 'finished' the county fair, insofar as a drawing power and the sweet jingling of many more dollars going into the tills of Anadarko's businesses are concerned."[20]

The 1934 Southwestern Indian Fair — described by the August 1 Anadarko *Tribune* as a "gala event with an unusual program" — was equal parts county agricultural fair and Craterville Park. "As an educational measure," the *Tribune* story disclosed, the Indians would receive "instructions on raising live stock, grain and farm products from authorities on these subjects." On the other hand, the five thousand to seven thousand Indians expected to attend were also going to be displaying their "native and picturesque attractions which . . . assures the fair board of having many white visitors." A parade with a "galaxy of colors and costumes" would open the event and mark the moment when the Indians would "fall back into native dress and custom for the duration of the fair." The Anadarko *Daily American-Democrat* repeated the same description line for line before adding that the participants would "revert to camp life" during the fair. The story also publicized that a "most beautiful Indian girl in modern costume will be chosen to reign over the fair" and "sports, which will occupy a great deal of their time during the encampment will include tribal dances of all sorts."[21]

One week before opening day, the *Tribune*'s August 8 edition predicted the fair would open "in a blaze of glory." The parade was all set, as were a round-robin baseball tournament and agricultural displays. Organizers had also arranged for public performances by the thirty-piece Southwestern Indian Band, and a carnival billed as the "Evangeline Shows" was already in place and open "for the diversion of the public." A week later, organizers told *Tribune* reporters that "those in charge feel that the Southwestern All-Indian Fair will be one of the foremost events of its kind ever attempted in this country," but failed to comment on any dancing. However, after reporting that the fair offered "everything reminiscent of early Indian life," the August 15 *Daily American-Democrat* reported that "tonight's program will consist of Indian dances; some of the best dancers in the country will take part." Two days later, the same paper noted that most local businesses were closed for the fair and that record crowds had taken in the band concerts, horse races, and an "interesting program depicting Indian customs" despite a heat wave with temperatures well over 100 degrees. At the fair's conclusion, the *Tribune* triumphantly reported that "All-Indian Fair Is Great Success From All Angles." "From every standpoint," said the accompanying story, "the Southwestern All-Indian Fair was a success. The officers were well-pleased with the way it went over, and the public avowed it a great exposition." Premium winners were listed in the *Tribune* and *Daily American-Democrat,* but neither newspaper indicated whether dance contests had been part of the program.[22]

By 1935 the fair was on steadier legs, yet had to weather what McKenzie described as "a temporary hindrance" when Malcolm Hazlett, who was irritated at his exclusion from the fair's board of directors, attempted to take control of the fair by having the state issue a charter in the name of the Southwestern Indian Fair Association to him and two others. McKenzie, Ware, and Bedoka, however, stole the march on their rivals by immediately having a charter issued in the name of the American Indian Exposition. As McKenzie later remembered it, "We then continued our business as if those other three gentlemen had never existed.[23] Internal squabbles notwithstanding, the 1935 fair began to take on the shape that would define it for years to come. No detail was overlooked. A princess contest was held (sponsored in part by the Anadarko *Daily American-Democrat,* which awarded cash prizes to readers who guessed the eventual winners and kept interest up by printing daily tallies of the votes), an ambitious promotional campaign took board members to Washington, D.C., to arrange for increased government funding, and a one-day whistle-top tour by the Exposition band visited seven towns in southwest Oklahoma. Moreover, the *Tribune* and *Daily American-Democrat* both reported that large contingents of dancers (and horse racers) from the Kaw and Ponca communities — including world champion fancy dancer Gus McDonald — were on their way "to take part in the many grandstand performances scheduled to visitors daily." The governors of Oklahoma and Texas, every member of the Oklahoma legislature's house and senate Indian committees, and "other important Indian officials" were on the guest list. Best of all, a Pathe newsreel team would be on hand to record the entire event.[24]

Still, there was much about the fair that seemed to contradict the celebration of Indian identity, which would in the very near future become one of its most enduring strengths. Maurice Bedoka, for example, reminded fair patrons that "the primary object of the exposition is that general improvement among the Indians should result from the exposition. . . . nothing is being undertaken that would be derogatory to government guardians' policies." And if Gus McDonald was coming, the local papers revealed that he was going to have to compete not only against other dancers but also against a host of decidedly non-Indian entertainments as well. These included a special display from the Emergency Conservation Works Project on " 'prairie dog warriors' illustrating their method of warfare on the prairie dogs," the "clean and wholesome entertainment" of a "monkey-goat rodeo," and "a colored minstrel show with two high class performers and funny comedians presenting coon shouting and buck-and-wing dancing." But the board's decision in 1939 to invite a Texas outfit specializing in Mexican bullfights was too much for some Anadarkoans, and a lively exchange of letters to the editor ensued in the newspapers. Writing under the pseudonym "Expo Joe," someone wrote a series of letters in broken English that McKenzie believed "managed to keep the upset readers from taking any drastic steps to stop the presentation." There was a bright spot to the controversy. "Due to the letters being published," McKenzie later recalled, "the exposition received a lot of free publicity."[25]

The fair came into its own in 1941–1942, and despite wartime restrictions on travel, Indian people flocked to the Expo, as it was commonly called by then. Indeed, it wasn't long before the Expo was being used to extol the bravery of Indians in the service and to suggest that the war against Hitler was bringing Indians ever closer to the mainstream. In 1942, for example, headlines announced "National War Dance Champs Show Tonight," but also noted that Saturday was "Army and Navy Day," and festivities would include "the induction of high army officials into native tribes." The evening pageant, a tradition begun in 1938, was entitled "War Drums Along The Washita," and carried program notes that read "the throb [of war drums] now echoes in the waste land of Australia, on the deserts of India, in the jungles of the Solomons. Soon the pulsating vibrations will throb on the ears of Germany." The pageant story was about a triumphant partnership between whites and Indians, who — risen from the depravity of savagery — were "inspired . . . to join the United States to keep this country free — forever."[26]

One year later, the fair opened with army units joining in the parade along with hundreds of dancers in a "million dollar array of new war dance costumes." Wednesday was "Indian Day," Thursday was "Oklahoma Day," Friday was "Army Day," and Saturday was "Navy Day." That year's pageant, "Signal Fires," was dedicated to Indians in the service and told "the tale of the Indian war effort as a tableaux of progress for natives, whose response to a Europe in flames was 'we are coming . . . we understand freedom. We were conquered and saved it. It rose from the ashes — from the fires of smoke signals.' " The commandant of Ft. Sill was made a "chief" of the Kiowas, and for virtually the only time during the entire war, the August 15, 1943, Anadarko *Daily News* column titled "Our Boys in Service" profiled Indian men in the service. But the Expo wasn't all seriousness; the T. J. Tidwell Show and Carnival was in town for the fair, and patrons could take in everything from elephant rides for the kids to "Fatima, Belle of the Follies."[27]

The Expo's role as a patriotic event peaked in 1945 when a "victory conscious crowd" joined in the combination VE Day and VJ Day parade and victory dance and jammed the evening show titled "Pageant of Indian Heroes." The pageant story, ironically enough, told of "white settlement as it parallels Indian history" (and for which the Expo board put out a call for at least thirty Indians needed to play white parts).[28] For many Indian people, the high point no doubt came when Corporal Lyndreth Palmer was awarded the Bronze Star posthumously. Palmer, who had died December 5, 1944, fighting in France, was a Kiowa and a well-known dancer who had performed at the Expo prior to entering the service.[29] As we'll see, this event gave the Expo a meaning that was often lost on outsiders.

By 1945, Anadarkoans were coming to think of the Expo as theirs, and as a sort of civic institution in which Indians and non-Indians alike could take great pride. Indeed, in its August 8, 1945, edition, the Anadarko *Daily News* reminded readers that "it is the time when our yards and houses should look their best, it is a time for Anadarko to 'strut her stuff' so that our many visitors will think well of us and like us. Each Anadarkoan has a duty to perform during exposition week. This is the time when the people of the state and nation come to see the Indians and they come to see our city. . . . The possibilities of the American Indian Exposition are unlimited, if Anadarkoans are on their toes. . . . Anadarko has an institution that is gaining in national recognition . . . that will in the years to come, bring a majority of the populations of the United States here for a visit. We must therefore become nationally minded and alert here at home as we support and promote the Indian fair."[30]

Here was small-town boosterism at its best; but all was not well in paradise. The editorial apparently struck some Expo officials as a little overbearing, and someone reminded the paper's editors that the Expo was operated by and for the benefit of Indians. And when people needed to know about the Expo, then its officials would take care of it. As a result, the paper ran a second editorial a week later that had a decidedly defensive tone. Gone was the "we're all in this together" attitude, replaced by something that had all the trappings of old-style paternalism. "Many people of the state are awakening to great possibilities of the American Indian Exposition," went the piece. "This is worthy indeed and here is hoping the Indians do not misunderstand when others want to help. Everyone wants the exposition to remain an all-Indian affair, for in this way alone will the event hold its own throughout the years to come. Our duty to the Indians is to help them publicize, they will plan and conduct."[31]

As Jethro Gaede notes in a perceptive essay on the Expo's deeper meaning, what occurred every August at the fair grounds did not necessarily promote the civic, social, and cultural assimilation that many reformers still hoped for a similar fairs and exhibitions. For if on the one hand the fair often seemed very much in the white mainstream with its agricultural shows, baked goods contests, baseball tournament, and 4-H demonstrations, on the other hand there was much about it that defied white, middle-class conventions. As briefly noted earlier, for example, the board of directors could hardly be saddled with the charge of being assimilationists, for in their personal lives they were striking

examples of cultural continuity and even of resistance. It simply does not follow, for example, that Jess Rowlodge would suddenly forsake his own heritage
for the privilege of sitting on the fair's board of directors. Far more likely, he,
like his colleagues, saw his appointment as an opportunity to work for the economic, political, and social advantage of his people. To modernize, moreover,
is not necessarily to Americanize, and to conflate the two terms is to miss the
deeply complicated cross-cultural encounters that typified not only the Expo,
but every powwow.

From its inception, the Expo reflected a level of agency that distinguished
twentieth-century shows, exhibitions, and contests from those of an earlier era.
The best example of this, of course, came in the wording of the 1932 resolution
creating the Southwestern Indian Fair Association. "Whereas we . . . realize the
necessity of depending upon ourselves in any line of endeavor in our contact
with the white people to be successful and fully enjoy the benefits resulting
therefrom. . . . Whereas, there has been held in the state of Oklahoma, various
events for the past several years designated as 'Indian Fair,' 'Indian Pow-wow,'
etc., which are not strictly Indian in their management although Indians participate. . . . it is the belief of this body that such events are merely money making ventures on the part of individuals or of groups, that the advancement of
the Indian in his industrial pursuits is not the paramount object of those responsible for these events, and that it is the belief of this body that in order for
the Indian to fully receive all benefits of such affairs, it must be his duty to participate in all phases of such an event — from the managing body on down."
These words claimed agency and self-determination, not to the complete exclusion of whites, but certainly in a fashion designed to leave little question as to
who was ultimately in charge of such events. As one longtime supporter of the
Expo put it to me, "Daddy and them they just up and went over to Anadarko,
where Indians were in charge."

Even in those areas of the Expo that seemed most like white fairs, Gaede discerned patterns of behavior and presentation that contradict the notion of its
being an engine of assimilation. To interpret the fair's canning programs, sewing
circles, garden exhibits, and the like as examples of how white notions of order
and value were imposed on Indian households, he argues, is to miss more subtle examples of subsistence practices and expressive arts. In his evaluation of
photographs of the fair's agricultural displays, for example, Gaede notes that
"one can see border designs comprised of geometric shapes, stacked produce
arranged with an assortment of ribbon-tied or metal-girded grain bundles. On
closer study, the design elements bear an uncanny resemblance to bead work,
parfleche designs, roach head pieces, and inverted tied hair braids or horse's tails.
The addition of shaped, colored pails, saucers, and metal pans accentuates and

segregates specific items, patterns, and colors. They have been deliberately oriented or combined to form contrasting bands of color, chevrons, triangles, diamond and boxed motifs. The same types of motifs regularly utilized by Indians in their traditional expressive arts. . . . the agricultural exhibits have [in] a distinctly Indian aesthetic."[32] Such subtle visual clues nevertheless powerfully reflected tribal arts.

Turning to what Indians chose to present, Gaede finds even more tangible evidence. Home economics projects were particularly rich in their evocation of an anti-assimilation ethic, for "their creativity and methods of production demonstrate not only a high degree of adaptability, but at the same time, maintain a discernible connection to their cultural traditions. Cloth napkins are embroidered with superimposed flatware that forms a star pattern. Other cloth items incorporate designs that can be associated with traditional Indian motifs. Even more telling are the numerous canned goods in glass jars. They are filled with choke cherries, uncooked corn meal, dried skunk berries, wild plums, pounded sun-cured meat, and other items. All of these were traditional food items. . . . It is clear that these meetings provided an important social context by which traditional activities could survive."[33] Even when foodstuffs were from sources familiar to whites, Indian people often used them in ways that reflected culturally significant practices. Eating parts of animals that whites found distasteful or preparing foods differently than whites were powerful markers of ethnicity. At the nearby Rainy Mountain Boarding School, for example, students often raided the kitchen out of sheer hunger, but also, as one student remembered, because "we wanted to cook it in our own way."[34]

In an essay on the American flag in Lakota beadwork, Howard Bad Hand observes that Indian innovations in the expressive arts must be seen through the cultural lens that produces them, otherwise they lose their context and meaning. Of the relationship between the flag and Lakota art, for example, Bad Hand notes that "to symbolize ideas and thoughts into images, the Lakota initially drew upon simple geometric symbols and designs to denote the human experience, history, stories, and meaning of life. In the flag, the Lakota saw visual simplicity and an attractive pattern. . . . It was easily adapted . . . and readily utilized . . . The flag crept into the material culture. . . . [and] enjoys widespread utilization as a symbol to show beauty and attractiveness, lend meaning to the warrior tradition, and more importantly, as a reminder of the relationship between the Lakota and American people."[35] Like Gaede's choke cherries and geometrically designed agricultural exhibits, Lakota art reveals a cultural template that is multidimensional.

Perhaps the Expo's most enduring example of its role as an agent of ethnic identity came in its dances. For if the theatrical pageants and parades wowed visitors, during the 1940s and 1950s, it was the singing and dancing that made events like the Expo increasingly noteworthy in the powwow world. Several aspects of the dancing merit attention. First, by the mid-1940s the Expo, like Craterville before it, was attracting the powwow scene's leading figures. Chester Lefthand and James White Buffalo were there, as were Jack Hokeah and Spencer Asah, all notable figures in fancy dance circles. World champion fancy dancer Gus McDonald made an appearance in 1935, and in 1945 fancy dance champion Steve Mopope led off the evening show. Also in 1945, Tony White Cloud, described by the Anadarko *Daily News* as "a world famous Indian hoop dancer," was a featured performer.[36] Photographs of the Expo from its first decades indicate the rising popularity of fancy dancing, and it is apparent by the number of such outfits that war dancing was all the rage at Anadarko by the 1930s, just as it was everywhere else on the Plains. The amount of time given to dancing also increased dramatically between the 1930s and the 1950s. In 1939, for example, the "All-tribes War Dance Contest" was the only dancing segment listed in four days of programming, and it lasted thirty minutes on Saturday afternoon. By comparison, there were four renditions of "Spirit of the Redman," eight band concerts (two per day), and two of the much debated Mexican bull fights that had prompted so many letters to the editor.[37]

But in the post-war years, dancing would come to dominate the Expo as never before. As chapters one and two affirm, because of dancing's implicit association with martial values, the war years exerted important influences on its shape and scope at events like the Expo. In 1945, for example, the huge victory dance that celebrated the end of the war was reminiscent of earlier society dances of the same name. Photos from the era clearly show that servicemen in uniform were asked to join in the dances. While it is impossible to know for sure what was going on, based on the comportment that one sees in the photographs, it is highly likely that those men and women were being asked to participate in songs honoring veterans. Moreover, when the Expo closed out its pageant on the last night, among those leading the dancing were members from each of Oklahoma's all-Indian War Mothers' clubs, as well as members of the Kiowa Victory Club and Purple Heart Club.[38] It can be said with complete certainty that their participation had nothing to do with a show or exhibition, but would have been taken as a moment of deep cultural importance in a way that profoundly and completely divorced it from any association with a public, performative exhibition.

A similar event occurred at the 1955 Expo when the Kiowa Gourd Dance was included in the pageant. Dormant since the 1920s, the dance was revived when Fred Tsoodle, the Kiowa Expo tribal director, invited a group of elders to make a special presentation. The demonstration was a striking success, and reports circulated widely that elders in the crowd had wept when they heard the songs and saw the dancing for the first time in three decades. Plans for a full-scale revival were underway within a year, and the first formal meeting of the revived Gourd Clan occurred in Carnegie Oklahoma, during the July 4 holiday in 1958.[39] In 1957, a similar set of circumstances occurred when the Kiowa Black Legs Society gave a performance at the Expo that Meadows writes was "well received and prompted further interest." Another performance followed in 1958, and three months later, in November 1958, Gus Palmer, Sr., called a meeting of Kiowa veterans to discuss reviving the society. Meadows reports that the first formal dance was held in June 1959. Notably, Palmer told Meadows that he had decided to revive the Black Legs to memorialize his brother Lyndreth, the man who had been honored at the 1945 Exposition with a posthumously awarded Bronze Star.[40] Here was a case of several threads running together; Lyndreth had been active in the Expo before entering the service, Expo officials chose the fair to honor one of their own, and Palmer's brother — also a well-known dancer and artisan — had been encouraged by a Black Legs demonstration at the Expo to attempt the revival.

There were other changes in the dances, and none more interesting than the appearance in the early 1940s of female fancy dancers. Wearing the same bustles and outfits as their male counterparts, these women caused quite a stir when they began entering contests at the American Indian Exposition and other large powwows. Shalah Rowlen, a Sac and Fox from a family with deep powwow roots, told me she and her sisters began wearing fancy dance clothes as teenagers in the early 1940s when they performed with their father's dance troupe. She remembered seeing women fancy dancers as early as 1938, but said, "It really got going in the war years. We were going to parades, war bond drives, performing at half-time for basketball and football games. The soldiers would come home, and we'd have dances for them, and some of us girls just began wearing the bustles and dancing fancy. I remember Daddy handing a set of bustles to me one day and telling me to put them on." When I asked her how many women were fancy dancing in the 1940s, she replied "I remember six or eight regulars. I'm sure there were more, of course, but I don't think there were ever more than a couple dozen."[41]

Audiences didn't quite know what to make of it. Shalah chuckled and said, "Well, at first they *just couldn't believe it,* but the crowds at the Expo liked it. First time I fancy danced there was in 1944, and nobody ever told us we couldn't do it. We could keep time, and we had to learn the songs the same as the guys. There was one girl who had studied ballet and who danced way up on her toes. She never could really war dance, couldn't get with it. But some of the others could go as fast as the guys. I guess the men thought I was a pretty good dancer and could probably outdance them. Maybe I could have back then, I don't know. But most of them sure didn't want to dance against me." A Kiowa man who recalled seeing Shalah and others at the Expo in the 1940s told me, "Those old people really liked it and got a kick out of it. But I'm not so sure some of the guys thought it was all that good an idea—a couple of those women could dance as good as the men. I mean, can you imagine the beating they'd have taken if they'd lost a contest to one of those young women? Oh man, it would've been rugged!"[42]

Shalah told me she never contested against the men at the Expo, but she did win an all-women's fancy dance contest at the 1945 Expo and took home $100, "all in one dollar bills." There were subsequent contests in 1946 and 1947, but by the 1950s "it started slowing down, and before long it died out. There were some girls who brought it back in the 1960s and 1970s—Gigi Palmer and some others, but I guess by then the women had their own fancy styles with shawl dancing and jingle dresses. But we sure did have a good time while it lasted."[43]

Jewel McDonald, sister to world champion fancy dancer Gus McDonald, also recalled fancy dancing, but she did so in a different context altogether. When her brother was not contesting at powwows, she said, he often entertained nightclub audiences in and around Pawhuska. Taking the stage between the house band's sets (and occasionally dancing as the band played), McDonald would give rousing performances that showcased his considerable talents. When he was too tired to go on stage, Jewel would step in and perform in his place, wearing his fancy dance outfit and doing her best to imitate her famous brother's routines. "The audience never knew the difference," she recalled.[44]

By the 1950s, dancing was becoming the Expo's most popular and visible component. In the early years and down through World War II, dancing was only one of many attractions, and but for the one evening given to the championship rounds was not especially prominent. The post-war years, however, saw an increase in the number of powwows across the Southern Plains and a generally rising interest in dance contests that were less dominated by the logistics and priorities of pageants and parades. In 1958, for example, dance contests or demonstrations were held every afternoon and during two evenings, including Friday night when the Expo hosted the "National Indian Championship War Dance Contest." On other evenings they gave way to the annual pageant, but that year's version, "The Song of the Redman," was a dance show during which contests and eighteen tribal dances were performed, including the Hoop Dance, Apache Fire Dance, Kiowa Gourd Dance, Kiowa Black Legs, Osage and Pawnee Straight Dance, and the Eagle Dance. Indeed, Jim Anquoe commented that the fair's intertribal nature helped to make it a success. "My dad, he had charge of the drum for years out there because the board knew he'd be able to get them guys to come and spend the week singing with him. So, when it came time, he'd call those Comanches, Pawnees, Osages, Poncas, people up there in Sac and Fox country—he'd just call them all and tell them to get ready to sing. And of course, those guys they'd bring their wives and kids, and they'd all dance every year, and some of 'em would win and they'd keep coming back. It was a good time to be around other dancers, you could learn a lot watching them Ponca boys kick it up."[45]

By the 1960s and 1970s, the dance contests had become so central to the fair that the programs included detailed schedules of categories and prize money. In 1978, the Expo hosted contests in thirteen divisions (all paying four places), from "Tiny Tots" to "Grandpa" and "Grandma" divisions (now known by the somewhat more elegant term "Golden Age"), and culminating on Friday evening with the "National War Dancing Contests." While all of this dancing delighted fair goers and contestants, some of the old-timers were ambivalent about what it had done to the character of the Expo. The fact that the 1978 fair's opening day was declared "Parker McKenzie Day," for example, was something of an irony given McKenzie's private lament at the direction the Expo had begun taking in the 1950s. Writing in 1988, McKenzie observed that the Indian fairs had "followed the same pattern for quite a number of years until WW II came around. . . . Many youths—both male and female—had gone to war and many of the older had gone into cities to work in war-time industries. . . . Indians who took part in them had made a dramatic change in their life style by concentrating on occupations other than farming so following the war, there were no more farm and garden products or livestock at their fairs. Even products of the household have disappeared, but these were entirely replaced with native arts and crafts as well as painting. The Exposition as of now is truly more native than it used to be," wrote McKenzie, but it is not altogether clear he considered that fact a good thing. In a separate essay, he noted somewhat more pessimistically that during the past thirty years the Expo had become "an Indian show extravaganza with no semblance left of its old-fashioned, county fair image, except for the carnival that annually makes its stand on the midway, until in 1989 when no carnival made an appearance."[46]

The emphasis on contests and championships continued so that the 2002 Expo was no different from its predecessors of the last two decades. With the heightened emphasis on dancing, the Expo dropped all pretense of being anything even remotely connected to a county fair. And McKenzie was correct about the Expo's image: the "old-fashioned, county fair image" is long gone, replaced by a program that celebrates Indian cultural heritage in the most dramatic fashion. Indeed, the first year I attended the fair, 1978, I was struck by the degree to which it resembled a typical powwow with a large encampment, lots of dancing and other entertainments, and plenty of good craft supplies. If earlier fairs were more deliberate about using the occasion to make connections to the non-Indian community, that emphasis has gone largely by the wayside.

The agricultural displays have given way to arts and crafts, the pageants no longer tell a more or less corny version of Indian history (and haven't since the 1960s), and the induction of whites as "chiefs" of the tribes has been replaced by the "Outstanding Indian of the Year" award. Given first to Jim Thorpe in 1951, the award has honored recipients as widely divergent as New York Yankees pitcher Allie P. Reynolds (1953), ballerina Maria Tallchief (1962), evangelist Oral Roberts (1963), writer N. Scott Momaday (1969), entertainer Willie Nelson (1982 and 1987), actor Claude Akins (1986), Apache tribal chair Mildred Cleghorn (1989), University of Oklahoma basketball coach Kelvin Sampson (1995), and tribal cultural leaders Leonard Cozad, Sr. (1999), Inman Gooday (2000), and Nelson Bigbow (2002).

The award sometimes prompts snorts of derision, as when Roy Rogers (1967), Jay Silverheels (1977), and Willie Nelson were honored. A Pawnee woman who was an undergraduate at Oklahoma State University when Nelson won for the second time in 1987 could not conceal her disgust one afternoon as we visited over a cup of coffee at the student union. "Wow, is that ever sad," she commented. "What, we can't go out to the community and find an elder who's teaching language or beadwork or just taking care of their grandkids? Do we really have to get some wannabe who thinks that because he likes turquoise he's one of us?" It also rankled her that in the years since its creation (thirty-six at the time of our conversation) the award had gone to Indian women only five times. In its fifty-one year history, women have been named only nine times. Other observers are less bothered by the Indian of the Year award. "You know," said one Delaware woman, "if this just gets other people to know about us, to see us as normal human beings, that's okay by me. Besides," she said with a hearty laugh, "who wouldn't want to come to Anadarko in August when it's 110 degrees to get this award?"[47]

In truth, some longtime participants believe that the Expo's best years are behind it. "It's an old pony now," said one white man who first attended the fair as a grade schooler in the mid-1950s. The encampments are smaller these days, the crowds are thinner, and the Expo has seen lean times since the 1980s. A Pawnee man commented just weeks after the 2002 Expo that "it's kind of sad. I remember when we'd all pile in the car and head to the fair for a week. We'd camp and raise a lot of hell, of course, we were kids after all. But you got to see those old people really enjoying themselves, and people just seemed to have more of a commitment. But times change — these days, who has time to camp for a week and stay out there?" Another longtime fair goer remembered that in the 1960s the crowds for the parade were "six and seven deep, it was just such a big deal. I mean you had to get there early to get your place — people staked a claim to certain places year after year. It was like going to an encampment — you just know where so-and-so is going to be. Since the 1970s, I guess it's gone downhill quite a bit. But you know, people can't get away like they used to, they don't camp and they don't like the heat. The people you see now are the hard-core Indian fair people; they'll just always be there. But the crowds, you don't get them anymore, not like in the old days, I'm talking about the 1960s."[48]

A number of publicly aired disagreements and charges of malfeascence marred the 1990s, and by 2001 there was serious talk of moving the Expo out of Anadarko. A story in the June 30, 2001, edition of *Native American Times* reported that "in the face of rising costs and dwindling city and county support, officials of the American Indian Exposition met in early May . . . to lay the cards on the table." Speaking for the Expo board, Alonzo Chalepah said that "attractive invitations" had come from Chickasha, Carnegie, and Lawton. Unless Anadarko and Caddo County officials addressed ongoing problems with facilities and funding, Chalepah said, the board would make "whatever adjustments we think are best for all of us . . . I do want you to realize the danger of our moving it out of Anadarko."[49]

As of 2002, the Expo was still in Anadarko, where it remains a viable and exciting event at which dancing remains the central attraction. The 2002 Expo ran for six days and featured a grand entry and dance sessions every evening, along with the usual assortment of dog and horse races, storytelling, flute playing, and contests for the best tipi and arbor, best fry bread, and most beautiful baby. If the canning and agricultural exhibits are long gone, they have been replaced by new traditions that affirm the Expo's continuing vitality. This is still a place that matters in the powwow world, and its advocates are determined that it remain that way for years to come.

It is important to acknowledge the Expo's influence on the powwow world as a model for others to follow. As Jim Anquoe suggested, by the time it was hitting its stride in the 1950s and 1960s, "the Expo had inspired Indian people all over the place to see if they couldn't come up with their own deal. My brother, Kenneth, he was Kiowa tribal director for a time at the Expo, and then he goes along with people like Charles Chibitty — another guy who went to the fair in those days — and creates the Tulsa Powwow, the best one of them all as far as I'm concerned. And it was the Expo that proved to people that they could make this 'powwow circuit' go. You combine that fair's ability to bring in the inter-tribal bunch — where we learned to get along and do each other's dances — you combine that with the fact that so many of our Indian people were living in those bigger places, I'm talking about Oklahoma City, Tulsa, Wichita, Dallas, and before long you had it everywhere. And man, it was exciting."[50] These dances were intertribal, often included contests, used committees and head staff structures that shortly became standardized, were often associated with families, communities, or dance grounds, and increasingly came to fill a cultural void that the warrior society dances did not. And by the 1950s their purposes would be similarly multidimensional. Homecomings, honorings, fund-raisers, holiday celebrations, birthdays, high school celebrations, and memorial dances would all find their niche.

Like many tribes, the Cheyennes and Arapahos saw an increase in dances by the 1950s and 1960s, and their experiences mirrored larger trends. As Loretta Fowler comments, during the 1950s "the powwow became a vehicle for individuals and families who had left the local communities to maintain or reestablish ties with their home communities of the Cheyenne-Arapaho community. Sometimes in the early years dances were referred to as 'homecomings.'" As dances "became an arena for the expression of self-determination and pride in Cheyenne and Arapaho heritage," they grew in number. Citing local newspapers and tribal publications, Fowler traces the evolution of several major powwows and points out that dances appeared with increasing frequency in the post–World War II years. The Clinton Powwow was mentioned in the press in 1947, and the Colony Powwow was mentioned in 1953. Arapahos in Canton began holding the annual Barefoot Powwow in 1954, and had previously sponsored dances it called powwows as early as 1943. Cheyennes in Kingfisher sponsored a local powwow in 1947, while the 1956 Cheyenne and Arapaho Powwow held in El Reno was run by a committee with members from every tribal district. The Canton *Record* carried powwow stories on no fewer than fourteen occasions between July 1942 and August 1959, and local papers mentioned individually sponsored dances no fewer than nine times between 1947 and 1955.[51]

Many powwow people point to World War II as the turning point for renewed interest in dances. The war years helped to revive dancing, especially in the context of veterans' associations and their dances, but it also created a new, urbanized Indian community eager for gatherings that would create and sustain pride in Indian culture and identity in ways that satisfied the new scene. Archie Mason, Jr., an Osage, recalled that in the 1940s "there was a great need to identify. . . . They saw they were absorbed in this urban setting, even in the 1940s, so they got together to begin something." Ed Red Eagle, Sr., also an Osage, recalled that "following World War II, the customs and the ways of our people were continued and from that time until the outbreak of the Korean Conflict, [people] began to . . . be encouraged to participate because of the men that had served in the armed forces . . . their children began to take part and have been since."[52] Kenneth Anquoe, a Kiowa who was one the originators of the Tulsa

Powwow, told Gloria Young that he and Charles Chibitty, a Comanche also living in the Tulsa area, were homesick for the kinds of dances they'd grown up with in southwest Oklahoma. Both had been longtime fixtures at the American Indian Exposition (Anquoe had served as director for the Kiowa tribe's participants), and both had deep roots in the powwow world. Anquoe told Young that when it came to powwowing, Chibitty "was in the same fix I was" and wanted to get a dance started in the Tulsa area.[53]

What they started was an intertribal powwow club that sponsored an annual dance that brought hundreds of Indian people and their dancing cultures together. In many ways, the Tulsa Powwow became the template for others to follow, for it showed the way toward an urbanized powwow culture that successfully negotiated the changing contours of Indian life in the decades after the war. "You know, it was a different kind of dance," one Pawnee woman told me. "By the 1940s and 1950s, of course, there were so many of us Indian people in the cities that we needed this kind of dance. Many people couldn't go for a week and camp like in the old days, but lots of people could sure drive down from Ft. Smith, or over from Stillwater, you know, to spend the weekend in Tulsa at that dance. Oh it was really wonderful, seeing all those people every year. Only bad thing was we always seemed to get rain, and so that hurt some years more than others. Still, I have such fond memories of that dance. We still went to Pawnee Powwow, of course, and over to the Osage dances every summer — that's where our people, our families were, so no way we'd miss those times. But Tulsa, and then Oklahoma City, IICOT, Indian Hills, all of those newer dances, they really added something to the powwows, I think." Angie Barnes, an Osage, believed that dances like the Tulsa Powwow filled an important void for her grandchildren. In a 1968 interview, she observed that her grandchildren would probably find jobs "in Dallas or someplace away from the Osages. . . . The people have to go to the larger cities to work. And I think that is why they have these clubs, these powwow clubs in larger cities for Indians. . . . I think it is a very good idea for Indians to get together and to enjoy their customs. It's a way of preserving them, I'd say. And I would encourage it for my children to attend if they were where they could. To actually take part in things. Seems like that way they mingle and they — maybe they may not learn the right customs, but it still would be a way of preserving some Indian customs, some Indian ways."[54]

Although most sources put the Tulsa dance's beginning in the late 1940s, Jim Anquoe told me, "If you really want to go back right to the beginning, it started in 1946 in Kenneth's backyard with the help of a few people he wanted to invite." With a chuckle, he added, "You couldn't hardly see your hand it was so dark those first few dances. We'd pop on all of the lights in the house, and pull a car into the driveway and turn on the high beams." The program for the powwow's twentieth annual dance included a history that put the official beginning at 1951 (when the first officers were elected) and stated: "In the fall of 1949 a small group of Indian people met together . . . to discuss the possibility of organizing an 'Indian gathering' on a regular basis. . . . Until this meeting, only 'Dance Shows' allowed a frequent opportunity to dance and put on 'those feathers' as powwows were not yet frequent enough throughout Oklahoma. . . . The need for a 'Plains Indian type' of culture for the Tulsa Area was soon to be fulfilled." Jim Anquoe told me that when the dance was in its formative years in the mid and late 1940s, "it was a situation where [Kenneth] wanted to give those urban Indians a place to get together." Kenneth Anquoe told Young that "we called the affair a dance. The powwow we stuck on there later as kind of an inside joke among us because the white people called them powwows. So we just kind of nicknamed it the powwow and it stuck." The twentieth anniversary program said that "several names were suggested but a rather tongue-in-cheek suggestion by Floyd Moses seemed to stick! So it was that the 'Tulsa Powwow Club' was born." The name was subsequently changed to the Tulsa Indian Club.[55]

With financial help from local families, the club managed to hold the dance annually, but by the early 1950s the need for better organization and more reliable funding led to a break between Chibitty and Kenneth Anquoe. Chibitty and a core of supporters began a dance at Lakeview Park, while Anquoe and his supporters moved to Mohawk Park.[56] Yet, even after the split, powwow people enthusiastically supported both dances. By the early 1950s, contests were part of the regular schedule, and large numbers of talented dancers from other regions began to attend regularly. "Tulsa was absolutely one of the most popular powwows in those days because of the intertribal character," said Jim Anquoe. "Kenneth made *everybody* feel at home [at Mohawk Park]. He gave rations when people camped, he sent us kids out to make sure that visitors were invited to the committee tent to get fed dinner. Kenneth loved people coming to Tulsa and enjoying themselves. They had to pay to get in, but they got their money's worth." When I asked Jim where Kenneth had found the inspiration for the way he ran his dance, he said, "My brother learned from those old people who had kept hold of their ways. You know, people who dance, they're generous. Way back there, why you just took care of people at those dances and ceremonies. Those societies, you know, they always fed the people, took care of their needs. That's where we learned this. Our family, we've been singing and dancing all our lives — so we grew up hearing Grandpa and Grandma tell us about these ways."[57]

A number of people confirmed what Jim Anquoe told me. One man said, "Well, this new way, this powwow, it wasn't all *that* new. We took what we'd always done and kept some of it more or less the same." Gloria Young's consultants told her the same thing. As powwows grew in size and complexity, they needed order and organization, and it wasn't long before powwow committees and head staffs became the solution. And as Young notes, this development followed "historic precedent. . . . The structure of committee, leaders of auxiliary events and head staff derives from the structure of historic tribal ceremonies and warrior societies." Daniel Gelo makes a similar argument about the role of the emcee, and Dennis Zotigh has commented on the parallels between head dancers and the whip men who had started each dance in the old days.[58]

Indeed, I was told during numerous conversations with powwow people on the Southern Plains that although these traditional duties were transferred to the powwow, they were not initially given a lot of emphasis, and head staffs were not common until the 1960s. Prior to that, as Harry Tofpi, Sr., put it, "We just all got together and danced. Nobody was in charge like today." Speaking at a 1971 Father's Day Powwow in Apache, Oklahoma, Yale Spotted Bird told the crowd that times had changed with the coming of the powwow. "Think of your father and my father. Just out on the prairie field, just out in the opening — they didn't have no benches or anything like that. They didn't have no loudspeaker. They don't get ready for a giveaway. Only time is when they want to give away, when one of their loved ones dances for the first time or is being honored in some way. They give what they have right at the moment. They don't prepare to give away. They don't look for shade. They just get out there, and just get around the drum, and the dancers get ready and they have a dance. We seen that . . . when the Gourd Clan used to have their dances way back there in 1915, 1910, and so forth."[59]

By the 1960s and 1970s, however, "head staff," as they came to be called, were a standardized part of the powwow, and appointing head dancers, head singers, and emcees had become routine. Over time, the list of head staff has grown to include all manner of notables: organization princesses, head fancy dancers, head straight dancers, head little boy dancers, head little girl dancers, and head judges, among others. With the change, however, came complaints that such things were unnecessarily complicating dances. It is not uncommon, for example, to hear people grumble at the perceived excesses that have accompanied the growth and complexity of head staffs, giveaways, and specials. At the 2002 Sac and Fox Powwow, for example, the Saturday evening session didn't get fully underway until well after 9 P.M. due to the large number of specials and giveaways. With so many specials to schedule, some dance sessions are virtually taken over by lengthy and sometimes extravagant giveaways. "These days, everyone and their cat have to have a big special," said one woman. "It's understandable that the committee and head dancers ought to do it, but when you start to get into head gourd dancers, two or three emcees, head little boy dancers, head singers, head little girl dancers, arena directors, princesses, last year's winner in the fancy dance contest — I mean there's some dances where it just doesn't end. And then they feel obligated to give something to every person within sight. Don't get me wrong, I know these things are important, but we've gotten carried away at some of these dances."[60]

Interestingly, Jim Anquoe remembers that when Kenneth told family members of his plans to have a head man and head lady dancer at the Tulsa Powwow in the early 1950s, their father asked, "What are they?" Anquoe said that his brother's immediate inspiration had come from the Cheyennes, but not necessarily from earlier society practices. "Kenneth said those old men, they used to select a gentleman to lead dances. And a woman too. So, Kenneth started all of this at Tulsa, and now everyone thinks powwows were invented that way!" Like every powwow committee today, Kenneth Anquoe knew that a well-known head staff would be a key to bringing in the dancers and crowds. But he didn't go for the top stars. "All the champion dancers come anyway," remarked Jim Anquoe. "What [Kenneth] wanted was someone he thought would *really* enjoy that position of being a head man, head lady, or head singer. He told us these people were really honored to be chosen." In some years, Kenneth "chose people you never heard of. But after you were on head staff at Tulsa Powwow, you were on the circuit."[61]

And after Tulsa, the circuit was more diverse and intertribal than ever before. Many observers credit Tulsa with opening powwow culture to tribes beyond Oklahoma. By the mid- and late 1960s, for example, Kenneth Anquoe was busily recruiting dancers from other regions to come to Tulsa. "Northern traditional, fancy shawl, grass dancing, jingle dress — you didn't see just a whole lot of that before the 1960s," said Jim Anquoe. A Sac and Fox woman said much the same thing. "I'd never seen a jingle dress before going to Tulsa and some of those bigger dances in the late 1960s and on into the 1970s. But when I saw it, I said, 'Wow, I have to get one of those.' I thought I'd win everywhere if I could get that jingle dress down. Not many girls had ever even seen it down here in those days. Of course," she laughed, "just as soon as I got mine, well, everybody else got it too. Didn't take long for me to go right back to my cloth dress."[62]

So, in many ways, Tulsa was the wave of the future. It was intertribal and urban, attracted the best contest dancers, hosted visitors from well outside of the region, was held annually, and featured an organizational structure that would become the model for all others. "Tulsa set the example for all the powwows in Oklahoma," says Jim Anquoe. But its innovations did not mean the dance wasn't grounded in traditional practices and values. The 1971 powwow program proudly stated that "the Tulsa Indian Club's aim in hosting this annual gathering is to preserve the traditions of the American Indian and to offer an insight into the many fine characteristics of the Indian people. The songs of many tribes are blended into the dances for all. The visitor will see the beauty and reverence and dignity and know something of the Indian spirit."[63] In time, this would come to be the touchstone for powwows across the region.

"My children and grandchildren, they've learned these ways, too, because it's good, it's powerful."

Like everything else in Indian country, conversations about powwows often fall on one side or another of several fault lines, the most noticeable of which is the one that divides powwow people from non-powwow people. At the risk of oversimplifying the issue, the notion that all (or most) Indian people attend, participate in, or support powwows is problematic. While it is impossible to say with certainty what percentage of Southern Plains Indian people regularly participate in powwows, most of my consultants agree that the number is, as one man put it, "somewhere south of ten percent." Others put the figure even lower. Jim Anquoe believes that out of twelve thousand Kiowas, "probably four hundred of them dance," meaning that fewer than four percent of the tribe are active powwowers. Whatever the numbers, powwow people are in the minority in most communities.[1]

But as Luke Eric Lassiter has observed, there are many ways to be Indian, and on the Southern Plains that includes groups who identify themselves as powwow people, peyote people, Stomp Dance people, Sun Dance people, church people (meaning one of the Christian denominations), even bingo and softball people.[2] Powwows, then, operate in the company of a multitude of other institutions that nurture and express identity, so the fact that a majority of Indian people in many places do not participate actively or regularly in powwows should not be taken as an indication that powwows are bit players. As Lassiter commented in a conversation with me, "The fact that most Indians might not go regularly doesn't mean that powwows don't exert wider influence. For example, every candidate in tribal elections makes the rounds these days to the dances because they recognize that there's a constituency there they need. And lots of these people have become powwowers themselves, much to the amazement of some powwow regulars."[3]

More important than the numbers game are two other considerations. The first is that powwows do not satisfy everyone's idea of what it means to be Indian. The second is that inside the powwow world, there are profound disagreements about what powwows are and what they mean. On the first point, during the early and mid-twentieth century, divisions occurred in many Indian communities concerning appropriate expressions of ethnic identity. Not surprisingly, powwows were part of the conversation from the beginning. One of the most obvious divisions occurred between Christian Indians, some of whom tended to regard powwows as morally and culturally dangerous, and dance advocates who saw these new traditions as arenas for the expression of identity.

Urged by missionaries during the late nineteenth and early twentieth centuries to give up dancing, some Indian people came to believe that dancing and Christianity were increasingly incompatible. In a 1967 interview, Reverend Cecil Horse (who was born in 1891) commented that during his career as a Kiowa Methodist Minister, powwows had hurt church attendance "a whole lot. . . . Let's say we have a camp meeting here. There's supposed to be a lot of people there and then here's a powwow over the hill about two miles. All of my church's young people and some of my church workers, weak ones, they go to the powwow before they come over here. . . . I'm just sitting over here and nobody comes into my church. That's a problem we have sometimes." When asked if that occurred often, Horse replied "pretty near all summer sometimes." Horse's wife, Jenny, added, "They have their powwows [on] a weekend and that's what makes it hard. . . . A long time ago when my father and the old folks was living, they believe in having powwow, but they have it once a year — that is, on the Fourth of July. They have a big gathering somewhere. The whole tribe comes. But now, I don't know why it is that the younger generation, they want to have powwows every weekend. It didn't used to be like that. The old Indians wasn't that way. . . . think the younger generation — I don't know. They have it every week. . . . The old people were, you know, they like Indian ways and all but they were more religious in the Christianity and they had that powwow and a Ghost Dance, they call it, once a year and that was the Fourth of July. But nowadays, it is different. I wonder why?" Cecil added that "in my old time days, it was better. The old people, not educated, they had long hair, they come in wagons, but they all was faithful ones. I have big crowd at that time."[4]

Thirty years later, Cy Hall Zotigh told me and Luke Eric Lassiter much the same thing. Indeed, he believed that the low number of young Indian people in churches was directly attributable to the influence of the powwow. "People will drive a long way to get to a powwow or a peyote meeting," he observed, "but not for church. I'm fighting the dance people. They let it get in the way of God." Helene Fletcher, the daughter of Ioleta McElhaney, a Kiowa woman who was a Baptist missionary, echoed the Horses during a 1998 interview with me. Speaking of the 1950s, she said, "It was a time when Christianity was important.

Everything was centered around the church. It was important — not the bingo hall, not the dances, not all that other stuff — the *church* was important." Zotigh and Fletcher both regretted what they perceived as the loss of faith in a younger generation of Indians to whom Christianity was less influential than for their parents and grandparents. And both mentioned powwows as one of the contributing factors. Benjamin Kracht makes a similar argument in a recent essay on Kiowa religion in which he says that some older people believe that "powwows serve as a religion for the youth." Vince Bointy, a Kiowa, suggested that after World War II, Indian people "got their prayers answered, and they didn't go back" to the churches. Powwows, on the other hand, became larger and ever more popular.[5]

As I noted earlier, Morris Foster has discussed the tension that appeared in Comanche communities when the Native American Church, Christian missions, a burgeoning powwow culture, and changing spatial relationships dictated by allotment affected how, when, and for what purpose Comanches gathered. It is important to remember, however, that whether Comanches were coming together for Christian services, peyote meetings, or powwows, their purpose was to maintain and negotiate different, but nonetheless concrete, visions of Comanche identity. With respect to dance, when communities began hosting annual encampments by the second decade of the twentieth century, these events reflected a growing generational and ritual schism in the community. Previously restricted from participating in dances, by the 1930s many young Comanches gained prominence in the dance crowd as well as in the Native American Church. Dancing and the use of peyote, Foster notes, had once been "elements of the same belief system." Rising generations of younger Comanches, however, assigned powwows a distinctly spiritual power, and thus fostered the rise of "two distinct 'religions'" in the Comanche community. As a result, "powwows provided these younger Comanches with their first opportunity to participate actively in a Comanche-derived . . . form of gathering. . . . Dance gatherings, which previously had had a carnival atmosphere, became more solemn occasions in the late 1930s."[6]

While there were discernible fault lines between powwow people, peyote people, and Christians in the post-war years, these days the dividing lines aren't always so sharply drawn. "In southwestern Oklahoma's Indian world," writes Lassiter, "tribal traditions are not necessarily mutually exclusive; they intersect in an intertribal social world. Therefore, we are no longer speaking of *aggregates* of individuals, but different worlds in which *individuals* participate. Powwow, hand-game, church, or peyote people, then, all take part in distinct but interrelated worlds defined by aesthetics, tradition, and history." As Danieala

Vickers put it to Lassiter, when it comes to these worlds, the issue is "how they overlap." Writing in 1998, Lassiter commented that "the inflexible stance against the dance crowd seems to have abated in the last several years, and open dialogues are the norm in some of the more conservative Christian congregations." Now, rather than seeing the Jesus Road and the Dance Road as opposites, many Indian people see them as things that need to be balanced. One individual confided to Lassiter, "I was just going to contest powwows all the time and neglecting my relationship with the Lord. So, I've just put off powwows for a while so I can concentrate on Him."[7]

In a world that has come to tolerate cultural diversity more fully than an earlier age, various forms of expression now tend to be seen as complementary in terms of their ability to reinforce certain values and ideals that remain important throughout Indian country, like shared histories, familial relations, and tribally specific practices. As Ralph Kotay, a Kiowa who has been singing powwow songs *and* Kiowa hymns for more than fifty years, has suggested, "When they become Christians . . . [some people] want Indians to do away with their traditions. . . . But for me, I won't say that. . . . We even have ministers who are shaking that gourd [gourd dancing at powwows]. You just can't get away from being an Indian."[8] Today, it is not uncommon to attend powwows at which Christian services are held on Sunday mornings; and some pastors have become ardent powwowers.

Scholars, too, disagree about what powwows mean. Much of the scholarly literature focuses on an overarching concern with the powwow's role as a Pan-Indian institution that will ultimately replace tribally specific dance culture. Among the first to suggest this were James H. Howard, William W. Newcomb, Jr., Samuel W. Corrigan, Robert K Thomas, and Nancy Lurie.[9] While Lurie was careful to distinguish between different types of powwow gatherings, she nonetheless agreed generally with Howard's observation that widely shared cultural traits and institutions — like the powwow — had become widely diffused by the 1950s. Pan-Indiansm, wrote Howard, was the "process by which sociocultural entities such as the Seneca, Delaware, Yuchi, Ponca, and Comanche are losing their distinctiveness and in its place are developing a non-tribal 'Indian' culture." Writing in 1965, Lurie noted that even though "at the inter-tribal level tribes are jealous of their identity and retain distinctive traits. . . . a generalized Indian identity which derives most of its external symbols of song, dance, costume, and ritual from the Plains area is indeed developing." Such traits, she commented, had been shared "from tribe to tribe so as to characterize virtually all Indian groups to some degree."[10] More recently, Barre Toelken has taken a similar position, writing about "the existence of a growing body of custom, observance, belief, propriety, and awareness which have superceded the specific tribal customs that once underscored the differences (often the open enmities) among the participating tribes. The emergence of this larger body of custom and observance . . . is an indication that specific tribal identity is being reassessed by many Native Americans and being replaced by a powerful synthesis of related traditions that can articulate Indianness."[11]

Yet, when Indian people talk about powwows and dance culture, they often make a clear distinction between intertribal powwows and tribal dances. Both satisfy important needs in the community, both appeal to many of the same values and priorities, and both play crucial roles in maintaining identity. But they are not the same thing. Indeed, to argue that the Pan-Indian powwow has replaced tribal notions of identity associated with dance is simply not borne out by the evidence. William K. Powers has noted somewhat forcefully that "it cannot be overemphasized that Pan-Indianism is simply a variation of acculturation and assimilation studies," which was reason enough for him to add that using it was not only problematic, but also misleading. "Although the idea that Pan-Indianism strives towards the creation of a new ethnic group, the American Indian, is novel and interesting," writes Powers, "it is unlikely that this definition can be regarded seriously, given what we know about the distinctiveness and variety of American Indian tribal cultures."[12]

Southern Plains Indian people, moreover, are quite conscious of the relationship between powwows, Pan-Indianism, and tribal identity. Sylvester Warrior, a Ponca, told an interviewer in 1968 that "when we perform our 'War Dance,' it isn't any Pow-wow dancing that one might see elsewhere. We dance strictly War dance all the way through. There is no other dances included. For instance you go to a powwow, you see round dance and snake dance and buffalo dance and what have you. But when we perform our war dance in this part of the country here among our people, it is strictly war dance all the way through. . . . these ways have been observed for many, many years." In a 1969 interview, Warrior addressed the Heluska specifically, not the powwow, when he said, "We of the younger generation [he was in his sixties] have fallen far short of the knowledge possessed by our forefathers. . . . we were ignorant in many ways in which they conducted this dance." Warrior was a well-known powwow singer, but when it came to his Ponca identity, it was clear that the dance tradition that mattered was the Heluska, not the powwow: "We know what we dance for, we know why we've organized — we're trying to preserve, perpetuate this dance for [the] sake of posterity. We want our children and our children's children, future generations to know how we used to dance this."[13] Warrior went on to say that "it is admirable to see these people teach their young men and women when they come home from school each spring. Some of their young people are in colleges . . . come home to put on their dancing clothes to dance the War

Dance. I've always admired these people for this." Ed Red Eagle, Sr., an Osage, was optimistic about the younger generation taking up Osage dances, especially the I'n-lon-schka. "Today [1967], it's gone to our grandchildren and they're actually taking an active part. They are very young today and we feel that the younger generations are the ones that is going to continue this as we did."[14]

It is clear that the generation of elders interviewed for the Doris Duke Oral History project understood their tribal dances to be a separate entity from the powwow culture that was beginning to sweep across the region in the 1960s and 1970s, when these interviews were conducted. In a 1969 interview, for example, William Collins, Sr., a Ponca, discussed the Heluska's continuing importance in his tribe and lamented that it was being overshadowed by the powwow. "This powwow dancing is common today," he said. "They pay no respect to this good old time ceremony." Another Ponca man told the crowd at the 1969 Ponca Heluska, "For you people who don't understand the Ponca language, I am taking these boys here around the drums — they need to know for now and all the days to come. . . . I want them to gather around these halls, all these days in your life." And in an interesting comment on the changes wrought by the powwow, Sylvester Warrior noted that "today, a lot of our Indian people have lost their traditional dances. You see all the Indians performing this [the war dance that began with the Heluska]. 'Course, some people have lost their traditional dances so completely that they have gone on and copied other tribal dances. They even went so far as to make up some dances. . . . That's kinda hard to believe."[15]

Lamont Brown was more emphatic about the consequences in a 1968 interview, and expressed concern that non-Indians were dominating some dances in Oklahoma. "This 'Pow-wow' world as they call it as of today, [it's] danced all over the State of Oklahoma . . . and on the east . . . and west coast. The white people are taking over. The Poncas are losing their ways. Maybe one of these days, the Ponca people will be paying admission to see the white people put on their Ponca dances for them." Brown's concerns about whites dancing at the Heluska were shared by other Poncas. By the 1980s, the issue led to a split that culminated in the creation of an all-Indian Heluska. As one member told me, "The hobs from Chicago and Dallas can still come out here and strut around like they're really keen Indians, but some of us have had enough of it." In a 1969 interview, John Blackowl, a Cheyenne, recounted a conversation he'd had with another man about whites — in this case Boy Scouts — who were becoming more and more interested in powwows. "These scouts . . . they go to some powwow — they've got a secret recorder, you know. Maybe they'll be parked where it's going on; they catch all that music and stuff. Well, there's some white boys [who] can really dance, and they do their own beadwork."[16]

The directors of the American Indian Exposition were also becoming sensitive to the participation of whites, and in 1961 the Exposition's president sent an appeal to *American Indian Tradition*, a magazine read largely by non-Indians, asking hobbyists to stay out of the Expo's dance arena. The magazine ran a column reporting the Expo president's wish "to mention that the Indian people request that no non-Indians try to participate in any of the public performances or private giveaways. . . . The Indian people feel that this is their fair, and that visitors come to see Indians dancing. . . . Hobbyists can learn most by just watching those performances."[17]

More recently, some people have taken stronger steps, including several attempts to create all-Indian dances and organizations. In 1983, for example, a group of Poncas who were worried by the high number of non-Indians participating in the tribe's Heluska dances established a new Heluska group limited only to Poncas. The organization sponsored dances between 1983 and 1985 but found it difficult to compete with other dance groups that allowed non-Indians to participate. A subsequent attempt in the mid-1990s also failed to gain momentum. (For their part, in conversations with me a number of white hobbyists seemed genuinely puzzled by the attempt to bar their attendance and participation.) In addition, a small number of powwow and dance organizations have become more explicit about prohibiting or discouraging participation by non-Indians.[18]

Not all Indians share this concern. Many non-Indians sing and dance regularly at Southern Plains dances of all kinds, including tribal ceremonials like the Osage I'n-lon-schka and Kiowa O-ho-mah, where they are treated in many cases with respect and affection. This is especially true at intertribal powwows, where many, many communities openly welcome non-Indian participants, and often invite them to serve as head dancers and head singers, especially when they are members of the community or have deep ties to local families or organizations. When I asked Jim Anquoe about this, he was quick to say that he didn't have a problem with non-Indians participating in powwows. "It's like this," he said, "if a non-Indian can sing and knows the songs I use, and knows how to behave at the drum, I don't see a problem. At the drum, my dad taught us that it's *singers*, not 'this one's Kiowa, that one's white, and the other one's Cheyenne.' I don't care if the guy sitting next to me is polka-dotted—if he can sing, I don't see a problem. Shoot, some of them guys know more songs than some of our regulars—and they take it seriously, they know what the drum is all about." Another Kiowa singer in his sixties was even more emphatic: "If those white kids want to be like us Indians, I think that's *great*. They want to learn to sing and dance and be like us, that's *great*."[19]

In 1967, Sylvester Warrior, a Ponca, told Tyrone Stewart that he was happy to help non-Indians learn Ponca songs and dances. "It makes me feel good to know that other people than the Indian are interested in this ancient dance of ours," Warrior said. "I was proud of the fact that they chose the Ponca way to conduct their War Dance. I feel we should give you this information in order that you boys might perform it in the right way. Follow it up and live up to its meanings and to the rules that govern this war dance." But the long-term effect of that relationship has troubled others. One Ponca man said that he understood why those first non-Indians were accepted into the Heluska, but added, "I'm not sure that our grandpas realized what would happen. Now we have dozens of those white guys here and because of it, my opinion is that we don't really have a Heluska anymore. We dance it, but it's diluted." The prevailing opinion in many corners, however, is that allowing non-Indians to participate in the Heluska and in powwows is a fact of life with which Indians have made their peace.[20]

Billy Evans Horse echoed this sentiment in his conversations with Luke Eric Lassiter. "A long time ago, my grandfather . . . said, 'You learn these songs, and these songs are going to go from one end of the world to the other. It's going to be a good dance, and there's going to be all kinds of people that will be gourd dancing.' He said, 'Not only the Indian people, but the black people, the Mexican people, and the white people will be gourd dancing.' " Another of Lassiter's consultants said, "As long as they [non-Indians] respect it, it's fine with me, because we're all intermarried. We can't bar nobody if they do it right. . . . But if you go out there and hop around and try to make fun of it, we'll throw you plumb out of there right now." When Lassiter expressed his nervousness at serving for the first time as a head singer at a dance in southwest Oklahoma, he recalled Billy Evans Horse telling him, "Remember . . . God blessed you with the talent of sound. That is the reason my people chose you to be their head singer, *not* the color of your skin."[21]

And it's not just non-Indians that prompt debates in the powwow world. In an especially dramatic turn of events in the late 1990s, the Potawatomi tribal council banned non-Potawatomis from participating in their annual powwow in Shawnee, Oklahoma. What had once been a thriving and very popular intertribal powwow that was a highlight of the spring season was suddenly reduced to a much smaller dance that, in the opinion of Indian people who had attended for years, is a shadow its former self. As one Sac and Fox woman described it, "You just have to wonder what they were thinking. I mean, it's not like they have enough people to pull this off. Who's going to sing for them? Who's going to be doing the dancing? But I'll tell you this — they're the ones who are missing out, not the rest of us. Their powwow is going to be dead in a couple of years because they've run off all of the other Indians by doing this. But we'll have plenty of other dances to go to."[22]

As these comments suggest, the relationship between powwow culture and tribal culture can be problematic. But while it is true that a generalized sense of powwow culture has emerged since the 1950s, the problem with the Pan-Indian argument is that it has tended to obscure the deeper complexities of powwow culture. It is simply not true, for example, that powwow culture is more or less the same thing across the Plains. (Even Lurie admitted that "to date, tribal identity takes precedence in many cases.") As a woman told me at the 2000 Kiowa Tiah-Piah Society dance, "Here, I remember what it means to be a member of this family, this tribe of people." She reminded me that the high point of the weekend would the singing of her family's song.[23] To borrow Loretta Fowler's very useful phrase, powwow culture is so thoroughly shot through with "shared symbols and contested meanings" that we should be immediately suspicious of attempts to interpret it according to a one-size-fits-all theory.[24] This is not to dismiss the notion that certain shared practices, assumptions, and values permeate powwow culture, only to observe that even at the most intertribal of powwows, there are actions taken, songs rendered, rituals engaged in, and beliefs affirmed that maintain their efficacy according to tribally specific ways.

In his work on Comanche powwows, for example, Thomas Kavanagh clearly demonstrates that many such gatherings maintain a close affinity to tribally specific practices, but that they also incorporate other elements of powwow culture that are not necessarily Comanche in origin or use. While acknowledging that the powwow's role in creating what Robert K. Thomas called " 'a new ethnic group' is partially correct," Kavanagh offers compelling evidence of how the same events also allow innovations that speak directly to tribally specific notions of identity. Writing in 1982, Kavanagh states that "the Comanche powwow is part of a wider network of pow-wows, and although this network includes many different cultural groups, the version of the pow-wow sponsored by Comanches does not exploit an 'Indian' identity function at the expense of a Comanche identity. In fact, several recent innovations in the Comanche powwow explicitly strengthen its tribal identity functions. It is through the identities created by and through participation in the pow-wow that a tribal identity gains political power."

Focusing on Comanche men's societies and descendants' organizations, Kavanagh observes that even at deeply intertribal events like Gourd Dances, Comanche organizations have adapted clothing and insignia that signal their identity as Comanches. The Comanche Gourd Dance group known as the Little Ponies, for example, wears distinctive pins as "a mark of identity." Similarly, the Gourd Dance outfits worn by members of the Comanche Indian Veterans Association include a red ribbon embroidered with the association's shield. "When a Little Pony dances," he notes, "whether or not other Little Ponies are present, he can be identified as a Little Pony, and thus as a Comanche, by the distinctive insignia of the society." Worried about losing their tribal identity in the large world of the Pan-Indian powwow, Comanches have seized on symbols that affirm their identity. "The participants in pow-wows, particularly in Oklahoma," Kavanaugh writes, "have realized that the symbols and signs through which they had identified themselves are now ambiguous and that those symbolic expressions of identity need tightening." Robert DesJarlait makes the same point in an essay on Northern Plains powwows when he notes that "although Northern Plains dance traditions seemingly predominate in the powwow, there are areas where they strongly conflict with Ojibwe-Anishinaabe dance traditions. . . . We need to make sure that our traditional powwows retain and express our tribal-centricity."[25]

Others expressed similar opinions about large contest powwows like Red Earth. Jim Anquoe, who helped lead the development of the first Red Earth festivals in 1986 and 1987, had hoped the event would bring Northern and Southern Plains people together "so we could learn each other's ways. Just like my brother Kenneth did with the Tulsa Powwow back there in the 1950s and 1960s, we thought this would be a good way to get together and learn about those other ways." Interestingly, Anquoe's choice of words suggested that he and some others saw this as a chance to emphasize tribally specific dances and songs, not to create a powwow "where it all looked alike." By its third year, however, Anquoe lost his enthusiasm when the festival turned into what he described as "more or less a money making spectacle that wasn't really about powwow ways. It was entertainment — the fine arts show, all the contests, tickets for every single event. I don't know, it just didn't seem like what I wanted to be doing. It serves a purpose, sure, and it helps some Indian people, but I wouldn't call it a powwow."[26]

Indeed, the Red Earth web page makes no bones about its purpose: "The Red Earth Festival was conceived in 1986 by local businessmen, civic leaders and government officials in cooperation with leaders of Oklahoma Indian tribes. Their goal was to preserve Native American cultures and create a major market for American Indian artists and crafts people. Their goals/dreams have been continued by the community and the current project is developed by a corps of 26 volunteer planning committees and over 1,000 volunteers, who devote their knowledge and time year-round."[27] Several of Lassiter's consultants clearly resented the tendency of such values to trump community and family traditions: "'It's a real shame that so many of them want the big powwows, the big money,' says one individual. 'They've forgotten. And it's a shame. That's not our ways. It's not Indian ways.'"[28]

At the other end of the spectrum, John Eastman wrote in a 1970 issue of *Natural History* that powwows were nothing more than crudely staged spectacles in which Indian people were "caught in their own stereotype and wrapped up in show biz." Eastman was appalled by what he considered the modern pow-wow's inherent lack of authentic culture, and concluded that "one cannot avoid the impression of almost desperate self-parody beneath the surface color and ceremony. . . . One cannot escape the sadness — for them, but also for us — of a people's faded richness."[29] As ridiculous as Eastman's argument is, he is hardly alone. At a powwow in North Carolina held during the late 1970s, for example, a well-intentioned but uninformed newspaper reporter expressed outrage that the Indians sponsoring the dance (including a large contingent of Poncas, Osages, and Comanches from Oklahoma) should be "forced" (her word) to dance under the flag of the United States. Even worse, she could not conceal her disappointment when she learned that Indians were cooking over gas camp stoves and sleeping in hotel rooms. It all seemed utterly inauthentic to her. When several of us tried to help her understand something of the complexities of contemporary powwow culture, she would have none of it, and shot back that we had all been duped. (When someone pointedly asked her "duped by whom," she derisively replied "by people who don't want to know the truth.")

Yet, the fabric of Southern Plains powwow culture is considerably more subtle and complicated than these interpretations suggest. Understanding the place and power of song and dance on the Southern Plains requires an understanding of the problematic, even antithetical forces that have shaped them. As Lassiter and I argue in a reply to Kracht, if powwows encourage a widely shared sense of unity and oneness among participants (and we agree that up to a point they do), they also impose order, have their own hierarchies, and make clear and meaningful distinctions concerning everything from the role of elders to gendered space to the power associated with knowledge of ritual and song. The emphasis on conformity and universally shared values is particularly problematic, if only because so many powwow people simply refute these ideals in practice. A Kiowa singer who has more than forty years of experience at the drum, for example, told me that when it comes to singing "our music," other Indians should be mindful of Kiowa practices and values. Of Kiowa songs he says, "Some of those songs are on the drum [i.e. can be sung by any group of singers], but not our O-ho-mah songs. Those are for *us*. The Poncas took two or three that they claim as theirs, but that's not right. The songs are ours."[30]

In a 1970 interview, Otis Russell, an Osage then in his late eighties, was agitated by the fact that some singers were too casual in their use and understanding of certain song traditions. On the one hand, he noted, misusing old ceremonial songs was "dangerous, you know. Take care of 'em. If you lose 'em, you might go blind or something will go wrong with you." On the other hand, misusing those same songs was an affront to his sense of history, and an insult to the power of the songs. Commenting on singers who couldn't speak the Osage language, Russell said, "Them Osage words, they tear them up, too. . . . When I hear some of them Poncas sing them songs, I told [several other Osage men] them songs don't belong in here. You can't tell Poncas nothing. They sing 'em. I hear 'em. I don't say nothing. If I say anything, [they're] liable to quarrel with me. Then Comanches, Kiowas — they got some songs Osages sing a long time ago. I hear 'em sing it out there. . . . What do they want to sing 'em for?" For his part, one Kiowa singer was dismissive of comments from a friend that he was mispronouncing the words in Ponca songs. "I don't really care," he said, "they aren't my songs."[31]

This attention to song is especially revealing, for it entails precisely the sort of power and knowledge that contradict the communitas and Pan-Indian arguments. As Lassiter points out in an important essay on the role of song in the Kiowa community, song is not an abstraction, but a tangible encounter with power.[32] To go back to a set of examples that appeared in chapter one, it is instructive to listen to the voices of people like Theresa Carter, a Kiowa. Powwow music is so important to her that she cannot "imagine being without it. . . . It's part of our everyday life . . . I get *tired* sometimes, and I *gripe*. . . . But, I need that music." Her comment is typical. At the 1996 Kiowa O-ho-mah dance, one man recounted publicly between sobs how his most precious memories were of his mother "who sang O-ho-mah songs to us kids while she did housework. I'll *always* protect these ways. My mom, my dad, all those old ones from a long time back — I can't ever forget how they loved this dance."[33]

And when people use a song inappropriately, it is not something to be taken lightly, or to be excused by an appeal to the "good feelings" that the communitas model suggests. When a visiting singer (a Sac and Fox) started a song at the 1996 Kiowa O-ho-mah that he thought was "on the drum," and thus available for use in any dance, he was quickly informed of his mistake. In fact, the song he led was the O-ho-mah Society's "tagging song," used only once a year when new members are identified and brought out of the crowd. Though some other powwow singers have used the song as an intertribal song, O-ho-mah members consider this an improper appropriation of the song. When the other singers recognized the song, they immediately pulled their sticks off the drum and let the man sing solo until one singer finally placed his drum stick across the visiting singer's stick and stopped him. It was an extraordinary moment, for it called attention to a situation that could not be politely excused. After some private discussions at the drum, the Sac and Fox man asked for the microphone and in a sincere speech apologized for his mistake, and pledged $100 and a side of beef for the following year's dance. By way of explanation, he told the crowd that he'd learned the song from his father in the 1940s when that man —

a widely respected singer — had often been a guest in Kiowa country. Invoking his father's name deflected some of the criticism and helped to explain his mistake, but it did not relieve him of the obligation to pay for his miscue.[34]

Another singer, who has spent nearly fifty years at the drum, told me of his experience at a large Gourd Dance during which the head singer, a Comanche, made a long speech in which he claimed the dance was a Comanche ceremony. This is deeply offensive to many Kiowas, whose claim to the dance is widely regarded as unassailable. "When that guy sat back down, I told him 'that was a mighty interesting speech about how you Comanches own this dance and all. So, seeing as how it's *yours,* let's have a set of Comanche Gourd Dance songs. I'd like to hear your songs — go ahead and start a couple up.' " In fact, the man couldn't do it, because as Gourd Dance singers will readily admit, all of the songs come from the Kiowas. Chagrined at being called on the carpet, the head singer quietly deferred to the Kiowas at the drum and asked my friend to start the next four songs. There was no public embarrassment, no calling attention to what Kiowas considered the head singer's misstep, but the point was made.[35]

The matter of song ownership and the responsibility it entails are not abstractions. An Osage woman put it to me this way, "An example of the strong sense of ownership over a particular song is at the Grayhorse I'n-Lon-Schka dances. One song that is sung in the memory of a man in our family originally belonged to a family that was not properly taking care of this song. The Grayhorse committee was considering throwing it out in order to make room for other songs, but another man told the committee that he would take it as his song because he did not want to see it forgotten. Now, the descendants of the original owner have come back to the dance and they want it back, but my family has a difficult time giving it back because we paid for it in the proper way and we feel that it now belongs to us. This has created a bit of tension between the two families."[36]

Yet if the powwow is complicated by issues of power and control, its appeal is almost impossible to overstate. Since its appearance in the 1920s, it has shown no sign of weakening, and there's every reason to believe that it will continue into the twenty-first century as a vibrant and dynamic expression of contemporary Indian culture, problems and all. Southern Plains powwow culture is an exhilarating thing full of vitality and joy; there are so many things to see and hear, so many experiences to take in, so many competing ideas to reconcile and balance. This was never clearer to me than in the summer of 1990 when I made the drive from Shawnee, Oklahoma, north to Tulsa for the Intertribal Indian Club of Tulsa's Powwow of Champions. In the car with me were Harry Tofpi, Sr., and his young grandson, Billy Bemo, who was about ten years old. I'd met them and their families a year or so earlier when I'd spent several nights with

Harry's son, JR, assembling a set of men's traditional dance clothes for Billy to wear at an upcoming dance in Meeker, Oklahoma. JR and I had met when we showed up on a rainy Saturday in late July to help the committee cut brush for the dance arbor. We hit it off right away and spent much of the next week visiting and getting to know one another. In the years to come, we all became good friends.

Some of the pictures from the trip to Tulsa show me and Billy leaning against a concrete wall before the first night's grand entry. Dressed in our dance clothes, we looked like the odd couple — me, a tall non-Indian, and Billy, a short chubby-faced Indian boy. In the pictures, I look a bit tired; Billy looks like the cat that just swallowed the canary. He was excited to be in Tulsa, looked forward to the dance, and was happy to be with friends and family. (So was I, but Billy had youth and an amazing ability to go without sleep on his side.) We had a fine time that weekend. Billy's Uncle JR was the head man dancer, so we had good hotel rooms and plenty of cold pop at our benches. Evenings we skipped out to eat pizza before coming back to put on our dance clothes in time for the grand entry. We visited aunts and uncles, got called up for giveaways, met good people, bought loads of craft supplies, and consumed our weight in funnel cake. We got almost no sleep, and nearly slept our way to an extra day's billing on the last morning in the hotel. And when it was over, we headed home and got ready to go to another dance the following weekend. It was during that trip that I first imagined writing this book. Other projects kept me from it, but it always lingered. Three years ago I looked at the pictures of Bill from that dance and figured it was time to get on with it.

The image of Bill leaning against that wall in his dance clothes has remained clear in my mind all these years. I have never forgotten his face, with his impish smile and fat cheeks grinning back at the camera. Even now, one of those photos is pinned to my office wall — next to his high school basketball photo, shots of graduation, pictures of his parents Ron and Jennie in their powwow clothes, and his wedding pictures. He isn't that chubby little kid anymore. Bill has outgrown two beadwork sets we've put together over the years, and he shows little sign of slowing down. Today, he and his wife Erin live in Shawnee not far from both sets of in-laws. Like their parents and many of their relatives, Bill and Erin are devoted powwowers. Between Bill's job at a local furniture store, and Erin's work as a nurse, their time is tight, but not so tight that they miss the dances that mean so much to them. They know that this way of life is important, and that the dances they attend are powerful shapers of their own history and heritage. Seeing them with their parents, siblings, nieces, nephews, aunts, uncles, grandmas, and grandpas reminds me that this way will endure as long as people like Bill and Erin find the will to take it up.

The powwow life is a hard way — you hear that sentiment often in Indian country; but it's a good way — you hear that a lot, too. When I see Bill and Erin dressed for a dance session, I can't help but recall what Bill's grandpa told me: "God gave us these ways. He gave us lots of ways to express ourselves, to keep our ways. One of them is these dances. When I go to them, whatever they are — powwow, Gourd Dance, Black Legs, whatever — I'm right where those old people were. Singing those songs, dancing *where they danced*. And my children and grandchildren, they've learned these ways, too, because it's good, it's powerful."

Notes

1 The Intertribal Indian Club of Tulsa's web page has links to the club's activities. URL http://www.iicot.org
2 Author's field notes, August 1990.
3 Author's field notes, July 2000. In Indian country, "ayyy" is a teasing term often used to suggest irony or humor in everyday situations.
4 Author's field notes, July 2000.
5 Author's field notes, August 2002.
6 Barre Toelken, "Ethnic Selection and Intensification in the Native American Pow-wow," in *Creative Ethnicity: Symbols and Strategies of Contemporary Ethnic Life,* Stephen Stern and John Allan Cicala, eds. (Logan: Utah State University Press, 1991): 138, 153. Emphasis in the original.
7 Angela Wilson, personal communication with the author, December 12, 2002.
8 Scott Tonemah, interview by the author, February 8, 1988, Norman, Okla.: author's field notes, July 2002.
9 Benjamin Kracht, "Kiowa Powwows: Continuity in Ritual Practice," *American Indian Quarterly* 18:3 (1994): 322; Jack Campisi, "Powwow: A Study in Ethnic Boundary Main-tenance," *Man in the Northeast* 9 (1975): 44. For a reply to Kracht, see Clyde Ellis and Luke Eric Lassiter, "Commentary: Applying Communitas to Kiowa Powwows," *American Indian Quarterly* 22:4 (1998): 485–491. For a recent account that emphasizes the role of the powwow as a positive form of generalized Indianness, see James Hamill, "Being Indian in Northeast Oklahoma," *Plains Anthropologist* 45:173 (2000): 291–303.
10 Mark Mattern, "The Powwow as a Public Arena for Negotiating Unity and Diversity in American Indian Life," *American Indian Culture and Research Journal* 20:4 (1996): 183.
11 Harry Tofpi, Sr., interview by the author, May 2, 1996, Shawnee, Okla.
12 Loretta Fowler, *Shared Symbols, Contested Meanings: Gros Ventre Culture and History, 1778–1985* (Ithaca, N.Y.: Cornell University Press, 1987): 9.
13 Gloria Alese Young, "Powwow Power: Perspectives on Historic and Contemporary Intertribalism" (Ph.D. diss., Indiana University, 1981): 68. Young's dissertation is a well-written, comprehensively framed discussion. Sharp and insightful, it is the fullest account of powwow culture on the Plains. Because it has never been pub-lished, and is now more than two decades old, it is not as well known as it deserves to be, and its influence has been largely limited to scholars working specifically on dance history and culture. Anyone working on powwow culture owes a large debt

to Young's research and analysis. Other sources that place the powwow in a larger context are Dennis Zotigh, *Moving History: The Evolution of the Powwow* (Oklahoma City: Center for the American Indian, 1991); Tara Browner, *Heartbeat of the People: Music and Dance of the Northern Powwow* (Urbana: University of Illinois Press, 2002); William Meadows, *Kiowa, Apache, and Comanche Military Societies: Enduring Veterans, 1800 to the Present* (Austin: University of Texas Press, 1999); and Loretta Fowler, *Tribal Sovereignty and the Historical Imagination: Cheyenne-Arapaho Politics* (Lincoln: University of Nebraska Press, 2002).

14 One exception is Charlotte Heth, ed., *Native American Dance: Ceremonies and Social Traditions* (Washington, D.C.: Smithsonian Institution Press, 1992). Heth's contributors do not focus exclusively on powwow culture, but the essays in this volume are notable for their attention to meaning and experience. Toelken, "Native American Powwow," 137.

15 Kenneth A. Ashworth, "The Contemporary Oklahoma Powwow" (Ph.D. diss., University of Oklahoma, 1986); Daniel J. Gelo, "Comanche Songs with English Lyrics: Context, Imagery, and Continuity," *Storia Nordamericana* 5:1 (1988): 137–146, and Gelo, "Powwow Patter: Indian Emcee Discourse on Power and Identity," *Journal of American Folklore* 112 (Winter 1999): 40–57; Thomas Kavanagh, "The Comanche Pow-wow: Pan-Indianism or Tribalism," *Haliksa'i*, University of New Mexico Contributions to Anthropology 1 (1982): 12–27; Luke Eric Lassiter, *The Power of Kiowa Song: A Collaborative Ethnography* (Tucson: University of Arizona Press, 1998), and Lassiter, "Charlie Brown: Not Just Another Essay on the Gourd Dance," *American Indian Culture and Research Journal* 21:4 (1997): 75–103; Meadows, *Military Societies;* Benjamin Kracht, "Kiowa Powwows: Continuity in Ritual Performance," *American Indian Quarterly* 18:3 (1994): 321–348; Jethro Gaede, "The American Indian Exposition, 1932–1950: Rejecting Assimilation Initiatives and Inverting Cultural Stereotypes," paper presented at annual meeting, American Society for Ethnohistory, 2000; Morris Foster, *Being Comanche: A Social History of an American Indian Community* (Tucson: University of Arizona Press, 1991); Stephanie Anna May, "Performance of Identity: Alabama-Coushatta Tourism, Powwows, and Everyday Life" (Ph.D. diss., University of Texas at Austin, 2001).

16 Author's field notes, August 1990.

1. AN OVERVIEW OF THE POWWOW'S HISTORY

1 Portions of this chapter appeared previously in Clyde Ellis, " 'We Don't Want Your Rations, We Want This Dance': The Changing Use of Song and Dance on the Southern Plains," *Western Historical Quarterly* 30:2 (1999): 133–154. Giveaway description from author's field notes, August 1996. Roaching refers to the act of tying a hair roach (a headdress made of porcupine hair) on a male dancer's head. "Paying for his seat" is a colloquialism used to describe the act of giving away that signifies one's payment for the privilege of dancing. Women, too, pay for their place in much the same fashion as the event recounted above.

General discussions of the contemporary powwow complex may be found in Charlotte Heth, ed., *Native American Dance: Ceremonies and Social Traditions* (Washington, D.C.: Smithsonian Institution Press, 1992); George P. Horse Capture, *Pow Wow*

(Cody, Wyo.: Buffalo Bill Historical Center, 1989); David Whitehorse, *Pow-wow: The Contemporary Pan-Indian Celebration*, Publications in American Indian Studies (San Diego: San Diego State University, 1988); Tara Browner, *Heartbeat of the People: Music and Dance of the Northern Pow-wow* (Urbana: University of Illinois Press, 2002); William K. Powers, *War Dance: Plains Indian Musical Performance* (Tucson: University of Arizona Press, 1990), and Powers, "Plains Indian Music and Dance," in *Anthropology on the Great Plains*, W. Raymond Wood and Margot Liberty, eds. (Lincoln: University of Nebraska Press, 1980): 212–229; Mark Mattern, "The Powwow as a Public Arena for Negotiating Unity and Diversity in American Indian Life," *American Indian Culture and Research Journal* 20:4 (1996): 183–201; James H. Howard, "Pan-Indianism in Native American Music and Dance," *Ethnomusicology* 27:1 (1983): 71–82; Joan D. Laxson, "Aspects of Acculturation among American Indians: Emphasis on Contemporary Pan-Indianism" (Ph.D. diss., University of California-Berkeley, 1972); Gloria Alese Young, "Powwow Power: Perspectives on Historic and Contemporary Intertribalism" (Ph.D. diss., Indiana University, 1981); Susan Applegate Krouse, "A Window into the Indian Culture: The Powwow as Performance" (Ph.D. diss., University of Wisconsin-Milwaukee, 1991); Ann Axtmann, "Dance: Celebration and Resistance, Native American Indian Intertribal Powwow Performance" (Ph.D. diss., New York University, 1999); Victoria Eugenie Sanchez, " 'As Long as We Dance, We Shall Know Who We Are': A Study of Off-Reservation Traditional Intertribal Powwows in Central Ohio" (Ph.D. diss., Ohio State University, 1995); Lita Mathews, "The Native American Powwow: A Contemporary Authentication of a Cultural Artifact" (Ph.D. diss., University of New Mexico, 1999); Kathleen Glenister Roberts, "Giving Away: The Performance of Speech and Sign in Powwow Ritual Exchange" (Ph.D. diss., Indiana University, 2001); Sarah Quick, "Powwow Dancing in North America: The Formation of an Indian Identity through Expressive Culture" (master's thesis, University of Missouri at Columbia, 2001).

For discussions of Southern Plains powwow and dance traditions, see Dennis Zotigh, *Moving History: The Evolution of the Powwow* (Oklahoma City: Center for the American Indian, 1991); Thomas W. Kavanagh, "Southern Plains Dance: Tradition and Dynamics," in *Native American Dance: Ceremonies and Social Traditions*, Charlotte Heth, ed., 105–123; William C. Meadows, *Kiowa, Apache, and Comanche Military Societies: Enduring Veterans, 1800 to the Present* (Austin: University of Texas Press, 1999); Luke Eric Lassiter, *The Power of Kiowa Song: A Collaborative Ethnography* (Tucson: University of Arizona Press, 1998), and Lassiter, " 'Charlie Brown': Not Just Another Essay on the Gourd Dance," *American Indian Culture and Research Journal* 21:4 (1997): 75–103; Maurice Boyd, *Kiowa Voices*, 2 vols. (Fort Worth: Texas Christianity University Press, 1981); Alice Anne Callahan, *The Osage Ceremonial Dance: I'n-Lon-Schka* (Norman: University of Oklahoma Press, 1990); Willie Smyth, ed., *Songs of Indian Territory: Native American Music Traditions of Oklahoma* (Oklahoma City: Center for the American Indian, 1989); Morris W. Foster, *Being Comanche: A Social History of an American Indian Community* (Tucson: University of Arizona Press, 1991), esp. 24–30, 123–153; Clyde Ellis, " 'Truly Dancing Their Own Way': Modern Revival and Diffusion of the Gourd Dance," *American Indian Quarterly* 14:1 (Winter 1990): 19–33, and Ellis, " 'There Is No Doubt . . . the Dances Should Be Curtailed': Indian Dances and Federal Policy on the Southern Plains, 1880–1930,"

Pacific Historical Review 70:4 (2001): 543–569; John H. Moore, "How Giveaways and Pow-wows Redistribute the Means of Subsistence," in *The Political Economy of North American Indians,* John H. Moore, ed. (Norman: University of Oklahoma Press, 1993): 240–269; Benjamin Kracht, "Kiowa Powwows: Continuity in Ritual Practice," *American Indian Quarterly* 18:3 (1994): 321–348; James H. Howard, "Pan-Indian Culture of Oklahoma," *Scientific Monthly* 18:5 (1955): 215–220, and Howard, "The Plains Gourd Dance as a Revitalization Movement," *American Ethnologist* 3:2 (1976): 243–259; Daniel J. Gelo, "Comanche Songs with English Lyrics: Context, Imagery, and Continuity," *Storia Nordamericana* 5:1 (1988): 137–146, and Gelo, "Powwow Patter: Indian Emcee Discourse on Power and Identity," *Journal of American Folklore* 112 (Winter 1999): 40–57; Young, "Powwow Power"; Sue Roark-Calnek, "Indian Way in Oklahoma: Transactions in Honor and Legitimacy" (Ph.D. diss., Bryn Mawr College, 1977); Kenneth Ashworth, "The Contemporary Oklahoma Powwow" (Ph.D. diss., University of Oklahoma, 1986); Andrew Wade Williams, "We Are All Warriors Now: Dancing the Future in the Contemporary Oklahoma Powwow" (senior honors thesis, Harvard University, 1997).

2 Lassiter, "Charlie Brown," 97; Kavanagh, "Southern Plains Dance," 105. Similar arguments have been made for other regions. Commenting on Northern Plains powwows, R. D. Theisz argues that song and dance are crucial for post–World War II Lakota identity. See his "Song Texts and Their Performers: The Centerpiece of Contemporary Lakota Identity Formulation," *Great Plains Quarterly* 7 (Spring 1987): 116–124. In "The Omaha Dance in Oglala and Sicangu Sioux History, 1883–1923," *Whispering Wind* 23:5 (Fall-Winter 1990), p. 4, Mark Thiel notes that "for generations the Omaha dance has been the most popular social and nationalistic celebration of the Oglala and Sicangu Sioux, thus serving as an obtrusive demonstration of tribal identity and cohesion."

3 Lassiter, "Charlie Brown," 75–76; Richard West, foreword, in *Native American Dance,* Charlotte Heth, ed., ix; Foster, *Being Comanche,* 153; Jeanne M. Devlin, "Oklahoma Tribesmen: Every Picture Tells a Story," *Oklahoma Today* 41:3 (May-June 1991): 22; Harry Tofpi, Sr., interview by the author, Shawnee, Okla., May 3, 1997; author's field notes, July 1996.

4 Francis Paul Prucha, *The Great Father: The United States Government and the American Indians* 2 vols. (Lincoln: University of Nebraska Press, 1984), 2: 800–801.

5 Prucha, *Great Father,* 2: 801–803; Lawrence C. Kelly, *The Assault on Assimilation: John Collier and the Origins of Indian Policy Reform* (Albuquerque: University of New Mexico Press, 1983): 304.

6 L. G. Moses, *Wild West Shows and the Images of the American Indians, 1883–1933* (Albuquerque: University of New Mexico Press, 1996): 253.

7 James H. Kyle, "How Shall the Indian Be Educated?" *North American Review* 159 (November 1894): 437; Heth quoted in Laurence F. Schmeckebier, *The Office of Indian Affairs: Its History, Activities, and Organization* (Baltimore: Johns Hopkins University Press, 1927): 72; Herbert Welsh quoted in Robert M. Utley, *The Last Days of the Sioux Nation* (New Haven, Conn.: Yale University Press, 1963): 38; Leonard D. White, *The Republican Era, 1869–1901: A Study in Administrative History* (New York: MacMillan, 1958): 175; Robert H. Keller, Jr., *American Protestantism and United States Indian Policy, 1869–82* (Lincoln: University of Nebraska Press, 1983): 10.

8 William T. Hagan, *United States-Comanche Relations: The Reservation Years* (Norman: University of Oklahoma Press, 1990): 42; see also Hagan, "The Reservation Policy: Too Little and Too Late," in *Indian-White Relations: A Persistent Paradox*, Jane F. Smith and Robert M. Kvasnicka, eds. (Washington, D.C.: Howard University Press, 1976), 157–169; Keller, *American Protestantism*, 11.

9 Quote on agencies as asylums from September 7, 1885, School Inspection Report, in "Agents' Reports," Records of the Kiowa Agency, Oklahoma Historical Society; Hagan, *United States-Comanche Relations*, esp. 166–200; Clyde Ellis, *To Change Them Forever: Indian Education at the Rainy Mountain Boarding School, 1893–1920* (Norman: University of Oklahoma Press, 1996): 32–34; John Jasper Methvin, "Reminiscences of Life Among the Indians," *Chronicles of Oklahoma* 5 (1927): 169–170. For comparisons of other agencies in the region, see Donald J. Berthrong, *The Cheyenne and Arapaho Ordeal: Reservation and Agency Life in the Indian Territory, 1875–1907* (Norman: University of Oklahoma Press, 1976).

10 Moses, *Wild West Shows*, 253, 73, and Moses, "Wild West Shows, Reformers, and the Image of the American Indian, 1887–1914," *South Dakota History* 14 (Fall 1984): 193–221; and Moses, "Indians on the Midway: Wild West Shows and the Indian Bureau at World's Fairs, 1893–1904," *South Dakota History* 21 (Fall 1991): 205–229. On the Miller Brothers, see Fred Gipson, *Fabulous Empire: Colonel Zack Miller's Story* (Boston: Houghton Mifflin Company, 1946); Michael Wallis, "The Miller Brothers and the 101 Ranch," *Gilcrease Journal* 1 (Spring 1993): 6–29; Barbara Williams Roth, "The 101 Ranch Wild West Show, 1904–1932," *Chronicles of Oklahoma* 43:4 (Winter 1965): 416–431.

11 Battice quoted in Moses, *Wild West Shows*, 180; Moses, "Interpreting the Wild West, 1883–1914," in *Between Indian and White Worlds: The Cultural Brokers*, Margaret Connell Szasz, ed. (Albuquerque: University of New Mexico Press, 1994): 161, 172; Thiel, "The Omaha Dance," 5; Sherrole Benton, "Grand Entry: A New Ceremony Derived from the Old West," *Tribal College Journal*, Winter 1992, 10–13.

12 Moses, *Wild West Shows*, 279, and Moses, "Interpreting the Wild West," 177–178; Thiel, "The Omaha Dance," 5–6.

13 Prucha, *Great Father*, 2: 951; Kenneth R. Philp, *John Collier's Crusade for Indian Reform, 1920–1954* (Tucson: University of Arizona Press, 1977): 55–70.

14 Harry Tofpi, Sr., interview by the author, May 3, 1997, Shawnee, Okla.

15 Lassiter, *Power of Kiowa Song*, 94; Carol Rachlin, "Tight Shoe Night: Oklahoma Indians Today," in *The American Indian Today*, Stuart Levine and Nancy O. Lurie, eds. (Baltimore: Pelican Books, 1970): 171, 182–183; Clifford Coppersmith, "Healing and Remembrance: The Chiricahua and Warm Springs Apache Mountain Spirit Dance in Oklahoma," manuscript in author's possession; Thiel, "The Omaha Dance," 5.

16 Lassiter, *Power of Kiowa Song*, 93–95, 119; Meadows, *Kiowa, Apache, and Comanche Military Societies*, 113–122, quote is on 121; author's field notes, Kiowa O-ho-mah Ceremonials, Anadarko, Okla., July 1996; Luke Eric Lassiter, telephone conversation with the author, July 30, 2002. The O-ho-mah song referenced here is often called the Resistance Song, and contains words that translate as "Do not hesitate to dance! Go ahead and be arrested and jailed." At the 1996 O-ho-mah dance, one speaker reminded the crowd that "O-ho-mah *never* stopped dancing." At the 2002 O-ho-mah dance, the Resistance Song was rendered along with a detailed explanation by Mac Whitehorse, the society's bustle keeper, of the song's history and meaning.

17 Kavanagh, "Southern Plains Dance," 109; James H. Howard, "Notes on the Dakota Grass Dance," *Southwest Journal of Anthropology* 8 (1951): 82. See Alice C. Fletcher and Francis LaFlesche, *The Omaha Tribe,* vol. 2 (Lincoln: University of Nebraska Press, 1972): 441–442, 459–480, for comments on the origin of the Omaha Dance and its diffusion, which led to the development of the O-ho-mah (Kiowa), Iruska (Pawnee), Hethu'shka (Omaha), Helushka (Ponca), and I'n-lon-schka (Osage) dance societies, among others; Clark Wissler, "General Discussion of Shamanistic and Dancing Societies," *Anthropological Papers of the American Museum of Natural History,* vol. XI, part XII: 859–860; Lassiter, *Power of Kiowa Song,* 80–98.

18 See Young, "Powwow Power," 129–153; Kavanagh, "Southern Plains Dance," 111.

19 Kavanagh, "Southern Plains Dance," 111; Nancy O. Lurie, "The Contemporary American Indian Scene," in *North American Indians in Historical Perspective,* Eleanor B. Leacock and Nancy O. Lurie, eds. (New York: Random House, 1971), 449–450; James H. Howard, *The Ponca Tribe,* Bureau of American Ethnology, Bulletin 195 (Lincoln: University of Nebraska Press, 1995), 107–108.

20 Foster, *Being Comanche,* 30.

21 Ibid., 123. Foster cites three reasons for the resurgence of Comanche dancing: 1. Concern among older Comanches for reviving traditional rituals; 2. The hiring of Comanches to perform at local civic functions and celebrations; 3. Requests by Comanches for surviving members of military societies to dance at intracommunity events. Reports of Quanah Parker's dances are in "Indian Celebrations and Dances, 1874–1917," Records of the Kiowa Agency, Oklahoma Historical Society; see also William T. Hagan, *Quanah Parker, Comanche Chief* (Norman: University of Oklahoma Press, 1993), 102–103.

22 Foster, *Being Comanche,* 126–127. Benjamin Kracht makes a similar argument in an essay on Kiowa religion, in which he says that some older people believe that "powwows serve as a religion for the youth"; Kracht, "Kiowa Religion in Historical Perspective," *American Indian Quarterly* 21:1 (1997): 28.

23 Kavanagh, "Southern Plains Dance," 105; author's field notes, July 1991; Scott Tonemah, interview by the author, February 8, 1988, Norman, Okla.; Lassiter, "Charlie Brown," 89.

24 Callahan, *Osage Ceremonial Dance,* 134.

25 Ralph Kotay, interview by the author, August 13, 2002, Apache, Okla. The best recent discussions of American Indians and military service are Thomas A. Britten, *American Indians in World War I: At Home and At War* (Albuquerque: University of New Mexico Press, 1997); Alison R. Bernstein, *American Indians and World War II: Toward a New Era in Indian Affairs* (Norman: University of Oklahoma Press, 1991); Tom Holm, *Strong Hearts, Wounded Souls: Native American Veterans of the Vietnam War* (Austin: University of Texas Press, 1996), esp. 66–102; Holm, "Fighting a White Man's War: The Extent and Legacy of American Indian Participation in World War II," in *The Plains Indians of the Twentieth Century,* Peter Iverson, ed. (Norman: University of Oklahoma Press, 1985), 149–167; Aaron McGaffey Beede, "The Dakota Indian Victory Dance," *North Dakota Historical Quarterly* 9 (April 1942): 167–178; James H. Howard, "The Dakota Victory Dance, World War II," *North Dakota History* 18 (1951): 31–40.

26 Britten, *American Indians in World War I,* 149.

27 Britten, *American Indians in World War I*, 149; Foster, *Being Comanche*, 125; *Annual Report of the Commissioner of Indian Affairs*, 1919, 12.

28 Britten, *American Indians in World War I*, 150–151. An essay titled "Lo, the Rich Indian, How He Blows His Coin!" *Literary Digest* 67:8 (November 20, 1920), 62–64, generally disparaged the oil-rich Osages as spendthrifts with little sense when it came to money, and recounted how Bacon Rind, a prominent Osage man, had spared no expense in sponsoring two dances in honor of his son, a returning World War I veteran. It is difficult to imagine that the *Literary Digest* would have made a similar editorial interpretation of white homecoming celebrations.

29 Britten, *American Indians in World War I*, 149–150; Beede, "Dakota Indian Victory Dance," 169–172; Frances Densmore, "The Songs of Indian Soldiers during the World War," *Musical Quarterly* 20 (October 1934): 419–435; R. D. Theisz, "The Bad Speakers and the Long Braids: References to Foreign Enemies in Lakota Song Texts," in *Indians and Europe: An Interdisciplinary Collection of Essays*, Christian Feest, ed. (Aachen, Ger.: RaderVerlag, 1987), 429–430; Harry Tofpi, Sr., interview by the author, May 2, 1996, Shawnee, Okla.

30 Tonemah interview; George "Woogie" Watchetaker from the video *Into the Circle: An Introduction to Oklahoma Powwows and Celebrations* (Tulsa: Full Circle Productions, 1992); Jim Anquoe, interview by the author, July 12, 2002, Stroud, Okla.; William C. Meadows and Gus Palmer, Sr., "Tonkonga: The Kiowa Black Legs Military Society," in *Native American Dance*, Heth, ed., 117; Boyd, *Kiowa Voices*, 1: 71, 73, 112; Kracht, "Kiowa Powwows," 339. Kracht's orthography is unnecessarily obscure; "dwdw" is pronounced "dawdaw."

31 Foster, *Being Comanche*, 145; Harry Tofpi, interview with the author, August 4, 1993, Seminole, Okla.; Tonemah interview; Parker McKenzie, interview by the author, August 1, 1990, Mountain View, Okla.

32 Program for the 59th Annual American Indian Exposition, August 20–25, 1990, in the possession of the author; *Ageless We Dance: A Photographic History of Kiowa Social Dancing from 1890–1940*, na, ca. 1995, a pamphlet printed in conjunction with an exhibit of historic photographs presented by the Oklahoma Historical Society, Museum of the Western Prairie, and the Kiowa Elders Center, pp. 3–4.

33 Luke Eric Lassiter, telephone conversation with the author, September 10, 1998.

34 Ibid.; see also Lassiter, *Power of Kiowa Song*, 241, n. 4; author's field notes, June 2001.

35 Meadows, *Military Societies*, 128. On War Mothers, see Marjorie Schweitzer, "The Oto-Missouria War Mothers: Women of Valor," *Moccasin Tracks* 7:1 (1981): 4–8, and "The War Mothers: Reflections of Space and Time," *Papers in Anthropology*, University of Oklahoma, 24:2 (1983): 157–171; Robert Anderson, "The Northern Cheyenne War Mothers," *Anthropological Quarterly* 29:3 (1956): 82–90.

36 Loretta Fowler, *Tribal Sovereignty and the Historical Imagination: Cheyenne-Arapaho Politics* (Lincoln: University of Nebraska Press, 2002): 94, see also her discussion at 266–269; Lassiter, *Power of Kiowa Song*, 246, n10. Gender remains a relatively rare topic in the literature on powwows and dances . Notable exceptions include Marla N. Powers, "Symbolic Representations of Sex Roles in the Plains War Dance," *European Review of Native American Studies* 2:2 (1988): 17–24; William K. Powers, "Echoing the Drum: The Place of Women in Lakota Song and Dance," *Whispering Wind* 31:1 (2000): 12–20; Orin T. Hatton, "In the Tradition: Grass Dance Musical Style and Female Pow-

wow Singers," *Ethnomusicology* 30:2 (1986): 197–221; Elizabeth Wyrick Thompson, "Pocahontas, Powwows, and Musical Power: Native American Women's Performances in North Carolina" (Master's thesis, University of North Carolina at Chapel Hill, 1998); Judith Ann Jones, "Women Never Used to Dance': Gender and Music in Nez Perce Culture Change" (Ph.D. diss., Washington State University, 1995).

37 Ralph Kotay, telephone conversation with the author, July 18, 1998; Howard, "Pan-Indianism in Native American Music and Dance," 71–82. Lassiter notes that "in southwestern Oklahoma's Indian world . . . tribal traditions are not necessarily mutually exclusive; they intersect in an intertribal social world. Therefore, we are no longer speaking of *aggregates* of individuals, but different worlds in which individuals participate. Powwow, hand-game, church, or peyote people, then, all take part in distinct but interrelated worlds defined by aesthetics, tradition, and history" (Lassiter's emphasis); *Power of Kiowa Song,* 77.

When the Peabody Museum returned the Sacred Pole to the Omaha Tribe in 1989 after an absence of nearly a century, for example, the tribe brought the Pole back into the community with emotional and ritually specific actions at its annual powwow in Macy, where later in the weekend dancers competed for monetary prizes. That this occurred at a contest powwow did not lessen the importance of the moment. See Robin Ridington and Dennis Hastings (In'aska), *Blessing for a Long Time: The Sacred Pole of the Omaha Tribe* (Lincoln: University of Nebraska Press, 1997): 170–189.

38 Kavanagh, "Southern Plains Dance," 121; Foster, *Being Comanche,* 131.

39 Lassiter, *Power of Kiowa Song,* 81–82; John Gamble, "Changing Patterns in Kiowa Dance," *International Congress of Americanists, Proceedings* 29:2 (1952), 100–105; Kracht, "Kiowa Powwows," 332–333.

40 Lassiter, *Power of Kiowa Song,* 90; Luke Eric Lassiter, telephone conversation with the author, July 16, 1998.

41 Lassiter, *Power of Kiowa Song,* 243.

42 David Rich Lewis, "Still Native: The Significance of Native Americans in the History of the Twentieth-Century American West," *Western Historical Quarterly* 24 (May 1993): 227.

43 Author's field notes, July 1996, August 1996.

2. NINETEENTH-CENTURY PLAINS SOCIETY DANCES AND THE ROOTS OF THE POWWOW

1 Morris Foster, *Being Comanche: A Social History of an American Indian Community* (Tucson: University of Arizona Press, 1991), 27–29.

2 James H. Howard, *The Ponca Tribe* Bureau of American Ethnology, Bulletin 195 (Lincoln: University of Nebraska Press, 1995): 102.

3 James Mooney, *Calendar History of the Kiowa Indians,* Seventeenth Annual Report of the Bureau of American Ethnology (Washington, D.C.: Smithsonian Institution Press, 1979): 229; Clark Wissler, "Societies of the Plains Indians — General Introduction," *Anthropological Papers of the American Museum of Natural History,* vol. XI, part I (1916): vi. For a more recent discussion that posits the existence of widely shared societies, see James H. Howard, "The Plains Gourd Dance as a Revitalization Movement," *American Ethnologist* 3:2 (1976): 243–259.

4 Mooney, *Calendar History*, 351, 352, 359, 379; William C. Meadows, *Kiowa, Apache, and Comanche Military Societies: Enduring Veterans, 1800 to the Present* (Austin: University of Texas Press, 1999), 55–56; Guy Quoetone, interview by Julia A. Jordan, September 19, 1967, Doris Duke Oral History Collection, Western History Collection, University of Oklahoma, Norman, Okla. (hereafter cited as DDOH). Quoetone was 81 years old at the time of the interview.

5 Alanson Skinner, "Societies of the Iowa," *Anthropological Papers of the American Museum of Natural History*, vol. XI, part IX (1915): 684, 690, 699.

6 Alanson Skinner, "Ponca Society and Dances," *Anthropological Papers of the American Museum of Natural History*, vol. XI, part IX (1915): 781, 783; Robert H. Lowie, "Dance Associations of the Eastern Dakota," *Anthropological Papers of the American Museum of Natural History*, vol. XI, part II (1913): 141, and Lowie, "Dances and Societies of the Plains Shoshone," *Anthropological Papers of the American Museum of Natural History*, vol. XI, part X (1915): 807; James R. Murie, "Pawnee Indian Societies," *Anthropological Papers of the American Museum of Natural History*, vol. XI, part VII (1914): 546; Clark Wissler, "Societies and Ceremonial Associations in the Oglala Division of the Teton-Dakota," *Anthropological Papers of the American Museum of Natural History*, vol. XI, part I (1912): 5, and Wissler, "Societies and Dance Associations of the Blackfoot Indians," *Anthropological Papers of the American Museum of Natural History*, vol. XI, part IV (1913): 363.

7 Howard, *The Ponca Tribe*, 102; James H. Howard and Gertrude P. Kurath, "Ponca Dance, Ceremonies, and Music," *Ethnomusicology* 3:1 (1959): 1. Ernest Wallace and E. Adamson Hoebel, *The Comanches: Lords of the South Plains* (Norman: University of Oklahoma Press, 1952): 252.

8 See, for example, Lynn F. Huenemann, "Northern Plains Dance," and Thomas W. Kavanagh, "Southern Plains Dance: Tradition and Dynamics," in *Native American Dance: Ceremonies and Social Traditions*, Charlotte Heth, ed. (Washington, D.C.: Smithsonian Institution, 1992): 125–147 (Huenemann), 105–123 (Kavanagh); Susan Applegate Krouse, "A Window into the Indian Culture: The Powwow as Performance," Ph.D. diss., University of Wisconsin-Milwaukee, 1991, 26–35. I am not criticizing these sources, which are sound and informative. I mean only to draw attention to the relatively brief attention that they (and many others) give to this issue.

   Interpretations that address the relationship between powwows and society dances include Abe Conklin, "Origin of the Powwow: The Ponca He-Thus-Ka Society Dance," *Native Americas: Hemispheric Journal of Indigenous Issues* (Fall/Winter 1994), 17–21; Gloria Young, "Dance as Communication," *Native Americas: Hemispheric Journal of Indigenous Issues* (Fall/Winter 1994), 9–15; Gloria Alese Young, "Powwow Power: Perspectives on Historic and Contemporary Intertribalism," Ph.D. diss., Indiana University, 1981; Foster, *Being Comanche;* and Meadows, *Military Societies.* Meadows does not write specifically about powwows, but his discussion of Southern Plains warrior societies and the twentieth century revivals of their rituals and dances is a nuanced and detailed account that demonstrates a clear connection to earlier practices. James H. Howard suggested a similar scenario in "The Plains Gourd Dance."

9 Aaron Fry, "Social Power and the Men's Northern Traditional Powwow Clothing Style," in *Painters, Patrons, and Identity: Essays in Native American Art to Honor J. J.*

Brody, Joyce M. Szabo, ed. (Albuquerque: University of New Mexico Press, 2001): 76, 91, n28, also 92, n37; author's field notes, May 1989, June 1990, May 2002, January 2003, April 2003.

10 Tara Browner, *Heartbeat of the People: Music and Dance of the Northern Powwow* (Urbana: University of Illinois Press, 2002): 4, 20–27. Taking Wissler and William K. Powers to task, Browner charges Wissler with failing to convincingly demonstrate that the choreography and accoutrement of late nineteenth-century Plains dance culture were rooted in the diffusion of the Omaha Society. Yet in her assessment of the Northern Plains powwow's origins, Browner ignores Goddard, Skinner, Lowie, Fletcher, LaFlesche, Denig, Dorsey, and Mooney, among others, whose works address her complaints and contradict her arguments. Browner ultimately resorts to the assertion that because Wissler's conclusions differ from selective oral accounts that support her interpretations, Wissler is unreliable and biased.

Her critique of Powers's comments on the Omaha/Grass Dance complex is a misreading of an essay published for a non-Indian hobbyist audience that was superseded by several important essays from Powers (that Browner does not cite) on various aspects of the history and diffusion of the Omaha Dance among the Lakota people. In response to my queries about this, Powers replied that in his estimation, Browner "is simply deficient in her reading of what Wissler said, what I said, and perhaps anyone else said in the last century"; William K. Powers, personal communication to the author, July 4, 2002.

11 Young, "Powwow Power," 103; Thomas W. Kavanagh, "The Comanche Pow-wow: Pan-Indianism or Tribalism," *Haliksa'i,* University of New Mexico Contributions to Anthropology 1 (1982): 13.

12 Howard, *The Ponca Tribe,* 102. For examples that illustrate this emphasis on style and spirituality, see Chris Roberts, *People of the Circle: Powwow Country* (Missoula, Mont.: Farcountry Press, 1998); Diane Morris Bernstein, *We Dance Because We Can: People of the Powwow* (Marietta, Ga.: Longstreet Press, 1996); David McCarl, "The Powwow Circle: Native American Dance and Dress," *TD&T* 32:3 (1996): 50–58; Ann Axtmann, "Performance Power in Native America: Powwow Dancing," *Dance Research Journal* 33:1 (Summer 2001): 7–22.

The tendency to emphasize dance steps and styles occasionally embraces theoretical musings that have little to do with how powwow people talk about their ways. For example, Axtmann has written in "Race, Persecution, and Persistence: Powwow Dancing," in *Dancing in the Millennium: Conference Proceedings* (Washington, D.C.: 2000): 23, 24, that among other things, she is "intrigued by *if* and *how* Native American powwow dancers express a distinctive performativity in relation to postcolonial life in Native America and the United States" (emphasis in the original). Convinced that they do, Axtmann adds that "the use of back space [*sic*] in many styles indicates an acute awareness of the past while polychronic time is reinforced in the circular shape of the arena," beliefs that she attributes to, among other things, "blood-memory." I showed this passage to a number of people who are regulars on the Southern Plains powwow circuit. To a person they either did not understand Axtmann's argument, or, in the case of one respondent, vehemently disagreed, saying "this is how academics talk, isn't it? Back space? Polychronic time? What the hell is that? The arena is circular because that's the way the old society dance halls were built — it isn't about 'polychronic time.' This arena looks like it does because that's the way they did it way back there." Author's field notes, March 2002.

13 Jim Charles, "Songs of the Ponca: Heluska," *Wicazo Sa Review* 5:2 (1989): 2–16; Luke Eric Lassiter, *The Power of Kiowa Song: A Collaborative Ethnography* (Tucson: University of Arizona Press, 1998), and Lassiter, "'Charlie Brown': Not Just Another Essay on the Gourd Dance," *American Indian Culture and Research Journal,* 21:4 (1997), 75–103; R. D. Theisz, "Song Texts and Their Performers: The Centerpiece of Contemporary Lakota Identity Formulation," *Great Plains Quarterly* 7 (Spring 1987): 116–124. See also Severt Young Bear and R. D. Theisz, *Standing in the Light: A Lakota Way of Seeing* (Lincoln: University of Nebraska Press, 1994), esp. 38–103.

14 Author's field notes, July 1996; Lassiter, *Power of Kiowa Song,* 95–96.

15 Conklin, "Origin of the Powwow," 18. He-thus-ka is also rendered as Heluska and Helushka. In "Songs of the Ponca," Jim Charles spells it Heluska, but he is referring to the same organization as Conklin.

16 James Mooney, "Military Societies," in *Handbook of American Indians North of Mexico,* Bulletin 30, Frederick W. Hodge, ed. (Washington, D.C.: Bureau of American Ethnology, 1912): 863.

17 Meadows, *Military Societies,* 1, 6. For an extended discussion, see ibid., 1–32.

18 J. Gilbert McAllister, "Kiowa-Apache Social Organization," Ph.D. diss., University of Chicago, 1935, 148–149, quoted in Meadows, *Military Societies,* 191–192. Willard H. Rollings, in *The Osage: An Ethnohistorical Study of Hegemony on the Prairie-Plains* (Columbia: University of Missouri Press, 1992), discusses societies more generally; see 14–66. See also Donald Berthrong, *The Southern Cheyennes* (Norman: University of Oklahoma Press, 1963): 50–75, esp. 67–71; Thomas W. Kavanagh, *Comanche Political History: An Ethnohistorical Perspective,* 1706–1875 (Lincoln: University of Nebraska Press, 1996): 48–51.

19 Wissler, "Societies and Ceremonial Associations in the Oglala Division of the Teton-Dakota," 9–10; Pliny Earle Goddard, "Dancing Societies of the Sarsi Indians," *Anthropological Papers of the American Museum of Natural History,* vol. XI, part V (1914): 465, 469; Meadows, *Military Societies,* 308–309.

20 Skinner, "Societies of the Iowa," 690, 699; Conklin, "Origin of the Powwow," 18.

21 Meadows, *Military Societies,* 53. See also Bernard Mishkin, *Rank and Warfare among the Plains Indians,* introduction by Morris Foster (Lincoln: University of Nebraska Press, 1992 [1940]), esp. 24–27, 35–56; and Jane Richardson, *Law and Status among the Kiowa Indians* (New York: American Ethnological Society, 1940).

22 See Victor Turner, *The Ritual Process: Structure and Anti-Structure* (Chicago: Aldine, 1969). On the powwow as a source of unity, see Benjamin Kracht, "Kiowa Powwows: Continuity in Ritual Practice," *American Indian Quarterly* 18:3 (1994): 321–348. For a reply to Kracht that challenges the communitas model as it pertains to the Kiowa Gourd Dance, see Clyde Ellis and Luke Eric Lassiter, Commentary: "Applying Communitas to Kiowa Powwows," *American Indian Quarterly* 22:4 (1998): 485–491.

23 Author's field notes, June 1990; Forrest Kassanavoid, conversation with the author, Llano, Texas, June 1990.

24 Mark Welch quoted in Victoria Sanchez, "Intertribal Dance and Cross Cultural Communication: Traditional Powwows in Ohio," *Communication Studies* 52:1 (Spring 2001): 59; Reverend Doctor Evelyn White Eye quoted in Suzanne Weatherly,

"Gathering of Nations," *News from Indian Country,* May 15, 2001, p. 4B; Patricia Barker Lerch and Susan Bullers, "Powwows as Identity Markers: Traditional or Pan-Indian?" *Human Organization* 55:4 (1996): 395.

25 Alice C. Fletcher and Francis LaFlesche, *The Omaha Tribe,* vol. II (Lincoln: University of Nebraska Press, 1972 [1911]): 459, 462; Edwin Thompson Denig, *The Assiniboine,* J. N. B. Hewitt, ed., introduction by David R. Miller (Norman: University of Oklahoma Press, 2000 [1928]): 556.

26 Meadows, *Military Societies,* 112–113, 197–198.

27 Murie, "Pawnee Indian Societies," 616–617; Skinner, "Societies of the Iowa," 687; Denig, *The Assiniboine,* 560.

28 Meadows, *Military Societies,* 40, 49, 212–214 (Klintidie), 268–269 (Los Lobos).

29 Robert H. Lowie, "Military Societies of the Crow Indians," *Anthropological Papers of the American Museum of Natural History,* vol. XI, part III (1913): 157–158; James R. Walker, *Lakota Belief and Ritual,* Raymond J. DeMallie and Elaine A. Jahner, eds. (Lincoln: University of Nebraska Press, 1991), 265; Wissler, "Societies and Ceremonial Associations in the Oglala Division of the Teton-Dakota," 49. For a more recent discussion, see William K. Powers, "Silhouettes of the Past: The Shape of Traditions to Come," *Whispering Wind* 27:2 (1995): 5–12, and Powers, "Innovation in Lakota Powwow Costumes," *American Indian Art* 19:4 (1994): 66–73, 103–104.

30 Robert H. Lowie, "The Assiniboine," *Anthropological Papers of the American Museum of Natural History,* vol. IV, part I (1909): 30; Meadows, *Military Societies,* 78; Wissler, "Societies and Ceremonial Associations in the Oglala Division of the Teton-Dakota," 15, and "Societies and Dance Associations of the Blackfoot Indians," 387; Orin Hatton, "'We Caused Them to Cry': Power and Performance in Gros Ventre War Expedition Songs" (Master's thesis, Catholic University of America, 1988).

31 Charles, "Songs of the Ponca," 12; Fletcher and LaFlesche, *The Omaha Tribe,* vol. II, 483–484. On contemporary song traditions that maintain these practices, see Lassiter *Power of Kiowa Song;* Meadows, *Military Societies,* 121–133. For especially good discussions from a Northern Plains perspective, see William K. Powers, *The Lakota Warrior Tradition: Three Essays on Lakotas at War* (Kendall Park, N.J.: Lakota Books, 2001); R. D. Theisz, "The Bad Speakers and the Long Braids: References to Foreign Enemies in Lakota Song Texts," in *Indians and Europe: An Interdisciplinary Collection of Essays,* Christian F. Feest, ed. (Aachen, Ger.: RaderVerlag, 1987): 427–434, and Theisz, "Acclamations and Accolades: Honor Songs in Lakota Society Today," *Kansas Quarterly* 13:2 (1981): 27–43. Theisz's essays are reprinted in R. D. Theisz, *Sending Their Voices: Essays on Lakota Musicology* (Kendall Park, N.J.: Lakota Books, 2001).

32 Meadows, *Military Societies,* 225; see also Lassiter, *Power of Kiowa Song,* 96, 242 n8.

33 Powers, *The Lakota Warrior Tradition,* 33.

34 Robert H. Lowie, "Social Life of the Crow Indians," *Anthropological Papers of the American Museum of Natural History,* vol. IX, part II (1912): 244.

35 Lowie, "The Assiniboine," 71–72; Goddard, "Dancing Societies of the Sarsi Indians,"470, 472. For an insightful discussion of giveaways and the role of generosity in powwow culture historically and contemporarily, see Kathleen Glenister Roberts, "Giving Away: The Performance of Speech and Sign in Powwow Ritual Exchange," Ph.D. diss., Indiana University, 2001; see also John H. Moore, "How Giveaways and Pow-wows Redistribute the Means of Subsistence," in *The Political Economy of North*

American Indians, John H. Moore, ed. (Norman: University of Oklahoma Press, 1993): 240–269.

36 Skinner, "Kansa Organizations," *Anthropological Papers of the American Museum of Natural History,* vol. XI, part IX (1915): 752–753; Wissler, "Societies and Ceremonial Associations in the Oglala Division of the Teton-Dakota," 18, 20–21, 65; Meadows, *Military Societies,* 58.

37 Wissler, "Societies and Ceremonial Associations in the Oglala Division of the Teton-Dakota," 64; Walker, *Lakota Belief and Ritual,* 269–270; Meadows, *Military Societies,* 201; Murie, "Pawnee Indian Societies," 580.

38 Skinner, "Ponca Society and Dances," 785; Conklin, "Origin of the Powwow," 19; Sylvester Warrior, interview by Leonard Maker, November 14, 1968, DDOH, 6; Howard, *The Ponca Tribe,* 106.

39 Browner, *Heartbeat of the People,* 96; Ed Red Eagle, Sr., interview by Robert L. Miller, May 17, 1967, DDOH, 7–8. Red Eagle was about 50 years old at the time of the interview.

40 Meadows, *Military Societies,* 370; Dennis Zotigh, *Moving History: The Evolution of the Powwow* (Oklahoma City: Center for the American Indian, 1991), np.

41 Young, "Powwow Power," 129–130. James S. Slotkin, *The Menomini Powwow: A Study in Cultural Decay,* Milwaukee Public Museum Publications in Anthropology (Milwaukee: Milwaukee Public Museum, 1957): 13, 165. Slotkin's account remains the most complete discussion of this dance in its twentieth-century form. See also S. A. Barrett, *Dream Dance of the Chippewa and Menominee Indians of Northern Wisconsin,* Milwaukee Public Museum Publications in Anthropology (Milwaukee: Milwaukee Public Museum, 1911); Michael A. Rynkiewich, "Chippewa Powwows," in *Anishinabe: 6 Studies of Modern Chippewa,* J. Anthony Paredes, ed. (Tallahassee: University of Florida Press, 1980): 31–100.

42 Young, "Powwow Power," 135, 151–153. Young's account of the Drum Dance is quite good; much of what follows relies on her analysis and description. For her extended discussion, see 129–153. See also Adriana Greci Green, "Performance and Celebrations: Displaying Lakota Indentity, 1880–1915," Ph.D. diss., Rutgers University, 2001: 23–24; Thomas Vennum, *The Ojibwa Dance Drum: Its History and Construction* (Washington, D.C.: Smithsonian Institution Press, 1982); Michael Reinschmidt, "The Drum Dance Religion of the Sauk: Historical and Contemporary Reflections," *European Review of Native American Studies* 8:1 (1994); 23–32.

43 Walter James Hoffman, "The Menomini Indians," Fourteenth Annual Report of the Bureau of American Ethnology (Washington, D.C.: Smithsonian Institution, 1893): 160–161.

44 James Mooney, *The Ghost Dance Religion and the Sioux Uprising of 1890,* Fourteenth Annual Report of the Bureau of American Ethnology (Washington, D.C.: Smithsonian Institution, 1896): 706. See also Young, "Powwow Power," 137–139.

45 Riggs quoted in Slotkin, *The Menomini Powwow,* 16–17; Young, "Powwow Power," 139–140.

46 Howard, *The Ponca Tribe,* 107; Young, "Powwow Power," 153; Kavanagh, "Southern Plains Dance," 111.

47 Slotkin, *The Menomini Powwow,* 16; Young, "Powwow Power," 139–140, 153; Kavanagh, "Southern Plains Dance," 111.

48 Young, "Powwow Power," 126. Because the Omaha Dance was so widespread, virtually every anthropologist working on the Plains in the late nineteenth and early twentieth centuries took note of it, especially Wissler, whose "General Discussion of Shamanistic and Dancing Societies," *Anthropological Papers of the American Museum of Natural History,* vol. XI, part XII (1916) formed the core of much of the literature that came out of the era.

49 Mooney, *Calendar History of the Kiowa Indians,* 358; Bill Meadows, personal communication with the author, August 21, 2002.

50 Wissler, "Shamanistic and Dancing Societies," 867.

51 Murie, "Pawnee Indian Societies," 608.

52 Wissler, "Shamanistic and Dancing Societies," 861.

53 Ibid., 859.

54 Young, "Powwow Power," 170–171; see also Murie, "Pawnee Indian Societies," 624.

55 Wissler, "Shamanistic and Dancing Societies," 865, 871–872; Skinner, "Kansa Organizations," 755; Fletcher and LaFlesche, *The Omaha Tribe,* vol. I, 460; Murie, "Pawnee Indian Societies," 624, 629; Alice Anne Callahan, *The Osage Ceremonial Dance: I'n-lon-schka* (Norman: University of Oklahoma Press, 1990): 24–25; Jimmy W. Duncan, "Hethuska Zani': An Ethnohistory of the War Dance Complex" (Master's thesis, Northeastern State University, 1997), 3.

56 Wissler, "Shamanistic and Dancing Societies," 862, 869; Skinner, "Kansa Organizations," 755; Lowie, "Dances and Societies of the Plains Shoshone," 833.

57 Green, "Displaying Lakota Identity," 42.

58 Regina Flannery, "The Changing Form and Functions of the Gros Ventre Grass Dance," *Primitive Man* 20:3 (July 1947): 63–65.

59 Callahan, *The Osage Ceremonial Dance,* 27; Otis Russell, interview by Leonard Maker, May 5, 1970, DDOH, 22; William K. Powers, "The Sioux Omaha Dance," *American Indian Tradition* 8:1 (1961): 27, 33.

60 Jim Anquoe, interview by the author, July 12, 2002, Stroud, Okla.; author's field notes, August 2002.

61 Meadows, *Military Societies,* 39, 216–217, 288; Young, "Powwow Power," 172.

62 Foster, *Being Comanche,* 123.

3. INDIAN DANCES AND FEDERAL POLICY ON THE SOUTHERN PLAINS, 1880–1930

1 Squirrel to Major Frank Baldwin, August 7, 1897, and October 2, 1897, "Indian Celebrations and Dances, 1874–1917," Records of the Kiowa Agency, Oklahoma Historical Society (hereafter cited as "Indian Celebrations and Dances," KA). There is no record of a reply from the agent. Portions of this chapter appeared previously in Clyde Ellis, "'There Is No Doubt . . . the Dances Should Be Curtailed': Indian Dances and Federal Policy on the Southern Plains, 1880–1930," *Pacific Historical Review* 70:4 (2001): 543–569.

2 Robert Utley, *The Indian Frontier of the American West, 1846–1890* (Albuquerque: University of New Mexico Press, 1984), 140, 142. On the distance between policy theory and reality, see Frederick E. Hoxie, "The Curious Story of Reformers and American Indians," in *Indians in American History,* 2d ed., Frederick E. Hoxie and Peter Iverson, eds. (Wheeling, Ill.: Harlan-Davidson, 1998), 177–197. For the Southern

Plains, see William T. Hagan, *United States-Comanche Relations: The Reservation Years* (Norman: University of Oklahoma Press, 1990), esp. chapters 3–8, and Hagan, *Quanah Parker: Comanche Chief* (Norman: University of Oklahoma Press, 1993), esp. chapters 4–6; Morris Foster, *Being Comanche: A Social History of an American Indian Community* (Tucson: University of Arizona Press, 1991), esp. chapter 3; Donald Berthrong, *The Cheyenne and Arapaho Ordeal: Reservation and Agency Life in the Indian Territory, 1875–1907* (Norman: University of Oklahoma Press, 1976), esp. chapters 5–8. For a compelling case study from the Northern Plains, see Hoxie "From Prison to Homeland: The Cheyenne River Reservation before World War I," in *The Plains Indians of the Twentieth Century,* Peter Iverson, ed. (Norman: University of Oklahoma Press, 1985), 55–75.

3 Francis Paul Prucha, ed., *Documents of United States Indian Policy* (Lincoln: University of Nebraska Press, 1990), 156, 177.

4 For an insightful reading of the relationship between missionaries and federal authorities concerning the dance issue, see David Wilson Daily, "Guardian Rivalries: G. E. E. Lindquist, John Collier, and the Moral Landscape of Federal Indian Policy, 1910–1950." Ph.D. diss., Duke University, 2000, esp. chapter two, "Missionaries, Bureaucrats, and the Politics of the Indian Dance Controversy, 1920–1923," 62–122.

5 Eugenia Mausape, interview with Julia A. Jordan, September 14, 1967, Doris Duke Oral History Collection, Western History Collection, University of Oklahoma, Norman, Okla. (hereafter cited as DDOH), 34–35; Mary Clouse to C. V. Stinchecum, September 15, 1915, and H. H. Clouse to C. V. Stinchecum, December 2, 1916, "Field Matrons' Files," Records of the Kiowa Agency, Oklahoma Historical Society, Oklahoma City, Okla.

6 Marvin Kroeker, *Comanches and Mennonites on the Oklahoma Plains: A. J. and Magdalena Becker and the Post Oak Mission* (Hillsboro, Kans.: Kindred Productions, 1997): 47, 77–79.

7 Isabel Crawford, *Kiowa: A Woman Missionary in Indian Territory* (Lincoln: University of Nebraska Press, 1998 [1915]), 27–28; Isabel Crawford Journal for 1898–1899, pp. 8–10, Samuel Colgate Historical Library, American Baptist Historical Society, Rochester, N.Y.

8 H. Brown to Captain A. E. Woodson, May 6, 1896, "Indian Celebrations and Dances," KA.

9 Ibid.; A. E. Woodson to Frank Baldwin, May 12, 1896, "Indian Celebrations and Dances," KA.

10 Report of the Secretary of the Interior, 1883, House Executive document no. 1, 48 Cong., 1 session, xi–xii; Francis Paul Prucha, *The Great Father: The United States Government and the American Indians,* 2 vols. (Lincoln: University of Nebraska Press, 1984), 2: 646–647.

11 David La Vere, *Life among the Texas Indians: The WPA Narratives* (College Station: Texas A & M Press, 1998), 131, 136, 210.

12 Ibid., 138–139.

13 Ibid., 185–186.

14 Mark G. Thiel, "The Omaha Dance in Oglala and Sicangu Sioux History," 1883–1923 *Whispering Wind* 23:5 (Fall/Winter 1990), 5–6.

15 "Report from St. Francis School, Rosebud Agency," *The Indian Sentinel* (Washington, D.C.: Bureau of Catholic Missions, 1907), 24, quoted in Emily Greenwald, "'Hur-

rah! 4th July': The Ironies of Independence Day on Western Reservations," draft in the possession of the author. See also William E. Farr, *The Reservation Blackfeet: A Photographic History of Cultural Survival* (Seattle: University of Washington Press, 1986), in which Farr notes one observer's discomfort upon realizing that during the 1910 July 4th Sun Dance, "the Blackfeet had become Indians again," 67.

16 Pawnee School Superintendent to Commissioner of Indian Affairs, May 27, 1920, "Dances," Records of the Pawnee Agency, Oklahoma Historical Society (hereafter cited as "Dances," PA); Gloria A. Young, "Powwow Power: Perspectives on Historic and Contemporary Intertribalism," Ph.D. diss., Indiana University, 1981, 211; Squirrel to Frank Baldwin, August 7, 1897, "Indian Celebrations and Dances."

17 H. A. Lewis to P. B. Hunt, July 18, 1884, and September 30, 1884, "Indians with Shows and Exhibitions, 1875–1924," Records of the Kiowa Agency, Oklahoma Historical Society (hereafter cited as "Indians with Shows and Exhibitions," KA).

18 Will Pyeatt to Comander [*sic*] In Chief, August 2, 1899, "Indian Celebrations and Dances," KA.

19 C. Thornburg to Anadarko Agency, November 16, 1894, "Indians with Shows and Exhibitions," KA; Peter Geller, " 'Hudson's Bay Company Indians': Images of Native People and the Red River Pageant, 1920," in *Dressing in Feathers: The Construction of the Indian in American Popular Culture,* S. Elizabeth Bird, ed. (Boulder, Colo.: Westview, 1996), 67.

On the role of such shows, see L. G. Moses, *Wild West Shows and the Images of the American Indians, 1883–1933* (Albuquerque: University of New Mexico Press, 1996); Moses, "Wild West Shows, Reformers, and the Image of the American Indian, 1887–1914," *South Dakota History,* 14 (1984), 193–221; Moses, "Indians on the Midway: Wild West Shows and the Indian Bureau at World's Fairs, 1893–1904," *South Dakota History,* 21 (1991), 205–229; Paul Reddin, *Wild West Shows* (Urbana: University of Illinois Press, 1999); Thomas L. Altherr, "Let 'er Rip: Popular Culture Images of the American West in Wild West Shows, Rodeos, and Rendezvous," in *Wanted Dead or Alive: The American West in Popular Culture,* Richard C. Aquila, ed. (Urbana: University of Illinois Press, 1996), 73–105; Michael Wallis, *The Real Wild West: The 101 Ranch and the Creation of the American West* (New York: St. Martin's Press, 1999); Wallis, "The Miller Brothers and the 101 Ranch," *Gilcrease Journal* 1 (Spring 1993), 6–29; Barbara Williams Roth, "The 101 Ranch Wild West Show, 1904–1932, *Chronicles of Oklahoma,* 43:4 (Winter 1965), 416–431.

20 W. A. Madaris to James Randlett, May 27, 1902, "Indian Celebrations and Dances," KA; W. A. Husted to Frank Baldwin, May 8, 1896, "Indians with Shows and Exhibitions," KA; W. F. Mull to Indian Agent, July 23, 1891, "Indians with Shows and Exhibitions," KA; William Newkirk to James Randlett, April 5, 1905, "Indians with Shows and Exhibitions."

21 House Executive Document, no. 1, 52 Cong., 2 session, 28–29; D. W. Browning to Frank Baldwin, August 4, 1896, "Indian Celebrations and Dances," KA.

22 Hiram Price to P. B. Hunt, October 24, 1884, "Kiowa Fairs, February 1, 1875–November 22, 1923," Records of the Kiowa Agency, Oklahoma Historical Society, Oklahoma City, Okla. (hereafter cited as "Kiowa Fairs," KA).

23 Moses, *Wild West Shows,* 73; *Annual Report of the Commissioner of Indian Affairs,* 1892, 105–106 (hereafter cited as *ARCIA*).

24 For official opposition to the Wild West, see Moses, *Wild West Shows,* esp. 106–128 and 195–222.

25 Prucha, *Great Father,* 2: 801–803; Lawrence C. Kelly, *The Assault on Assimilation: John Collier and the Origins of Indian Reform* (Albuquerque: University of Oklahoma Press, 1983), 300–306; Supplement to Circular 1665, February 14, 1923, "Dances"; Circular 1604 in "Extracts from Annual Reports of Superintendents, 1920, On Dancing," Central Classified Files, 1907–1939, Record Group 75 National Archives, Washington, D.C. (hereafter cited as "Extracts from Annual Reports of Superintendents, 1920").

26 Moses, *Wild West Shows,* 253–255, Burke quoted at 255, emphasis in the original; Burke, Supplement to Circular 1665, February 14, 1923, "Dances," KA.

27 Stinchecum to Cato Sells, August 1, 1915, "Indian Celebrations and Dances," KA.

28 Moses, *Wild West Shows,* 212; Muriel H. Wright, "The American Indian Exposition in Oklahoma," *Chronicles of Oklahoma* 24:2 (1946), 158–165; Wright, "The Indian International Fair at Muskogee," *Chronicles of Oklahoma* 49:1 (1971), 14.

29 La Vere, *Life among the Texas Indians,* 107.

30 Moses, *Wild West Shows,* 207–218, Valentine quoted at 210; William C. Meadows, *Kiowa, Apache, and Comanche Military Societies: Enduring Veterans, 1800 to the Present* (Austin: University of Texas Pres, 1999): 124–125.

31 Acting Commissioner to E. E. White, August 17, 1888, "Kiowa Fairs"; Acting Commissioner to U.S. Indian Agents of Indian Territory and Oklahoma, August 30, 1892, ibid.

32 Benjamin Kracht, "Kiowa Religion: An Ethnohistorical Analysis of Ritual Symbolism, 1832–1987," Ph.D. diss., Southern Methodist University, 1989, 836; George W. Mills to Robert Valentine, November 10, 1909, "Dances," PA.

33 Circular 836, Sells to Superintendents, March 18, 1914, "Kiowa Fairs," emphasis in the original.

34 Circular 896, Sells to Superintendents, September 2, 1914, and Circular 1079, Sells to Superintendents, January 26, 1916, ibid.

35 Circular 1079, Sells to Superintendents, January 26, 1916, ibid.; Moses, *Wild West Shows,* 218.

36 F. E. Ferrell to George W. Mullis, January 18, 1913, "Kiowa Fairs"; Ferrell to Oklahoma Superintendents, January 15, 1913, concerning "Indian State Fair of Oklahoma Indians," ibid.

37 Moses, *Wild West Shows,* 212, 218; Stinchecum to Sells, April 15, 1916, August 6, 1917, "Kiowa Fairs."

38 Scott Tonemah, interview by the author, February 4, 1988, Norman, Okla.

39 E. H. Bowman to P. B. Hunt, May 23, 1882, "Indian Celebrations and Dances," KA; Lauretta Ballew to Captain Frank Baldwin, July 22, 1895, ibid.

40 Report of the Ponca Subagency, Nebraska, *ARCIA,* 1893: 201–202. The Winnebagos apparently caused headaches for a number of agencies. In 1894 the Santee agent reported he successfully discouraged dancing until "a large band of Winnebagos came to visit and that started the dance.... there is more or less drunkenness, and sometimes they break up with a fight," Report of Santee Agency, *ARCIA,* 1894: 192.

41 Report of the Ponca Subagency, Nebraska, *ARCIA,* 1893: 202.

42 Report of the Otoe Subagency, *ARCIA,* 1894: 250–251; *ARCIA,* 1903: 8.

43 Benjamin Kracht, "Kiowa Powwows: Continuity in Ritual Practice," *American Indian*

Quarterly 18:3 (1994): 329, 330–331; Meadows, *Military Societies,* 119, 121; Young, "Pow-wow Power," 236–239.

44 Colonel Mizner to P. B. Hunt, June 23, 1881, John Oberly to W. D. Myers, June 4, 1889, Thomas Morgan to Myers, August 9, 1889, Frank Baldwin to Myers, June 17, 1889, all in "Indian Celebrations and Dances," KA; James Mooney, *Calendar History of the Kiowa Indians,* Seventeenth Annual Report of the Bureau of American Ethnology (Washington, D.C.: Smithsonian Institution, 1979), 341–344, 358–359.

45 E. L. Clark to Hunt, July 20, 26, 1881, "Indian Celebrations and Dances," KA.

46 James Deere to C. E. Adams, December 29, 1890, "Indian Celebrations and Dances," KA.

47 Big Tree to Frank Baldwin, August 10, 1895, and April 19, 1896, "Indian Celebrations and Dances," KA.

48 Lucius Aitson to Major W. T. Walker, October 31, 1898, "Indian Celebrations and Dances," KA.

49 Luke Eric Lassiter, Clyde Ellis, and Ralph Kotay, *The Jesus Road: Kiowas, Christianity, and Indian Hymns* (Lincoln: University of Nebraska Press, 2002), 55.

50 La Vere, *Life Among the Texas Indians,* 134–135; L. G. Moses, *The Indian Man: A Biography of James Mooney* (Urbana: University of Illinois Press, 1984), 58–60.

51 Stinchecum to James Tonkeamah, June 22, 1917, and Stinchecum to John Law, June 22, 1917, "Indian Celebrations and Dances," KA.

52 Stinchecum to Sells, February 18, 1920, "Establishment and Abolition of Agencies and Schools," Kiowa Agency Classified Files, 1907–1939, Record Group 75, National Archives, Washington, D.C.

53 Thomas Morgan to Indian Agents and Superintendents of Indian Schools, October 22, 1891, "Indian Celebrations and Dances," KA; Moses, *Wild West Shows,* 219–222; *ARCIA,* 1903: 9.

54 *ARCIA,* 1919: 9.

55 "Indians Use Human Scalps in Dance," *American Indian Magazine,* 7 (1919): 184; Thomas A. Britten, *American Indians in World War I: At Home and at War* (Albuquerque: University of New Mexico Press, 1997), 150–151; Meadows, *Military Societies,* 122–126.

56 Sells to J. C. Hart, May 25, 1920, "Dances," CAA; Jess Rowlodge, interview by Julia A. Jordan, June 4, 1969, DDOH, 8.

57 *ARCIA,* 1919: 12; Meadows, *Military Societies,* 124.

58 Stinchecum to Ahpeahtone, et al., April 9, 1917, "Indian Celebrations and Dances," KA.

59 "Report of the Board of Indian Commissioners," *ARCIA,* 1901: 810.

60 Report of the Navajo Agency, *ARCIA,* 1892: 208; Report of the School at Seger, Okla., ibid., 1893: 445; "Extracts from Annual Reports of Superintendents, 1920."

61 "Extracts from Annual Reports of Superintendents, 1920."

62 David Wooley and William T. Waters, "Waw-no-she's Dance," *American Indian Art Magazine,* 23 (Winter 1998), 45; Lassiter, *The Power of Kiowa Song,* 81–82.

63 Loretta Fowler, *Shared Symbols, Contested Meanings: Gros Ventre Culture and History,* 1778–1984 (Ithaca, N.Y.: Cornell University Press, 1987): 9; See also Clyde Ellis, " 'Truly Dancing Their Own Way,': Modern Revival and Diffusion of the Gourd Dance," *American Indian Quarterly* 14: (Winter 1990): 22–23; Lassiter, *Power of Kiowa Song,* 119–120; Meadows, *Military Societies,* 110–112.

64 Foster, *Being Comanche,* esp. 24–30, 123–153. For discussions of these adaptations,

see also Meadows, *Military Societies;* Kavanagh, "Southern Plains Dance"; Ellis, " 'We Don't Want Your Rations, We Want This Dance': The Changing Use of Song and Dance on the Southern Plains," *Western Historical Quarterly* 30:2 (1999): 133–154. Kracht, "Kiowa Powwows"; Lassiter, *Power of Kiowa Song;* Callahan, *The Osage Ceremonial Dance.*

65 L. G. Moses, "Interpreting the Wild West, 1883–1914," in *Between Indian and White Worlds: The Cultural Broker,* Margaret Connell Szasz, ed. (Albuquerque: University of New Mexico, 1994), 177; Ralph Kotay, telephone interview by the author, July 18, 1998.

4. SHOWS, EXHIBITIONS, AND THE ECONOMICS OF INDIAN DANCING, 1880–1930

1 This paragraph is based on L. G. Moses, *Wild West Shows and the Images of American Indians, 1883–1933* (Albuquerque: University of New Mexico Press, 1996), 101–103. Portions of this essay appeared previously in Clyde Ellis, "Five Dollars a Week to Be 'Regular Indians': Shows, Exhibitions, and the Economics of Indian Dancing, 1880–1930," in *Native Pathways: Economic Development and American Indian Culture,* Brian Hosmer and Colleen O'Neil, eds. (Boulder: University Press of Colorado, forthcoming).

2 Moses addresses this, but his concern is with a larger story. John H. Moore, "How Giveaways and Pow-wows Redistribute the Means of Subsistence," in *The Political Economy of North American Indians,* John H. Moore, ed. (Norman: University of Oklahoma Press, 1993), 240–269, and Kenneth Ashworth, "The Contemporary Oklahoma Powwow," Ph.D diss., University of Oklahoma, 1986, discuss economic issues, but neither addresses the formative era of shows and exhibitions, and Ashworth badly overstates the economic imperatives at work in contemporary Oklahoma powwows.

3 Moses, *Wild West Shows,* 101; Michael Wallis, *The Real Wild West: The 101 Ranch and the Creation of the American West* (New York: St. Martin's Press, 1999), 141.

4 Rita G. Napier, "Across the Big Water: American Indians' Perceptions of Europe and Europeans, 1887–1906," in *Indians and Europe: An Interdisciplinary Collection of Essays,* Christian F. Feest, ed. (Lincoln: University of Nebraska Press, 1999), 385; Joy S. Kasson, *Buffalo Bill's Wild West: Celebrity, Memory, and Popular History* (New York: Hill and Wang, 2000), 174, 181; Robert M. Utley, *The Lance and the Shield: The Life and Times of Sitting Bull* (New York: Henry Holt, 1993), 260; Raymond J. DeMallie, ed., *The Sixth Grandfather: Black Elk's Teachings Given to John G. Neihardt* (Lincoln: University of Nebraska Press, 1984), 245–246; Moses, *Wild West Shows,* 44–45, 279.

See also David Blanchard, "Entertainment, Dance, and Northern Mohawk Showmanship," *American Indian Quarterly* 7:1 (1983): 2–26, in which Blanchard notes that during the 1860s Mohawk men and women who signed on with the native-owned dance shows that came out of Kahnawake "were able to find employment in work that was economically rewarding as well as intrinsically satisfying," 19.

5 Wallis, *The Real Wild West,* 425; Kasson, *Buffalo Bill's Wild West,* 190–191.

6 Vine Deloria quoted in Kasson, *Buffalo Bill's Wild West,* 163–164; Napier, "Across the Big Water," 400; Moses, *Wild West Shows,* 188, 279; Adriana Greci Green, "Perfor-

mances and Celebrations: Displaying Lakota Identity, 1880–1915," Ph.D. diss., Rutgers University, 2001, 124–125.

7 Wallis, *The Real Wild West,* 390–391; U.S. Indian Agent, Osage Indian Agency to Samuel McCowan, June 24, 1903, Records of Chilocco School, Oklahoma Historical Society, "Fairs, June 1895–June 1903"; Ned P. DeWitt, "Behind the Scenes of the Old '101,' " March 24, 1929, Pawneee Agency Files, Section X, Miller Brothers 101 Ranch, OHS.

8 Teller quoted in Jacqueline Fear-Seagal, "Nineteenth-Century Indian Education: Universalism versus Evolutionism," *Journal of American Studies* 33:2 (1999): 332; Ireland quoted in the *Annual Report of the Superintendent of Indian Schools,* in *Annual Report of the Commissioner of Indian Affairs,* 1902, 420–421.

9 Cato Sells to Superintendents, September 2, 1914, Circular 896, Records of the Kiowa Agency, Oklahoma Historical Society, "Kiowa Fairs, February 1, 1875–November 22, 1923," (hereafter cited as "Kiowa Fairs"); Charles Burke to Superintendents, June 12, 1922, Records of the Pawnee Agency, Oklahoma Historical Society, "Indian Celebrations and Dances," (hereafter cited as "Indian Celebrations and Dances," PA); Charles Shell to Commissioner of Indian Affairs, August 25, 1909, Records of the Cheyenne and Arapaho Agency, Oklahoma Historical Society, "Indian Dances," (hereafter cited as "Indian Dances," CAA); Hubert E. Collins to Joseph Thoburn, August 8, 1932, Records of the Pawnee Agency, Oklahoma Historical Society, Section X, "Miller Brothers 101 Ranch"; Edgar Barnett to U. S. Indian Agent, February 13, 1919, Records of the Cheyenne and Arapaho Agency, Oklahoma Historical Society, "Indians with Shows and Exhibitions" (hereafter cited as "Indians with Shows and Exhibitions," CAA).

10 John Whitewell to U.S. Indian Agent, September 3, 1902, "Indian Dances," CAA; L. S. Bonnin to Little Snake, June 13, 1924, Records of the Cheyenne and Arapaho Agency, Oklahoma Historical Society, "Acculturation."

11 Chauncey Yellow Robe, "The Menace of the Wild West Show," *Quarterly Journal of the Society of American Indians* 2:3 (September 1914): 223–224. It is worth noting the irony that Yellow Robe appeared in precisely the kind of films that he charged were misrepresenting Indians. He appeared in buckskins and a wig, for example, to introduce *Silent Enemy,* a 1930 film starring the Indian imposter Long Lance that relied on virtually every stereotype associated with Indians and nature.

12 E. H. Gohl, "The Effect of Wild Westing," *Quarterly Journal of the Society of American Indians* 2:3 (September 1914): 226–228. Emphasis in the original.

13 Transcripts of the Carlisle student papers courtesy of Barbara Landis.

14 Ibid.

15 *Annual Report of the Secretary of the Interior,* 1883, House Executive Document no. 1, 48th Congress, 1st session, xi–xii.

16 *Annual Report of the Superintendent of Indian Schools,* 1893, in *Annual Report of the Commissioner of Indian Affairs,* 1893 (Washington, D.C.: Government Printing Office): 395–396.

17 Ibid.

18 Edward P. Smith to Agents, Circular 3, February 1, 1875, "Kiowa Fairs"; W. A. Mercer to U. S. Indian Agent, July 19, 1898, ibid.; *Annual Report of the Commissioner of Indian Affairs,* 1892, 61; W. A. Mercer to James Randlett, January 18, 1905, Records of the Kiowa Agency, Oklahoma Historical Society, "Quanah Parker."

19 H. A. Hall to Colonel James Randlett, August 3, 1905, Records of the Kiowa Agency,

Oklahoma Historical Society, "Indians with Shows and Exhibitions" (hereafter cited as "Indians with Shows and Exhibitions," KA); Handbill for "Great Extra Attractions"; Ed Basye to Quapaw Agent, February 14, 1882, Records of the Quapaw Agency, Oklahoma Historical Society, "Indians with Shows and Exhibitions" (hereafter cited as "Indians with Shows and Exhibitions," QA), emphasis in the original.

20 Mark David Spence, *Dispossessing the Wilderness: Indian Removal and the Making of the National Parks* (New York: Oxford University Press, 1999), 116–120; Robert H. Keller, Jr., and Michael Turek, *American Indians and National Parks* (Tucson: University of Arizona Press, 1998), 39, 56–59; John Finger, *Cherokee Americans: The Eastern Band of the Cherokee Indians in the Twentieth Century* (Lincoln: University of Nebraska Press, 1991), 98–100. The idea of an outdoor drama was revived in 1950 as "Unto These Hills," which remains a staple of the summer tourist season at the Eastern Cherokee reservation in western North Carolina.

21 William D. Murray, *The History of the Boy Scouts of America* (New York: Boy Scouts of America, 1937), 385–386.

22 John Seger to Byron White, July 20, 1903, "Indian Dances," CAA 45.

23 William Freer to Commissioner of Indian Affairs, January 5, 1912, Records of the Cheyenne-Arapaho Agency, Oklahoma Historical Society, "Indian Councils."

24 John W. Troutman, " 'Tell Us More About Handling Poisonous Snakes': The Politics of Dance, Indianness, and Citizenship in Indian Country, 1900–1930," paper presented at the annual meeting of the American Society for Ethnohistory, 2002, unpublished ms. in the author's possession, 7.

25 Napier, "Across the Big Water," 385; Troutman, " 'Tell Us More About Handling Poisonous Snakes," 7–8; Moses, *Wild West Shows*, 8.

26 J. B. Dickinson to Pawnee Agent, August 8 and 13, 1907, "Indian Celebrations and Dances," PA.

27 L. G. Moses, "Interpreting the Wild West, 1883–1914," in *Between Indian and White Worlds: The Cultural Broker*, Margaret Connell Szasz, ed. (Norman: University of Oklahoma Press, 1994), 165–166; Moses, *Wild West Shows*, 116.

28 C. Thornburg to Unknown, November 16, 1894, "Indians with Shows and Exhibitions," KA.

29 C. F. Larrabee to Lt. Colonel G. W. H. Stouch, March 29, 1905, and May 20, 1905, "Indians with Shows and Exhibitions," CAA; Zack Mulhall to John Blackmon, June 9, 1907, "Indians with Shows and Exhibitions," KA.

30 W. B. Garnett to Major James Randlett, September 28, 1901, "Kiowa Fairs"; G. C. Brewer to Major James Randlett, September 29, 1901, ibid.; M. F. Wren to Principal of Cantonment Schools, June 6, 1905, "Indians with Shows and Exhibitions," CAA; Charles Grant to William B. Freer, July 5, 1910, Records of the Cheyenne and Arapaho Agency, Oklahoma Historical Society, "Indian Fairs" (hereafter cited as "Indian Fairs," CAA). S. W. Morris to Walter Dickens, March 23, 1910, "Indian Fairs," CAA.

31 William A. Jones to Lee Patrick, March 22, 1898, Records of the Sac and Fox and Shawnee Agency, Oklahoma Historical Society, "Indian Fairs" (hereafter cited as "Indian Fairs," SF); Samuel McCowan to T. W. Potter, January 25, 1904, Records of the Chilocco School, Oklahoma Historical Society, "Fairs, January 16, 1904–January 31, 1904"; Frank A. Thackery to S. M. McCowen [*sic*], November 11, 1903, ibid., "Fairs, November 1903"; Reverend Henry Gibbs to S. M. McCowan, July 21, 1903, and

S. M. McCowan to Reverend Henry Gibbs, December 11, 1903, Records of the Chilocco School, Oklahoma Historical Society, "Fairs, July 1903."

32 B. F. Bennett to L. S. Bonnin, June 27, 1923, "Indian Dances," CAA.

33 Newspaper clipping, "Indian Features," 1909, and Charles Shell to L L. Legtees, August 17, 1909, both in "Indian Fairs," CAA; Hoxie, *A Final Promise*, 5; Moses, *Wild West Shows*, 39.

34 Cato Sells to Superintendents, March 18, 1914, "Kiowa Fairs."

35 "Statement of expenditures under various heads," ca. 1900, and "Program and Premium list for the Indian fair at Weatherford, October 18–20, 1910," "Indian Fairs," CAA.

36 *Wichita Eagle*, August 28, 1902, in "Indian Dances," CAA.

37 Kasson, *Buffalo Bill's Wild West*, 174; Utley, *The Lance and the Shield*, 261, 264.

38 Farrand Sayre to S. M. McCowan, September 20, 1903, Records of the Chilocco School, Oklahoma Historical Society, "Fairs, October 1903."

39 N. F. Shabert and W. R. Haynes to Commissioners of the Louisiana Exposition, April 25, 1903, Records of the Chilocco School, Oklahoma Historical Society, "Fairs, June 1895–June 1903."

40 Wallis, *The Real Wild West*, 247–248.

41 Sarah J. Blackstone, *Buckskins, Bullets, and Business: A History of Buffalo Bill's Wild West* (Westport, Conn.: Greenwood Press, 1986), 87.

42 W. A. Husted to Frank Baldwin, May 8, 1896, "Indians with Shows and Exhibitions," KA; D. Bigman to Byron White, September 7, 1903, "Indian Fairs," CAA; Wallis, *The Real Wild West*, 273, 341; Gloria Alese Young, "Powwow Power: Perspectives on Historic and Contemporary Intertribalism," Ph.D. diss., Indiana University, 1981, 260.

43 Moses, *Wild West Shows*, 181–182; J. G. Collins to R. P. Stamon, March 7, 1914, Records of the Pawnee Agency, Oklahoma Historical Society, "Indians with Shows and Exhibitions"; L. G. Moses, personal communication with the author, August 28, 2001.

44 Kasson, *Buffalo Bill's Wild West*, 188–189; D. Bigman to Byron White, September 3, 1903, "Indian Fairs," CAA; Julia Roy to Unknown, May 1, 1914, "Indians with Shows and Exhibitions," PA.

45 Moses, *Wild West Shows*, 182–183, 265.

46 Elmer Sugar Brown, interview by Sandy Rhoades and the author, January 20, 2003, Tulsa, Okla.

47 Ibid.

48 Wallis, *The Real Wild West*, 174, 256, 431–432, 444; Moses, *Wild West Shows*, 85.

49 Moses, *Wild West Shows*, 173–174.

50 Miller Brothers to Cheyenne and Arapaho Agent, February 2, 1908, "Indians with Shows and Exhibitions," CAA; Moses, *Wild West Shows*, 122, 256.

51 Young, "Powwow Power," 239–240.

52 DeWitt, "Behind the Scenes of the Old '101'; High Chief to Charles Shell, March 12, 1907, and Lillard High Chief to Unknown, September 30, 1914, "Indians with Shows and Exhibitions," CAA; Agency Farmer to W. W. Scott, March 1, 1915, "Indians with Shows and Exhibitions," CAA.

53 Mack Hagg, Coyote, Red Cloud, et al. to agent, November 23, 1910; Sam Grayson to agent, November 25, 1910; William Freer to Sam Grayson, December 7, 1910, all in "Indians with Shows and Exhibitions," CAA; telegram from San Antonio International Fair Association to United States Indian agent, November 22, 1923, "Kiowa Fairs."

54 Anne M. Butler, "Selling the Popular Myth," in *The Oxford History of the American West,* Clyde A. Milner II, Carol A. O'Connor, and Martha Sandweiss, eds. (New York: Oxford University Press, 1994), 780; Moses, *Wild West Shows,* 277.

55 Blackstone, *Buckskins, Bullets, and Business,* 88; Joe Starita, *The Dull Knifes of Pine Ridge: A Lakota Odyssey* (New York: G. P. Putnam's and Sons, 1995), 138.

56 Henry Pahocscut to John Blackmon, April 14, 1906, "Indians with Shows and Exhibitions," KA.

5. THE POWWOW COMES INTO VIEW

1 James H. Howard, *The Ponca Tribe* (Lincoln: University of Nebraska Press, 1995): 107; Jim Charles, "The History in Ponca *Heluska* Songs," unpublished ms. in the author's possession, 3–4; William Collins, Sr., Ponca Oral History Material, October 23, 1969, Doris Duke Oral History, Western History Collection, University of Oklahoma, Norman, OK, 14–15 (hereafter cited as DDOH).

2 Luke Eric Lassiter, *The Power of Kiowa Song: A Collaborative Ethnography* (Tucson: University of Arizona Press, 1998); Morris W. Foster, *Being Comanche: A Social History of an American Indian Community* (Tucson: University of Arizona Press, 1991); William C. Meadows, *Kiowa, Apache, and Comanche Military Societies: Enduring Veterans,* 1800 *to the Present* (Austin: University of Texas Press, 1999); Benjamin Kracht, "Kiowa Powwows: Continuity in Ritual Practice." *American Indian Quarterly* 18:3 (1994): 321–348; Thomas W. Kavanagh, "Southern Plains Dance: Tradition and Dynamics," in *Native American Dance: Ceremonies and Social Traditions,* Charlotte Heth, ed. (Washington, D.C.: Smithsonian Institution, 1992): 105–123, and Kavanagh, "The Comanche Pow-wow: Pan-Indianism or Tribalism," *Haliksa'i,* University of New Mexico Contributions to Anthropology 1 (1982): 12–27; Gloria Alese Young, "Powwow Power: Perspectives on Historic and Contemporary Intertribalism," Ph.D. diss., Indiana University, 1981; Adriana Greci Green, "Performances and Celebrations: Displaying Lakota Identity, 1880–1915," Ph.D. diss., Rutgers University, 2001, iii.

3 Meadows, *Military Societies,* 122–123.

4 Frances Densmore, *Pawnee Music,* Bureau of American Ethnology, Bulletin 93 (Washington, D.C.: Smithsonian Institution, 1929): 65.

5 Young, "Powwow Power," 258–259; Josephine Walker, interview by Leonard Maker, December 31, 1968, DDOH, 5–6.

6 Meadows, *Military Societies,* 123.

7 George W. Nellis to Robert G. Valentine, November 10, 1909, "Indian Dances, 1909–1924," Records of the Pawnee Agency, Oklahoma Historical Society; Young, "Powwow Power," 205–206.

8 Young, "Powwow Power," 229, 235.

9 Young, "Powwow Power," 231, 236–238; Meadows, *Military Societies,* 113–118.

10 Young, "Powwow Power, 212–219.

11 J. L. Suffecool to Charles Burke, July 28, 1923, "Dances, November 22, 1890–April 19, 1924," Records of the Sac and Fox and Shawnee Agency, Oklahoma Historical Society.

12 Jess Rowlodge, interview by Julia A. Jordan, June 4, 1969, DDOH, 8, 11, 13–14.

13 Young, "Powwow Power," 267. For an informed discussion of the dance controversy in a different context, see Margaret D. Jacobs, *Engendered Encounters: Feminism and*

Pueblo Cultures, 1879–1920 (Lincoln: University of Nebraska Press, 1999), esp. chapter 5, "The 1920s Controversy over Indian Dances," 106–148.

14 John W. Troutman, " 'Tell Us More About Handling Poisonous Snakes': The Politics of Dance, Indianness, and Citizenship in Indian Country, 1900–1930," paper presented at the annual meeting of the American Society for Ethnohistory, 2002, unpublished ms. in the author's possession, 8–9, 12 n.27.

15 The potential for abusing those same rights, of course, was equally strong, and courts systematically gutted the provisions of Indian citizenship in case after case between 1880 and 1920. For an analysis of the barriers to meaningful citizenship created by courts and government agencies, see Frederick E. Hoxie, *A Final Promise: The Campaign to Assimilate the Indians,* 1880–1920 (Cambridge, Mass.: Cambridge University Press, 1984): 211–238. In this environment of disfranchisement and legally sanctioned discrimination, powwows could soften the worst of the consequences.

16 Young, "Powwow Power," 261–262, 267; Troutman, " 'Tell Us More About Handling Poisonous Snakes,' " 3, 4.

17 Superintendent Pawnee Agency to Charles Burke, October 25, 1921, "Dances," Records of the Pawnee Agency, Oklahoma Historical Society.

18 Oklahoma City *Daily Oklahoman,* June 18, 1928.

19 Young, "Powwow Power," 275–279.

20 Ibid., 238–239, 255.

21 Author's field notes, September 2000, May 2001, January 2003, February 2003; Elmer Sugar Brown, interview by Sandy Rhoades and the author, January 20, 2003, Tulsa, Okla.

22 Brown interview; "Indian Fancy Dance Style on TV Friday," Ponca City *News,* October 7, 1998; Reginald and Gladys Laubin, *Indian Dances of North America: Their Importance to Indian Life* (Norman: University of Oklahoma Press, 1977): 465; author's field notes, January 2003. For discussions of the evolution of fancy dance, see William K. Power, *Feathers Costume* (Kendall Park, N.J.: Lakota Books, 1996); C. Scott Evans, *The Modern Fancy Dancer* (Pottsboro, Tex.: Crazy Crow Trading Post, 1998).

23 Carter Revard, *Ponca War Dancers* (Norman, Okla.: Point Rider's Press, 1980): 53–54, 59.

24 Meadows, *Military Societies,* 340–342.

25 Foster, *Being Comanche,* 126.

26 Meadows, *Military Societies,* 217–218.

27 Foster, *Being Comanche,* 124.

28 Ibid., 123–124; Meadows, *Military Societies,* 340–341; Sylvester Warrior, interview by Leonard Maker, November 14, 1968, DDOH, 1–2; Otis Russell, interview with Leonard Maker, May 14, 1969, DDOH, 15.

29 Young, "Powwow Power," 177, 181.

30 Meadows, *Military Societies,* 105–107; author's field notes, August 2002; Luke Eric Lassiter, telephone conversation with the author, September 1, 2002.

31 Marriott quoted in Meadows, *Military Societies,* 112.

32 Author's field notes, July 2002.

33 Author's field notes, January 2003. My thanks to Sandy Rhoades and Scott Swearingen, who made portions of their interview with Leonard Cozad, Sr., available to me for this work. See also William R. Kennan and L. Brooks Hill, "Kiowa Forty-Nine

Singing: A Communication Perspective," *International Journal of Intercultural Relations* 4 (1980): 149–165; Joseph E. DeFlyer, "From Creation Stories to '49 Songs: Cultural Transactions with the White World as Portrayed in Northern Plains Indian Story and Song," *Studies in American Indian Literature* 2:1 (1990): 11–27.

34 Kennan and Hill, "Kiowa Forty-Nine Singing," 150.

35 Sylvester Warrior, interview by Leonard Maker, November 14, 1968, DDOH, 5–6.

36 Young, "Powwow Power," 249; Meadows, *Military Societies,* 125.

37 Young, "Powwow Power," 263.

38 See http://opera.stanford.edu/opera/cadman/shanewis/libretto.html for the full script [accessed September 21, 2002]. My thanks to Phil Deloria, who told me about Cadman.

39 Foster, *Being Comanche,* 127.

40 Young, "Powwow Power," 275–276.

41 Ibid., 264.

42 Muriel Wright, "The American Indian Exposition in Oklahoma," *Chronicles of Oklahoma* 24:2 (1946): 159 n.4; Young, "Powwow Power," 283–284; Loretta Fowler, *Tribal Sovereignty and the Historical Imagination: Cheyenne-Arapaho Politics* (Lincoln: University of Nebraska Press, 2002): 66.

43 Leonard Maker, interview by Katherine Maker, November 14, 1968, DDOH, 1–2, 6.

44 Young, "Powwow Power," 269–272.

45 Ibid., 273–274.

46 Will H. Spindler, *Tragedy Strikes at Wounded Knee and Other Essays on Indian Life in South Dakota and Nebraska* (Vermillion, S.D.: Dakota Press, 1972): 71–77.

47 Charles Chibitty, interview by Mary Jane Warde and Jim Anquoe, February 17, 2000, Tribal Songs Collection, Oklahoma Historical Society; Young, "Powwow Power," 274.

48 John Bloom, *To Show What an Indian Can Do: Sports at Native American Boarding Schools* (Minneapolis: University of Minnesota Press, 2000), 11, 35. See also John Bloom, " 'There Is Madness in the Air': The 1926 Haskell Homecoming and Popular Representations of Sports in Federal Indian Boarding Schools," in *Dressing in Feathers: The Construction of the Indian in American Popular Culture,* S. Elizabeth Bird, ed. (Boulder, Colo.: Westview Press, 1996): 97–110.

49 Bloom, *To Show What an Indian Can Do,* 41–42.

50 Young, "Powwow Power," 270–271; Mark G. Thiel, "The Powwow: Development of the Contemporary American Indian Celebration," part 3, *Whispering Wind* 15:4 (1982), 13, n.80b.

51 *The Indian Leader,* October 15, 1926, p. 1; ibid., October 22, 1926, pp. 1, 20, courtesy of Sandy Rhoades; Thiel, "The Powwow," 13, n.80b.

52 Bloom, *To Show What an Indian Can Do,* 46, 47–48.

53 And as John Bloom and David Wallace Adams have noted, winning the football game that weekend also sent a not so subtle signal to observers that Indian school teams could use cultural icons like football to assert their own identity as Indians. See Bloom, *To Show What an Indian Can Do;* David Wallace Adams, "More Than a Game: The Carlisle Indians Take to the Gridiron, 1893–1917," *Western Historical Quarterly* 32:1 (Spring 2001): 25–53.

54 Young, "Powwow Power," 270.

55 Frank Turley, "Ponca Fair and Powwow," *American Indian Tradition* 7:5 (1961): 180.

56 Ponca City *News,* August 26 and 28, 1938.

57 Ponca City *News,* August 23, 1940.

58 Ponca City *News,* August 28, 1930; Alfred Chalepah, Evelyn Chalepah, interview by Julia A. Jordan, May 3, 1967, DDOH, 5, 29–30.

59 Ibid.

60 Mary Belle Curtis Lonebear, interview by Mary Jane Warde and Jim Anquoe, July 30, 1999, Cheyenne/Washita Oral History Project, Oklahoma Historical Society.

61 Madeline Hamilton, interview by the author, February 7, 2003, Anadarko, Okla.

62 Ibid.

63 Jim Anquoe interview, July 12, 2002; Mary Belle Curtis Lonebear, interview.

64 Jim Anquoe interview, July 12, 2002.

65 Ibid.

66 C. V. Stinchecum to Charles Burke, December 20, 1921, "Kiowa Fairs, February 1, 1875–November 22, 1923," Records of the Kiowa Agency, Oklahoma Historical Society.

67 Lawton *Constitution,* July 24, 1924.

68 Lawton *Constitution,* July 3, 1924.

69 Lawton *Constitution,* July 31, 1925.

70 Lawton *Constitution,* August 2, 1925.

71 Young, "Powwow Power," 250.

6. CRATERVILLE PARK AND THE AMERICAN INDIAN EXPOSITION

1 Lawton *Constitution,* August 15, 1924; Muriel H. Wright, "The American Indian Exposition in Oklahoma," *Chronicles of Oklahoma* 24:2 (1946), 159.

2 Lawton *Constitution,* August 15, 1924.

3 Lawton *Constitution,* August 8 and 17, 1924.

4 Lawton *Constitution,* August 23 and 26, 1925.

5 Lawton *Constitution,* August 19, 1930; Gloria Alese Young, "Powwow Power: Perspectives on Historic and Contemporary Intertribalism," Ph.D. diss., Indiana University, 1981, 281–282; Wright, "American Indian Exposition in Oklahoma," 160; Oklahoma City *Daily Oklahoman,* August 26, 1931.

6 Lawton *Constitution,* August 31, 1931. The August 24 edition announced that "each night weird Apache Indian ghost dances will be held," while on August 25 it reported that "thousands of red men from all over the state" would appear for the evening shows "dressed in their gaudy costumes, their faces painted in bright colors, [to] excecute their age-old dances."

7 Lawton *Constitution,* August 26, 1932; author's field notes, August 2002.

8 Lawton *Constitution,* August 24, 1933.

9 Oklahoma City *Daily Oklahoman,* April 8 and 10, 1933; Lawton *Constitution,* April 7 and 10, 1933; Wright, "American Indian Exposition in Oklahoma," 160–161, 161 n9.

10 Oklahoma City *Daily Oklahoman,* April 8, 1933; Lawton *Constitution,* April 8, 1933.

11 Lawton *Constitution,* April 8 and 10, 1933; Oklahoma City *Daily Oklahoman,* April 10, 1933.

12 Author's field notes, July 2002.

13 Jethro Gaede, "The American Indian Exposition, 1932–1950: Rejecting Assimilation

Initiatives and Inverting Cultural Stereotypes," paper presented at the annual meeting of the American Society for Ethnohistory, 2000, unpublished ms. in the author's possession, 3.

14 Parker Paul McKenzie, "Brief History of the American Indian Exposition," 1, ca. 1990, American Indian Exposition File, Parker McKenzie Collection, Oklahoma Historical Society (hereafter cited as McKenzie Collection); Parker Paul McKenzie to Richard Tartsah, October 23, 1993, ibid.; Parker McKenzie, "First Years of the Expo," ibid.; Anadarko *Daily News,* August 5 and 6, 1989.

15 McKenzie, "Brief History of the American Indian Exposition," 1–2, McKenzie Collection; Jeanne M. Devlin, "American Indian Exposition," *Oklahoma Today* 40:4 (July-August 1990): 45–46.

16 Devlin, "American Indian Exposition," 45–46.

17 Anadarko *Tribune,* September 21, 1932.

18 Anadarko *Tribune,* August 10, 1932.

19 Anadarko *Tribune,* August 31, 1932.

20 McKenzie, "Brief History of the American Indian Exposition," 2–3, McKenzie Collection.

21 Anadarko *Tribune,* August 1, 1934, Anadarko *Daily American-Democrat,* August 1, 1934.

22 Anadarko *Tribune,* August 8, 15, and 22, 1934; Anadarko *Daily American-Democrat,* August 15, 17, and 18, 1934.

23 McKenzie, "Brief History of the American Indian Exposition," 3, McKenzie Collection; Parker McKenzie letter to the editor, typescript copy, August 11, 1986, Anadarko *Daily News* File, McKenzie Collection; Parker McKenzie, interview by the author, August 1, 1990, Mountain View, Okla.

24 Anadarko *Tribune,* August 14, 21, and 22, 1935; Anadarko *Daily American-Democrat,* August 13, 15, and 16, 1935.

25 Anadarko *Tribune,* August 28, 1935; Anadarko *Daily American-Democrat,* August 21, 1935; Parker McKenzie, published letter to the editor, December 24, 1990, Anadarko *Daily News* File, McKenzie Collection; 1939 American Indian Exposition program, American Indian Exposition File, McKenzie Collection.

26 Anadarko *Daily News,* August 21 and 23, 1942.

27 Anadarko *Daily News,* August 10, 15, 18, and 19, 1943.

28 Anadarko *Daily News,* August 12 and 19, 1945; July 22, 1945.

29 Anadarko *Daily News,* July 19, 1945.

30 Anadarko *Daily News,* August 8, 1945.

31 Anadarko *Daily News,* August 19, 1945.

32 Gaede, "American Indian Exposition," 3–4.

33 Gaede, "American Indian Exposition," 4–5.

34 Clyde Ellis, *To Change Them Forever: Indian Education at the Rainy Mountain Boarding School,* 1893–1920 (Norman: University of Oklahoma Press, 1996): 126–127; Jim Whitewolf, *The Life of a Kiowa-Apache Man,* Charles Brant, ed. (New York: Dover, 1969), 96.

35 Howard Bad Hand, "The American Flag in Lakota Tradition," in *The Flag in American Indian Art,* Toby Herbst and Joel Kopp, eds. (Cooperstown, N.Y.: New York State Historical Association, 1993), 12.

36 Wright, "American Indian Exposition in Oklahoma," 164; Anadarko *Daily News,* July 22, 1945.

37 1939 American Indian Exposition program, American Indian Exposition File, McKenzie Collection.

38 Wright, "American Indian Exposition in Oklahoma," 164.

39 William Meadows, *Kiowa, Comanche, and Apache Military Societies: Enduring Veterans, 1800 to the Present* (Austin: University of Texas Press, 1999), 136–137; Clyde Ellis, " 'Truly Dancing Their Own Way': Modern Revival and Diffusion of the Gourd Dance," *American Indian Quarterly* 14:1 (Winter 1990): 19–33; Scott Tonemah, interview by the author, February 8, 1988, Norman, Okla.

40 Meadows, *Military Societies,* 139–140.

41 Shalah Rowlen, interview by the author, January 21, 2003, Meeker, Okla,

42 Rowlen interview; author's field notes, February 2003.

43 Rowlen interview.

44 Jewel McDonald, interview by Sandy Rhoades and Scott Swearingen, courtesy of Sandy Rhoades.

45 1958 American Indian Exposition program, American Indian Exposition File, McKenzie Collection; Jim Anquoe, interview with the author, July 12, 2002, Stroud, OK.

46 McKenzie, "Reminiscing of Old Times," 1988, American Indian Exposition File, McKenzie Collection; McKenzie, "Brief History of the American Indian Exposition," ibid.

47 "Outstanding Indians of the Year" listed in the 2002 American Indian Exposition program, p. 5, in the possession of the author; author's field notes, September 1987; author's field notes April 1995.

48 Author's field notes, July 2002 and August 2002.

49 *Native American Times,* June 30, 2001.

50 Jim Anquoe, interview by the author, August 15, 2002, Oklahoma City, Okla.

51 Loretta Fowler, *Tribal Sovereignty and the Historical Imagination: Cheyenne-Arapaho Politics* (Lincoln: University of Nebraska Press, 2002): 95, 312–313, n.7.

52 Young, "Powwow Power," 292–293; Ed Red Eagle, Sr., interview by Robert L. Miller, May 17, 1967, Doris Duke Oral History Collection, Western History Collection, University of Oklahoma, Norman, Okla. 7 (hereafter cited as DDOH).

53 Young, "Powwow Power," 295–297.

54 Author's field notes, October 1989; Angie Barnes, interview by Leonard Maker, December 26, 1968, 13–14, DDOH.

55 Jim Anquoe interview, August 15, 2002; Young, "Powwow Power," 296–297; 20th Annual Tulsa Powwow Program, August 6–8, 1971, American Indian Exposition File, Parker McKenzie Collection.

56 Young, "Powwow Power," 294.

57 Jim Anquoe interview, July 12, 2002; Jim Anquoe interview, August 15, 2002;

58 Young, "Powwow Power," 352–355; Daniel J. Gelo, "Powwow Patter: Indian Emcee Discourse on Power and Identity," *Journal of American Folklore* 112 (Winter 1999):40–57; Dennis Zotigh, *Moving History: The Evolution of the Powwow* (Oklahoma City: Center for the American Indian, 1991), 8.

59 Harry Tofpi, Sr., interview by the author, August 4, 1993, Seminole, Okla.; "Father's Day Dance," recorded by Boyce Timmons, June 19, 1971, DDOH, 10.

60 Author's field notes, June 2000 and July 2002. Others have made similar observations. Writing in 1981, Bea Medicine commented "the 'giveaway' among the Lakota is now merely a prestige seeking, wealth displaying, ethnic marker among many of its practitioners. It has become a mirror image of the Northwest Coast 'potlatch' rather than an accepted and institutionalized way of honoring someone by giving to the less fortunate, the mourners, or the ill and infirm in the local community"; "American Indian Family: Cultural Change and Adaptive Strategies," *Journal of Ethnic Studies* 8:4 (Winter 1981): 14.

61 Jim Anquoe interview, July 12, 2002.

62 Jim Anquoe interview, August 15, 2002; author's field notes, April 1998.

63 Jim Anquoe interview, August 15, 2002; 20th Annual Tulsa Powwow program, August 6–8, 1971.

CONCLUSION

1 Author's field notes, June 2001; Jim Anquoe, interview by the author, July 13, 2002, Stroud, Okla. The matter of how many people are regular powwowers is difficult to assess. The issue has never been systematically researched, so the estimates offered here are about as subjective as it gets. Estimates from friends who are regulars on the Southern Plains powwow circuit ranged from ten to twenty-five percent of the Indian community. No one was willing to go any higher than thirty percent, and most observed that while it's hard to be sure, the consensus is that the numbers fall "somewhere in the twenty percent range," as one woman put it. Most agreed that gender lines were about evenly divided, and all agreed that while young people are a larger and larger component of the powwow crowd, positions of authority and control continue to be lodged with older people. Outside of the Plains, the majority of powwowers are young, and it seems that men generally outnumber women. For the only attempt to quantify powwow attendance, see Karl Eschbach and Kalman Applbaum, "Who Goes to Powwows? Evidence from the Survey of American Indians and Alaska Natives," *American Indian Culture and Research Journal* 24:2 (2000): 65–83.

2 Luke Eric Lassiter, *The Power of Kiowa Song: A Collaborative Ethnography* (Tucson: University of Arizona Press, 1998), 76.

3 Luke Eric Lassiter, telephone conversation with the author, September 17, 2002.

4 Cecil Horse and Jenny Horse, interview by Julia A. Jordan, June 21, 1967, Doris Duke Oral History Collection, Western History Collection, University of Oklahoma, Norman, Okla. 29–31 (hereafter cited as DDOH).

5 Cy Hall Zotigh, interview by Luke Eric Lassiter and Clyde Ellis, June 11, 1998, Saddle Mountain, Okla.; Helene Fletcher, telephone conversation with Clyde Ellis, July 20, 1998; Vincent Bointy, interview by Luke Eric Lassiter and Clyde Ellis, June 12, 1998, Carnegie, Okla., all cited in Luke Eric Lassiter, Clyde Ellis, and Ralph Kotay, *The Jesus Road: Kiowas, Christianity, and Indian Hymns* (Lincoln: University of Nebraska Press, 2002), 66; Benjamin Kracht, "Kiowa Religion in Historical Perspective," *American Indian Quarterly* 21:1 (1997): 28.

6 Morris W. Foster, *Being Comanche: A Social History of an American Indian Community* (Tucson: University of Arizona Press, 1991): 126–127.

7 Lassiter, *Power of Kiowa Song,* 77–79, emphasis in the original.

8 Lassiter, Ellis, and Kotay, *The Jesus Road,* 62–63.

9 James H. Howard, "The Pan-Indian Culture of Oklahoma," *Scientific Monthly* 18:5 (1955): 215–220; William W. Newcomb, Jr., "A Note on Cherokee-Delaware Pan-Indianism," *American Anthropologist* 57 (1955): 1041–1045; Samuel W. Corrigan, "The Plains Indian Pow-wow: Cultural Integration in Manitoba and Saskatchewan," *Anthropologica* 12 (1970): 253–277; Robert K. Thomas, "Pan-Indianism," in *The American Indian Today,* Stuart Levine and Nancy O. Lurie, eds. (Baltimore: Pelican Books, 1970), 128–140; Nancy O. Lurie, "An American Indian Renascence?" in *The American Indian Today,* Stuart Levine and Nancy O. Lurie, eds. (Baltimore: Pelican Books, 1970), 295–327. See also James H. Howard, "Pan-Indianism in Native American Music and Dance," *Ethnomusicology* 27:1 (1983): 71–82.

     For extended discussions of the relationship between powwows and Pan-Indianism, see Joan D. Laxson, "Aspects of Acculturation among American Indians: Emphasis on Contemporary Pan-Indianism," Ph.D. diss., University of California-Berkeley, 1972, 46–100; Susan Applegate Krouse, "A Window into the Indian Culture: The Powwow as Performance," Ph.D. diss., University of Wisconsin-Milwaukee, 1991, 9–25; Gloria Alese Young, "Powwow Power: Perspectives on Historic and Contemporary Intertribalism," Ph.D. diss., Indiana University, 1981, 69–81.

10 Howard, "Pan-Indian Culture of Oklahoma," 215; Nancy O. Lurie, "The Contemporary American Indian Scene," in *North American Indians in Historical Perspective,* Nancy O. Lurie and Eleanor B. Leacock, eds. (New York: Random House, 1971), 419; Lurie, "An American Indian Renascence?" 315.

11 Barre Toelken, "Ethnic Selection and Intensification in the Native American Powwow," in *Creative Ethnicity: Symbols and Strategies of Contemporary Ethnic Life,* Stephen Stern and John Allan Cicala, eds. (Logan: Utah State University Press, 1991): 140.

12 William K. Powers, *War Dance: Plains Indian Musical Performance* (Tucson: University of Arizona Press, 1990): 87, 108.

13 Sylvester Warrior, interview by Leonard Maker, November 14, 1968, DDOH, 6–7, 11; Sylvester Warrior quoted in "Ponca Indian Haylonska," May 3, 1969, DDOH, 5–6.

14 Lamont Brown, interview by Leonard Maker, December 1, 1968, DDOH, 13; Ed Red Eagle, Sr., interview by Robert L. Miller, May 17, 1967, DDOH, 7.

15 William Collins, Sr., interview in "Ponca Oral History Material," October 23, 1969, DDOH, 18; Warrior interview, DDOH, 4.

16 Brown interview, DDOH, 13; John Blackowl, interview by Kirk Kickingbird, January 1, 1969, DDOH, 13; author's field notes, May 1995.

17 "American Indian Expo," *American Indian Tradition* 7:5 (1961): 179.

18 Author's field notes, January 2003, February 2003.

19 Jim Anquoe, interview by the author, August 15, 2002, Oklahoma City, Okla.; author's field notes, August 2000.

20 Sylvester Warrior quoted in Jimmy W. Duncan, "Hethuska Zani': An Ethnohistory of the War Dance Complex," master's thesis, Northeastern State University, 1997: 106; author's field notes, January 2003.

21 Lassiter, *Power of Kiowa Song,* 62, 122–123; see also 22–29 for Lassiter's account of his own experiences in the hobbyist world. The participation of non-Indians in powwow culture has attracted surprisingly little interest from scholars. One of the first to address it was William K. Powers, "The Indian Hobbyist Movement in North Amer-

ica," in *Handbook of North American Indians,* vol. 4, *History of Indian-White Relations,* William C. Sturtevant, ed. (Washington, D.C.: Smithsonian Institution Press, 1988): 557–561. Philip J. Deloria has an informed and wideranging discussion of the movement in *Playing Indian* (New Haven, Conn.: Yale University Press, 1998). For an insightful account of one non-Indian's life in the Southern Plains powwow world, see Robert J. Stahl, "Joe True: Convergent Needs and Assumed Identity," in *Being and Becoming Indian: Biographical Studies of North American Frontiers,* James Clifton, ed. (Prospect Heights, Ill: Waveland Press, 1993): 276–289. For a discussion of hobbyist powwows in the Great Lakes region, see Sharon M. Hansen, "Culture of Choice: An Ethnography of a Hobbyist Powwow," master's thesis, University of Wyoming, 1986.

22 Author's field notes, August 2002.

23 Author's field notes, July 2000.

24 Loretta Fowler, *Shared Symbols, Contested Meanings: Gros Ventre Culture and History,* 1778–1985 (Ithaca, N.Y.: Cornell University, 1987). Fowler notes that at the Fort Belknap Reservation, "an array of symbols — political, ritual, sacred — have meaning and emotional impact for all, yet people disagree over the interpretation of these symbols." Of powwows, she notes that to "Gros Ventres youths, the powwow and dance committee of today represent traditions perpetuated; to elders they are innovations," 2, 157. For her insightful discussion of contemporary powwow culture at Fort Belknap, see 156–178.

25 Thomas W. Kavanagh, "The Comanche Pow-wow: Pan-Indianism or Tribalism," *Haliksa'i,* University of New Mexico Contributions to Anthropology 1 (1982): 12–13, 18–19, 21; Robert DesJarlait, "The Contest Powwow versus the Traditional Powwow and the Role of the Native American Community," *Wicazo Sa Review* 12:1 (Spring 1997): 124, 126.

26 Anquoe interview, August 15, 2002.

27 Red Earth Festival homepage, http://www.redearth.org/festival.htm [September 16, 2002].

28 Lassiter, *Power of Kiowa Song,* 98.

29 John Eastman, "Powwow," *Natural History* 79 (1970): 24.

30 Clyde Ellis and Luke Eric Lassiter, "Commentary: Applying Communitas to Kiowa Powwows," *American Indian Quarterly* 22:4 (1998): 487; author's field notes, August 2002.

31 Otis Russell, interview by Leonard Maker, May 5, 1970, DDOH, 12–14; author's field notes, July 1999.

32 Luke Eric Lassiter, " 'Charlie Brown': Not Just Another Essay on the Gourd Dance," *American Indian Culture and Research Journal* 21:4 (1997): 75–103.

33 Lassiter, " 'Charlie Brown,' " 75–76; author's field notes, July 1996.

34 Author's field notes, July 1996.

35 Author's field notes, August 2002.

36 Author's field notes, March 2002. See also Lassiter, " 'Charlie Brown' "; Tara Browner, "Making and Singing Pow-wow Songs: Text, Form, and the Significance of Culture-Based Analysis," *Ethnomusicology* 44 (2): 214–233; Severt Young Bear and R. D. Theisz, *Standing in the Light: A Lakota Way of Seeing* (Lincoln: University of Nebraska Press, 1994), 38–103.

Bibliography

UNPUBLISHED PRIMARY SOURCES

American Baptist Historical Society, Rochester, N.Y.
    Isabel Crawford Collection, Samuel Colgate Historical Library
        Isabel Crawford Journal for 1898–1899
National Archives, Record Group 75, Washington, D.C.
Kiowa Agency Classified Files, 1907–1939
Oklahoma Historical Society, Oklahoma City, Okla.
Records of the Chilocco School
    "Fairs, June 1895–June 1903"
    "Fairs, July 1903"
    "Fairs, October 1903"
    Records of the Cheyenne and Arapaho Agency
        "Indian Councils"
        "Indian Dances"
        "Indians with Shows and Exhibitions"
        "Acculturation"
        "Indian Fairs"
    Records of the Kiowa Agency
        "Indian Celebrations and Dances," 1874–1917
        "Agents' Reports"
        "Field Matrons' Files"
        "Indians with Shows and Exhibitions, 1875–1924"
        "Kiowa Fairs, February 1, 1875–November 22, 1923"
        "Quanah Parker"
    Records of the Pawnee Agency
        "Dances"
        "Indian Celebrations and Dances"
        "Indians with Shows and Exhibitions"
    Records of the Quapaw Agency
        "Indians with Shows and Exhibitions"
    Records of the Sac and Fox and Shawnee Agency
        "Indian Fairs"
    Parker McKenzie Collection
        "American Indian Exposition File"
        "Anadarko *Daily News* File"

Tribal Songs Collection
   Charles Chibitty, interview by Mary Jane Warde and Jim Anquoe, February 17, 2000
Cheyenne/Washita Oral History Project
   Mary Belle Curtis Lonebear, interview by Mary Jane Warde and Jim Anquoe, July 30, 1999

Western History Collection, University of Oklahoma, Norman, Okla.
Doris Duke Oral History Collection
   Angie Barnes, interview by Leonard Maker, December 26, 1968
   John Blackowl, interview by Kirk Kickingbird, January 1, 1969
   Lamont Brown, interview by Leonard Maker, December 1, 1968
   Alfred Chalepah and Evelyn Chalepah, interview by Julia A. Jordan, May 3, 1967
   William Collins, Sr., Ponca Oral History Material, October 23, 1969
   "Father's Day Dance," recorded by Boyce Timmons, June 19, 1971
   Bert Geikoumah, interview by Julia A. Jordan, July 28, 1967
   Ralph Goodman, interview by Julia A. Jordan, June 4, 1969
   Cecil Horse and Jenny Horse, interview by Julia A. Jordan, June 21, 1967
   Leonard Maker, interview by Katherine Maker, November 14, 1968
   Eugenia Mausape, interview by Julia A. Jordan, September 14, 1967
   Ponca Indian Haylonska, recorded by Leonard Maker, May 3, 1969
   Guy Quoetone, interview by Julia A. Jordan, September 19, 1967
   Guy Quoetone, interview by Julia A. Jordan, March 23, 1971
   Ed Red Eagle, Sr., interview by Robert L. Miller, May 17, 1967
   Jess Rowlodge, interview by Julia A. Jordan, June 4, 1969
   Otis Russell, interview by Leonard Maker, May 14, 1969
   Otis Russell, interview by Leonard Maker, May 5, 1970
   Josephine Walker, interview by Leonard Maker, December 31, 1968
   Sylvester Warrior, interview by Leonard Maker, November 14, 1968

Interviews and Personal Communications
Jim Anquoe, interview by the author, July 12, 2002, Stroud, Okla.
Jim Anquoe, interview by the author, August 15, 2002, Oklahoma City, Okla.
Vincent Bointy, interview by Luke Eric Lassiter and the author, June 12, 1998, Carnegie, Okla.
Helene Fletcher, telephone conversation with the author, July 20, 1998.
Madeline Hamilton, interview by the author, February 7, 2003, Anadarko, Okla.
Forrest Kassanavoid, conversation with the author, June 1990, Llano, Tex.
Ralph Kotay, telephone interview with the author, July 18, 1998.
Ralph Kotay, interview by the author, August 12, 2002, Apache, Okla.
Luke Eric Lassiter, telephone conversation with the author, July 16, 1998, September 10, 1998, September 1, 2002, and September 17, 2002.
Ray Littleturtle, interview by the author, June 23, 2001, Pembroke, NC.
Derek Lowry, interview by the author, June 9, 2001, Greensboro, NC.
Jewel McDonald, interview by Sandy Rhoades and Scott Swearingen.
Parker McKenzie, interview by the author, August 1, 1990, Mountain View, Okla.
Bill Meadows, personal communication to the author, August 21, 2002.

L. G. Moses, personal communication to the author, August 28, 2001.

William K. Powers, personal communication to the author, July 4, 2002.

Shalah Rowlen, interview by the author, January 21, 2003, Meeker, Okla.

Elmer Sugar Brown, interview by Sandy Rhoades and the author, January 20, 2003, Tulsa, Okla.

Harry Tofpi, Sr., interview by the author, August 4, 1993, Seminole, Okla.; May 2, 1996, and May 3, 1997, Shawnee, Okla.

Scott Tonemah, interview by the author, February 8, 1989, Norman, Okla.

George "Woogie" Watchetaker comments. *Into the Circle: An Introduction to Oklahoma Powwows and Celebrations.* Tulsa: Full Circle Productions, 1992. Videorecording.

Angela Wilson, personal communication to the author, December 12, 2002.

Cy Hall Zotigh, interview by Luke Eric Lassiter and the author, June 11, 1998, Saddle Mountain, Okla.

PUBLISHED PRIMARY SOURCES

Annual Report of the Commissioner of Indian Affairs, 1892, 1893, 1894, 1895, 1901, 1902, 1903, 1919

Annual Report of the Secretary of the Interior, 1883

Annual Report of the Superintendent of Indian Schools, 1893

Newspapers

Anadarko, Okla., *Daily American-Democrat*

Anadarko, Okla., *Daily News*

Anadarko, Okla., *Tribune*

Lawton, Okla., *Constitution*

Native American Times

News from Indian Country

Oklahoma City, Okla., *Daily Oklahoman*

Ponca City, Okla., *News*

Online Sources

Intertribal Indian Club of Tulsa (IICOT). http://www.iicot.org [April 11, 2002].

Shanewis opera libretto. http://opera.stanford.edu/opera/cadman/shanewis/libretto.html [September 21, 2002].

Red Earth Festival home page. http://www.redearth.org/festival.htm [September 16, 2003].

Books

Barrett, S. A. *Dream Dance of the Chippewa and Menominee Indians of Northern Wisconsin.* Milwaukee Public Museum Publications in Anthropology. Milwaukee: Milwaukee Public Museum, 1911.

Bernstein, Alison R. *American Indians and World War II: Toward a New Era in Indian Affairs.* Norman: University of Oklahoma Press, 1991.

Bernstein, Diane Morris. *We Dance Because We Can: People of the Powwow.* Marietta, Ga.: Longstreet Press, 1996.

Berthrong, Donald J. *The Cheyenne and Arapaho Ordeal: Reservation and Agency Life in the Indian Territory, 1875–1907.* Norman: University of Oklahoma Press, 1976.

———. *The Southern Cheyennes.* Norman: University of Oklahoma Press, 1963.

Blackstone, Sarah J. *Buckskins, Bullets, and Business: A History of Buffalo Bill's Wild West.* Westport, Conn.: Greenwood Press, 1986.

Bloom, John. *To Show What an Indian Can Do: Sports at Native American Boarding Schools.* Minneapolis: University of Minnesota Press, 2000.

Boyd, Maurice. *Kiowa Voices,* 2 vols. Fort Worth: Texas Christianity University Press, 1981.

Britten, Thomas A. *American Indians in World War I: At Home and at War.* Albuquerque: University of New Mexico Press, 1997.

Browner, Tara. *Heartbeat of the People: Music and Dance of the Northern Powwow.* Urbana: University of Illinois Press, 2002.

Callahan, Alice Anne. *The Osage Ceremonial Dance: I'n-Lon-Schka.* Norman: University of Oklahoma Press, 1990.

Crawford, Isabel. *Kiowa: A Woman Missionary in Indian Territory.* Lincoln: University of Nebraska Press, 1998 (1915).

Deloria, Philip J. *Playing Indian.* New Haven, Conn.: Yale University Press, 1998.

DeMallie, Raymond J., ed. *The Sixth Grandfather: Black Elk's Teachings Given to John G. Neihardt.* Lincoln: University of Nebraska Press, 1984.

Denig, Edwin Thompson. *The Assiniboine.* J. N. B. Hewitt, ed.; introduction by David R. Miller. Norman: University of Oklahoma Press, 2000 (1928).

Densmore, Frances. *Pawnee Music.* Bureau of American Ethnology, Bulletin 93. Washington, D.C.: Smithsonian Institution, 1929.

Ellis, Clyde. *To Change Them Forever: Indian Education at the Rainy Mountain Boarding School, 1893–1920.* Norman: University of Oklahoma Press, 1996.

Evans, C. Scott. *The Modern Fancy Dancer.* Pottsboro, Tex.: Crazy Crow Trading Post, 1998.

Farr, William E. *The Reservation Blackfeet: A Photographic History of Cultural Survival.* Seattle: University of Washington Press, 1986.

Finger, John. *Cherokee Americans: The Eastern Band of the Cherokee Indians in the Twentieth Century.* Lincoln: University of Nebraska Press, 1991.

Fletcher, Alice C., and Francis LaFlesche. *The Omaha Tribe.* 2 vols. Lincoln: University of Nebraska Press, 1972 (1911).

Foster, Morris W. *Being Comanche: A Social History of an American Indian Community.* Tucson: University of Arizona Press, 1991.

Fowler, Loretta. *Shared Symbols, Contested Meanings: Gros Ventre Culture and History, 1778–1985.* Ithaca, N.Y.: Cornell University, 1987.

———. *Tribal Sovereignty and the Historical Imagination: Cheyenne-Arapaho Politics.* Lincoln: University of Nebraska Press, 2002.

Gipson, Fred. *Fabulous Empire: Colonel Zack Miller's Story.* Boston: Houghton Mifflin Company, 1946.

Hagan, William T. *Quanah Parker, Comanche Chief.* Norman: University of Oklahoma Press, 1993.

———. *United States-Comanche Relations: The Reservation Years.* Norman: University of Oklahoma Press, 1990.

Heth, Charlotte, ed. *Native American Dance: Ceremonies and Social Traditions.* Washington, D.C.: Smithsonian Institution Press, 1992.

Holm, Tom. *Strong Hearts, Wounded Souls: Native American Veterans of the Vietnam War.* Austin: University of Texas Press, 1996.

Horse Capture, George P. *Pow Wow.* Cody, Wyo.: Buffalo Bill Historical Center, 1989.

Howard, James H. *The Ponca Tribe.* Bureau of American Ethnology, Bulletin 195. Lincoln: University of Nebraska Press, 1995.

Hoxie, Frederick E. *A Final Promise: The Campaign to Assimilate the Indians, 1880–1920.* Cambridge, Mass.: Cambridge University Press, 1984.

Jacobs, Margaret D. *Engendered Encounters: Feminism and Pueblo Cultures, 1879–1920.* Lincoln: University of Nebraska Press, 1999.

Kasson, Joy S. *Buffalo Bill's Wild West: Celebrity, Memory, and Popular History.* New York: Hill and Wang, 2000.

Kavanagh, Thomas W. *Comanche Political History: An Ethnohistorical Perspective, 1706–1875.* Lincoln: University of Nebraska Press, 1996.

Keller, Jr., Robert H. *American Protestantism and United States Indian Policy, 1869–82.* Lincoln: University of Nebraska Press, 1983.

Keller, Jr., Robert H., and Michael Turek. *American Indians and National Parks.* Tucson: University of Arizona Press, 1998.

Kelly, Lawrence C. *The Assault on Assimilation: John Collier and the Origins of Indian Policy Reform.* Albuquerque: University of New Mexico Press, 1983.

Kroeker, Marvin. *Comanches and Mennonites on the Oklahoma Plains: A. J. and Magdalena Becker and the Post Oak Mission.* Hillsboro, Kans.: Kindred Productions, 1997.

Lassiter, Luke Eric. *The Power of Kiowa Song: A Collaborative Ethnography.* Tucson: University of Arizona Press, 1998.

Lassiter, Luke Eric, Clyde Ellis, and Ralph Kotay. *The Jesus Road: Kiowas, Christianity, and Indian Hymns.* Lincoln: University of Nebraska Press, 2002.

Laubin, Reginald and Gladys. *Indian Dances of North America: Their Importance to Indian Life.* Norman: University of Oklahoma Press, 1977.

La Vere, David. *Life among the Texas Indians: The WPA Narratives.* College Station: Texas A & M Press, 1998.

Meadows, William C. *Kiowa, Apache, and Comanche Military Societies: Enduring Veterans, 1800 to the Present.* Austin: University of Texas Press, 1999.

Mishkin, Bernard. *Rank and Warfare among the Plains Indians.* Introduction by Morris Foster. Lincoln: University of Nebraska Press, 1992 (1940).

Mooney, James. *Calendar History of the Kiowa Indians.* Seventeenth Annual Report of the Bureau of American Ethnology. Reprint, Washington, D.C.: Smithsonian Institution Press, 1979.

———. *The Ghost Dance Religion and the Sioux Uprising of 1890.* Fourteenth Annual Report of the Bureau of American Ethnology. Washington, D.C.: Smithsonian Institution, 1896.

Moses, L. G. *The Indian Man: A Biography of James Mooney.* Urbana: University of Illinois Press, 1984.

———. *Wild West Shows and the Images of the American Indians, 1883–1933.* Albuquerque: University of New Mexico Press, 1996.

Murray, William D. *The History of the Boy Scouts of America.* New York: Boy Scouts of America, 1937.

Philp, Kenneth R. *John Collier's Crusade for Indian Reform, 1920–1954.* Tucson: University of Arizona Press, 1977.

Powers, William K. *Feathers Costume.* Kendall Park, N.J.: Lakota Books, 1996.

———. *The Lakota Warrior Tradition: Three Essays on Lakotas at War.* Kendall Park, N.J.: Lakota Books, 2001.

———. *War Dance: Plains Indian Musical Performance.* Tucson: University of Arizona Press, 1990.

Prucha, Francis Paul. *The Great Father: The United States Government and the American Indians.* 2 vols. Lincoln: University of Nebraska Press, 1984.

Prucha, Francis Paul, ed. *Documents of United States Indian Policy.* Lincoln: University of Nebraska Press, 1990.

Reddin, Paul. *Wild West Shows.* Urbana: University of Illinois Press, 1999.

Revard, Carter. *Ponca War Dancers.* Norman, Okla.: Point Rider's Press, 1980.

Richardson, Jane. *Law and Status among the Kiowa Indians.* New York: American Ethnological Society, 1940.

Ridington, Robin, and Dennis Hastings (In'aska). *Blessing for a Long Time: The Sacred Pole of the Omaha Tribe.* Lincoln: University of Nebraska Press, 1997.

Roberts, Chris. *People of the Circle: Powwow Country.* Missoula, Mont.: Farcountry Press, 1998.

Rollings, Willard H. *The Osage: An Ethnohistorical Study of Hegemony on the Prairie-Plains.* Columbia: University of Missouri Press, 1992.

Schmeckebier, Laurence F. *The Office of Indian Affairs: Its History, Activities, and Organization.* Baltimore: Johns Hopkins University Press, 1927.

Slotkin, James S. *The Menomini Powwow: A Study in Cultural Decay.* Milwaukee Public Museum Publications in Anthropology. Milwaukee: Milwaukee Public Museum, 1957.

Smyth, Willie, ed. *Songs of Indian Territory: Native American Music Traditions of Oklahoma.* Oklahoma City: Center for the American Indian, 1989.

Spence, Mark David. *Dispossessing the Wilderness: Indian Removal and the Making of the National Parks.* New York: Oxford University Press, 1999.

Spindler, Will H. *Tragedy Strikes at Wounded Knee and Other Essays on Indian Life in South Dakota and Nebraska.* Vermillion, S.D.: Dakota Press, 1972.

Starita, Joe. *The Dull Knifes of Pine Ridge: A Lakota Odyssey.* New York: G. P. Putnam's and Sons, 1995.

Theisz, R. D. *Sending Their Voices: Essays on Lakota Musicology.* Kendall Park, N.J.: Lakota Books, 2001.

Turner, Victor. *The Ritual Process: Structure and Anti-Structure.* Chicago: Aldine, 1969.

Utley, Robert M. *The Indian Frontier of the American West, 1846–1890.* Albuquerque: University of New Mexico Press, 1984.

———. *The Lance and the Shield: The Life and Times of Sitting Bull.* New York: Henry Holt, 1993.

———. *The Last Days of the Sioux Nation.* New Haven, Conn.: Yale University Press, 1963.

Vennum, Thomas. *The Ojibway Dance Drum: Its History and Construction.* Washington, D.C.: Smithsonian Institution Press, 1982.

Walker, James R. *Lakota Belief and Ritual.* Raymond J. De Mallie and Elaine A. Jahner, eds. Lincoln: University of Nebraska Press, 1991.

Wallace, Ernest, and E. Adamson Hoebel. *The Comanches: Lords of the South Plains.* Norman: University of Oklahoma Press, 1952.

Wallis, Michael. *The Real Wild West: The 101 Ranch and the Creation of the American West.* New York: St. Martin's Press, 1999.

White, Leonard D. *The Republican Era, 1869–1901: A Study in Administrative History.* New York: MacMillan, 1958.

Whitehorse, David. *Pow-wow: The Contemporary Pan-Indian Celebration.* Publications in American Indian Studies. San Diego: San Diego State University, 1988.

Whitewolf, Jim. *The Life of a Kiowa-Apache Man.* Charles Brant, ed. New York: Dover, 1969.

Young Bear, Severt, and R. D. Theisz. *Standing in the Light: A Lakota Way of Seeing.* Lincoln: University of Nebraska Press, 1994.

Zotigh, Dennis. *Moving History: The Evolution of the Powwow.* Oklahoma City: Center for the American Indian, 1991.

Theses and Dissertations

Ashworth, Kenneth A. "The Contemporary Oklahoma Powwow." Ph.D. diss., University of Oklahoma, 1986.

Axtmann, Ann. "Dance: Celebration and Resistance, Native American Indian Intertribal Powwow Performance." Ph.D. diss., New York University, 1999.

Daily, David Wilson. "Guardian Rivalries: G. E. E. Lindquist, John Collier, and the Moral Landscape of Federal Indian Policy, 1910–1950." Ph.D. diss., Duke University, 2000.

Duncan, Jimmy W. "Hethuska Zani': An Ethnohistory of the War Dance Complex." Master's thesis, Northeastern State University, 1997.

Green, Adriana Greci. "Performances and Celebrations: Displaying Lakota Identity, 1880–1915." Ph.D. diss., Rutgers University, 2001.

Hansen, Sharon M. "Culture of Choice: An Ethnography of a Hobbyist Powwow." Master's thesis, University of Wyoming, 1986.

Hatton, Orin. " 'We Caused Them to Cry': Power and Performance in Gros Ventre War Expedition Songs." Master's thesis, Catholic University of America, 1988.

Jones, Judith Ann. " 'Women Never Used to Dance': Gender and Music in Nez Perce Culture Change." Ph.D. diss., Washington State University, 1995.

Kracht, Benjamin. "Kiowa Religion: An Ethnohistorical Analysis of Ritual Symbolism, 1832–1987." Ph.D. diss., Southern Methodist University, 1989.

Krouse, Susan Applegate. "A Window into the Indian Culture: The Powwow as Performance." Ph.D. diss., University of Wisconsin-Milwaukee, 1991.

Laxson, Joan D. "Aspects of Acculturation among American Indians: Emphasis on Contemporary Pan-Indianism." Ph.D. diss., University of California-Berkeley, 1972.

Mathews, Lita. "The Native American Powwow: A Contemporary Authentication of a Cultural Artifact." Ph.D. diss., University of New Mexico, 1999.

May, Stephanie Anna. "Performance of Identity: Alabama-Coushatta Tourism, Powwows, and Everyday Life." Ph.D. diss., University of Texas at Austin, 2001.

Quick, Sarah. "Powwow Dancing in North America: The Formation of an Indian Identity Through Expressive Culture." Master's thesis, University of Missouri at Columbia, 2001.

Roark-Calnek, Sue. "Indian Way in Oklahoma: Transactions in Honor and Legitimacy." Ph.D. diss., Bryn Mawr College, 1977.

Roberts, Kathleen Glenister. "Giving Away: The Performance of Speech and Sign in Powwow Ritual Exchange." Ph.D. diss., Indiana University, 2001.

Sanchez, Victoria Eugenie. " 'As Long as We Dance, We Shall Know Who We Are': A Study of Off-Reservation Traditional Intertribal Powwows in Central Ohio." Ph.D. diss., Ohio State University, 1995.

Thompson, Elizabeth Wyrick, "Pocahontas, Powwows, and Musical Power: Native American Women's Performances in North Carolina." Master's thesis, University of North Carolina at Chapel Hill, 1998.

Williams, Andrew Wade. "We Are All Warriors Now: Dancing the Future in the Contemporary Oklahoma Powwow." Senior honors thesis, Harvard University, 1997.

Young, Gloria Alese. "Powwow Power: Perspectives on Historic and Contemporary Intertribalism." Ph.D. diss., Indiana University, 1981.

Articles

Adams, David Wallace. "More Than a Game: The Carlisle Indians Take to the Gridiron, 1893–1917." *Western Historical Quarterly* 32:1 (Spring 2001): 25–53.

Altherr, Thomas L. "Let 'er Rip: Popular Culture Images of the American West in Wild West Shows, Rodeos, and Rendezvous," in *Wanted Dead or Alive: The American West in Popular Culture*, Richard C. Aquila, ed. (Urbana: University of Illinois Press, 1996): 73–105.

"American Indian Expo," *American Indian Tradition* 7:5 (1961): 179.

Anderson, Robert. "The Northern Cheyenne War Mothers." *Antropological Quarterly* 29:3 (1956): 82–90.

Axtmann, Ann. "Performance Power in Native America: Powwow Dancing." *Dance Research Journal* 33:1 (Summer 2001): 7–22.

———. "Race, Persecution, and Persistence: Powwow Dancing." In *Dancing in the Millennium: Conference Proceedings* (Washington, D.C.: 2000): 23–27.

Bad Hand, Howard. "The American Flag in Lakota Tradition." In *The Flag in American Indian Art,* Toby Herbst and Joel Kopp, eds. (Cooperstown, N.Y.: New York State Historical Association, 1993): 11–13.

Beede, Aaron McGaffey. "The Dakota Indian Victory Dance." *North Dakota Historical Quarterly* 9 (April 1942): 167–178.

Benton, Sherrole. "Grand Entry: A New Ceremony Derived from the Old West." *Tribal College Journal* (Winter 1997): 10–13.

Blanchard, David. "Entertainment, Dance, and Northern Mohawk Showmanship." *American Indian Quarterly* 7:1 (1983): 2–26.

Bloom, John. " 'There Is Madness in the Air': The 1926 Haskell Homecoming and Popular Representations of Sports in Federal Indian Boarding Schools." In *Dressing in Feathers: The Construction of the Indian in American Popular Culture,* S. Elizabeth Bird, ed. (Boulder, Colo.: Westview Press, 1996): 97–110.

Browner, Tara. "Making and Singing Pow-wow Songs: Text, Form, and the Significance of Culture-Based Analysis." *Ethnomusicology* 44 (2): 214–233.

Butler, Anne M. "Selling the Popular Myth." In *The Oxford History of the American West,* Clyde A. Milner II, Carol A. O'Connor, and Martha Sandweiss, eds. (New York: Oxford University Press, 1994): 771–801.

Campisi, Jack. "Powwow: A Study of Ethnic Boundary Maintenance." *Man in the Northeast* 9 (1975): 33–36.

Charles, Jim. "The History in Ponca *Heluska* Songs." Unpublished ms. in the author's possession.

———. "Songs of the Ponca: Heluska." *Wicazo Sa Review* 5:2 (1989): 2–16.

Conklin, Abe. "Origin of the Powwow: The Ponca He-Thus-Ka Society Dance." *Native Americas: Hemispheric Journal of Indigenous Issues* (Fall/Winter 1994): 17–21.

Coppersmith, Clifford. "Healing and Remembrance: The Chiricahua and Warm Springs Apache Mountain Spirit Dance in Oklahoma." Unpublished ms. in the author's possession.

Corrigan, Samuel W. "The Plains Indian Pow-wow: Cultural Integration in Manitoba and Saskatchewan." *Anthropologica* 12 (1970): 253–277.

De Flyer, Joseph E. "From Creation Stories to '49 Songs: Cultural Transactions with the White World as Portrayed in Northern Plains Indian Story and Song." *Studies in American Indian Culture and Research Journal* 24:2 (2000): 65–83.

Densmore, Frances. "The Songs of Indian Soldiers during the World War." *Musical Quarterly* 20 (October 1934): 419–435.

DesJarlait, Robert. "The Contest Powwow versus the Traditional Powwow and the Role of the Native American Community." *Wicazo Sa Review* 12:1 (Spring 1997): 115–127.

Devlin, Jeanne M. "American Indian Exposition." *Oklahoma Today* 40:4 (July-August 1990): 45–46.

———. "Oklahoma Tribesmen: Every Picture Tells a Story." *Oklahoma Today* 41:3 (May-June 1991): 22–24.

Eastman, John. "Powwow." *Natural History* 79 (1970): 24–26.

Ellis, Clyde. "Five Dollars a Week to Be 'Regular Indians': Shows, Exhibitions, and the Economics of Indian Dancing, 1880–1930." In *Native Pathways: Economic Development and American Indian Culture,* Brian Hosmer and Colleen O'Neil, eds. (Boulder: University Press of Colorado, forthcoming).

———. "'A Gathering of Life Itself': The Kiowa Gourd Dance." In *Native American Values: Survival and Renewal,* Thomas E. Schirer and Susan M. Branstner, eds. (Sault Ste. Marie, Mich.: Lake Superior State University Press, 1993): 365–375.

———. "'There Is No Doubt . . . the Dances Should Be Curtailed': Indian Dances and Federal Policy on the Southern Plains, 1880–1930." *Pacific Historical Review* 70:4 (2001): 543–569.

———. "'There's a Dance Every Weekend': Powwow Culture in North Carolina." In *Southern Heritage on Display: Public Ritual and Ethnic Diversity within Southern Regionalism,* Celeste Ray, ed. (Tuscaloosa: University of Alabama Press, 2003): 79–105.

———. "'Truly Dancing Their Own Way': Modern Revival and Diffusion of the Gourd Dance." *American Indian Quarterly* 14:1 (Winter 1990): 19–33.

———. "'We Don't Want Your Rations, We Want This Dance': The Changing Use of Song and Dance on the Southern Plains." *Western Historical Quarterly* 30:2 (1999): 133–154.

Ellis, Clyde, and Luke Eric Lassiter. "Commentary: Applying Communitas to Kiowa Powwows." *American Indian Quarterly* 22:4 (1998): 485–91.

Eschbach, Karl, and Kalman Applbaum. "Who Goes to Powwows? Evidence from the Survey of American Indians and Alaska Natives." *American Indian Culture and Research Journal* 24:2 (2000): 65–83.

Fear-Seagal, Jacqueline. "Nineteenth-Century Indian Education: Universalism versus Evolutionism." *Journal of American Studies* 33:2 (1999): 323–341.

Flannery, Regina. "The Changing Form and Functions of the Gros Ventre Grass Dance." *Primitive Man* 20:3 (July 1947): 39–70.

Fry, Aaron. "Social Power and the Men's Northern Traditional Powwow Clothing Style." In *Painters, Patrons, and Identity: Essays in Native American Art to Honor J. J. Brody,* Joyce M. Szabo, ed. (Albuquerque: University of New Mexico Press, 2001): 71–93.

Gaede, Jethro. "The American Indian Exposition, 1932–1950: Rejecting Assimilation Initiatives and Inverting Cultural Stereotypes." Paper presented at the annual meeting of the American Society for Ethnohistory, 2000. Unpublished ms. in the author's possession.

Gan.ble, John. "Changing Patterns in Kiowa Dance." In *International Congress of Americanists, Proceedings* 29:2 (1952): 100–105.

Geller, Peter. " 'Hudson's Bay Company Indians': Images of Native People and the Red River Pageant, 1920." In *Dressing in Feathers: The Construction of the Indian in American Popular Culture,* S. Elizabeth Bird, ed. (Boulder, Colo.: Westview, 1996): 65–77.

Gelo, Daniel J. "Comanche Songs with English Lyrics: Context, Imagery, and Continuity." *Storia Nordamericana* 5:1 (1988): 137–146.

———. "Powwow Patter: Indian Emcee Discourse on Power and Identity." *Journal of American Folklore* 112 (Winter 1999): 40–57.

Goddard, Pliny Earle. "Dancing Societies of the Sarsi Indians." *Anthropological Papers of the American Museum of Natural History,* vol. XI, part V (1914): 461–474.

Gohl, E. H. "The Effect of Wild Westing." *Quarterly Journal of the Society of American Indians* 2:3 (September 1914): 226–228.

Greenwald, Emily. " 'Hurrah! 4th July': The Ironies of Independence Day on Western Reservations." Unpublished ms. in the author's possession.

Hagan, William T. "The Reservation Policy: Too Little and Too Late." In *Indian-White Relations: A Persistent Paradox,* Jane F. Smith and Robert M. Kvasnicka, eds. (Washington, D.C.: Howard University Press, 1976): 157–169.

Hamill, James. "Being Indian in Northeast Oklahoma." *Plains Anthropologist* 45:173 (2000): 291–303.

Hatton, Orin T. "In the Tradition: Grass Dance Musical Style and Female Pow-wow Singers." *Ethnomusicology* 30:2 (1986): 197–221.

Hoffman, Walter James. "The Menomini Indians." Fourteenth Annual Report of the Bureau of American Ethnology (Washington, D.C.: Smithsonian Institution, 1893): 11–328.

Holm, Tom. "Fighting a White Man's War: The Extent and Legacy of American Indian Participation in World War II." In *The Plains Indians of the Twentieth Century,* Peter Iverson, ed. (Norman: University of Oklahoma Press, 1985): 149–167.

Howard, James H. "The Dakota Victory Dance, World War II." *North Dakota History* 18 (1951): 31–40.

———. "Notes on the Dakota Grass Dance." *Southwest Journal of Anthropology* 8 (1951): 82–85.

———. "The Pan-Indian Culture of Oklahoma." *Scientific Monthly* 18:5 (1955): 215–220.

———. "Pan-Indianism in Native American Music and Dance." *Ethnomusicology* 27:1 (1983): 71–82.

———. "The Plains Gourd Dance as a Revitalization Movement." *American Ethnologist* 3:2 (1976): 243–259.

Howard, James H., and Gertrude Kurath. "Ponca Dances, Ceremonies, and Music." *Ethnomusicology* 3:1 (1959): 1–14.

———. "The Curious Story of Reformers and American Indians." In *Indians in American History,* 2d ed., Frederick E. Hoxie and Peter Iverson, eds. (Wheeling, Ill.: Harlan-Davidson, 1998).

Hoxie, Frederick E. "From Prison to Homeland: The Cheyenne River Reservation before World War I." In *The Plains Indians of the Twentieth Century,* Peter Iverson, ed. (Norman: University of Oklahoma Press, 1985): 55–75.

Huenemann, Lynn F. "Northern Plains Dance." In *Native American Dance: Ceremonies and Social Traditions,* Charlotte Heth, ed. (Washington, D.C.: Smithsonian Institution, 1992): 125–127.

"Indians Use Human Scalps in Dance." *American Indian Magazine* 7 (1919): 184.

Kavanagh, Thomas W. "The Comanche Pow-wow: Pan-Indianism or Tribalism." *Haliksa'i,* University of New Mexico Contributions to Anthropology 1 (1982): 12–27.

———. "Southern Plains Dance: Tradition and Dynamics." In *Native American Dance: Ceremonies and Social Traditions,* Charlotte Heth, ed. (Washington, D.C.: Smithsonian Institution, 1992): 105–123.

Kennan, William R., and L. Brooks Hill. "Kiowa Forty-Nine Singing: A Communication Perspective." *International Journal of Intercultural Relations* 4 (1980): 149–165.

Kracht, Benjamin. "Kiowa Powwows: Continuity in Ritual Practice." *American Indian Quarterly* 18:3 (1994): 321–348.

———. "Kiowa Religion in Historical Perspective." *American Indian Quarterly* 21:1 (1997): 15–33.

Kyle, James H. "How Shall the Indian Be Educated?" *North American Review* 159 (November 1894): 434–447.

Lassiter, Luke Eric. " 'Charlie Brown': Not Just Another Essay on the Gourd Dance." *American Indian Culture and Research Journal* 21:4 (1997): 75–103.

Lerch, Patricia Barker, and Susan Bullers. "Powwows as Identity Markers: Traditional or Pan-Indian?" *Human Organization* 55:4 (1996): 395.

Lewis, David Rich. "Still Native: The Significance of Native Americans in the History of the Twentieth-Century American West." *Western Historical Quarterly* 24 (May 1993): 203–227.

"Lo, the Rich Indian How He Blows His Coin!" *Literary Digest* 67:8 (November 20, 1920): 62-64.

Lowie, Robert H. "The Assiniboine." *Anthropological Papers of the American Museum of Natural History,* vol. IV, part I (1909): 5–265.

———. "Dance Associations of the Eastern Dakota." *Anthropological Papers of the American Museum of Natural History,* vol. XI, part II (1913): 101–142.

———. "Dances and Societies of the Plains Shoshone." *Anthropological Papers of the American Museum of Natural History,* vol. XI, part X (1915): 803–835.

———. "Military Societies of the Crow Indians." *Anthropological Papers of the American Museum of Natural History,* vol. XI, part III (1913): 143–358.

————. "Social Life of the Crow Indians." *Anthropological Papers of the American Museum of Natural History,* vol. IX, part II (1912): 181–247.

Lurie, Nancy O. "An American Indian Renascence?" In *The American Indian Today,* Stuart Levine and Nancy O. Lurie, eds. (Baltimore: Pelican Books, 1970): 295–327.

————. "The Contemporary American Indian Scene." In *North American Indians in Historical Perspective,* Nancy O. Lurie and Eleanor B. Leacock, eds. (New York: Random House, 1971): 418–480.

Mattern, Mark. "The Powwow as a Public Arena for Negotiating Unity and Diversity in American Indian Life." *American Indian Culture and Research Journal* 20:4 (1996): 183–201.

McCarl, David. "The Powwow Circle: Native American Dance and Dress." *TD&T* 32:3 (1996): 50–58.

Meadows, William C., and Gus Palmer, Sr. "Tonkonga: The Kiowa Black Legs Military Society." In *Native American Dance: Ceremonies and Social Traditions,* Charlotte Heth, ed. (Washington, D.C.: Smithsonian Institution, 1992): 116–117.

Medicine, Bea. "American Indian Family: Cultural Change and Adaptive Strategies." *Journal of Ethnic Studies* 8:4 (Winter 1981): 13–23.

Methvin, John Jasper. "Reminiscences of Life Among the Indians." *Chronicles of Oklahoma* 5 (1927): 166–179.

Mooney, James. "Military Societies." In *Handbook of American Indians North of Mexico,* Bulletin 30, Frederick W. Hodge, ed. (Washington, D.C.: Bureau of American Ethnology, 1912): 861–863.

Moore, John H. "How Giveaways and Pow-wows Redistribute the Means of Subsistence." In *The Political Economy of North American Indians,* John H. Moore, ed. (Norman: University of Oklahoma Press, 1993): 240–269.

Moses, L. G. "Indians on the Midway: Wild West Shows and the Indian Bureau at World's Fairs, 1893–1904." *South Dakota History* 21 (Fall 1991): 205–229.

————. "Interpreting the Wild West, 1883–1914." In *Between Indian and White Worlds: The Cultural Brokers,* Margaret Connell Szasz, ed. (Albuquerque: University of New Mexico Press, 1994): 158–178.

————. "Wild West Shows, Reformers, and the Image of the American Indian, 1887–1914." *South Dakota History* 14 (Fall 1984): 193–221.

Murie, James R. "Pawnee Indian Societies." *Anthropological Papers of the American Museum of Natural History,* vol. XI, part VII (1914): 543–644.

Napier, Rita G. "Across the Big Water: American Indians' Perceptions of Europe and Europeans, 1887–1906." In *Indians and Europe: An Interdisciplinary Collection of Essays,* Christian F. Feest, ed. (Lincoln: University of Nebraska Press, 1999): 383–401.

Newcomb, Jr., William W. "A Note on Cherokee-Delaware Pan-Indianism." *American Anthropologist* 57 (1955): 1041–1045.

Paredes, J. Anthony. "Federal Recognition and the Poarch Creek Indians." In *Indians of the Southeastern United States in the Late 20th Century,* J. Anthony Paredes, ed. (Tuscaloosa: University of Alabama Press, 1992): 120–139.

Parezo, Nancy J., and John W. Troutman. "The 'Shy' Cocopa Go To The Fair." In *Selling the Indian: Commercializing and Appropriating American Indian Cultures,* Carter Jones Meyer and Diana Royer, eds. (Tucson: University of Arizona Press, 2001): 3–43.

Powers, Marla N. "Symbolic Representations of Sex Roles in the Plains War Dance." *European Review of Native American Studies* 2:2 (1988): 17–24.

Powers, William K. "Contemporary Oglala Music and Dance: Pan-Indianism versus Pan-Tetonism." *Ethnomusicology* 12:3 (1968): 352–372.

———. "Echoing the Drum: The Place of Women in Lakota Song and Dance." *Whispering Wind* 31:1 (2000): 12–20.

———. "The Indian Hobbyist Movement in North America." In *Handbook of North American Indians*, vol. 4, *History of Indian-White Relations*, William C. Sturtevant, ed. (Washington, D.C.: Smithsonian Institution Press, 1988): 557–561.

———. "Innovation in Lakota Powwow Costumes." *American Indian Art* 19:4 (1994): 66-73, 103–104.

———. "Plains Indian Music and Dance." In *Anthropology on the Great Plains*, W. Raymond Wood and Margot Liberty, eds. (Lincoln: University of Nebraska Press, 1980): 212–229.

———. "Silhouettes of the Past: The Shape of Traditions to Come." *Whispering Wind* 27:2 (1995): 4–12.

———. "The Sioux Omaha Dance." *American Indian Tradition* 8:1 (1961): 24–33.

Rachlin, Carol K. "Powwow." *Oklahoma Today* 15:2 (Spring 1964): 18–22.

———. "Tight Shoe Night: Oklahoma Indians Today." In *The American Indian Today*, Stuart Levine and Nancy O. Lurie, eds. (Baltimore: Pelican Books, 1970): 160–183.

Reinschmidt, Michael. "The Drum Dance Religion of the Sauk: Historical and Contemporary Reflections." *European Review of Native American Studies* 8:1 (1994): 23–32.

Roth, Barbara Williams. "The 101 Ranch Wild West Show, 1904–1932." *Chronicles of Oklahoma* 43:4 (Winter 1965): 416–431.

Roth, George. "Overview of Southeastern Tribes Today." In *Indians of the Southeastern United States in the Late 20th Century*, J. Anthony Paredes, ed. (Tuscaloosa: University of Alabama Press, 1992): 183–202.

Rountree, Helen C. "Indian Virginians on the Move." In *Indians of the Southeastern United States in the Late 20th Century*, J. Anthony Paredes, ed. (Tuscaloosa: University of Alabama Press, 1992): 9–28.

Rynkiewich, Michael A. "Chippewa Powwows." In *Anishinabe: 6 Studies of Modern Chippewa*, J. Anthony Paredes, ed. (Tallahassee: University of Florida Press, 1980): 31–100.

Sanchez, Victoria. "Intertribal Dance and Cross Cultural Communication: Traditional Powwows in Ohio." *Communication Studies* 52:1 (Spring 2001): 51–69.

Schweitzer, Marjorie. "The Oto-Missouria War Mothers: Women of Valor." *Moccasin Tracks* 7:1 (1981): 4–8.

———. "The War Mothers: Reflections of Space and Time." *Papers in Anthropology*, University of Oklahoma, 24:2 (1983): 157–171.

Skinner, Alanson. "Kansa Organizations." *Anthropological Papers of the American Museum of Natural History*, vol. XI, part IX (1915): 745–775.

———. "Ponca Society and Dances." *Anthropological Papers of the American Museum of Natural History*, vol. XI, part IX (1915): 779–801.

———. "Societies of the Iowa." *Anthropological Papers of the American Museum of Natural History*, vol. XI, part IX (1915): 679–739.

Stahl, Robert J. "Joe True: Convergent Needs and Assumed Identity." In *Being and Becoming Indian: Biographical Studies of North American Frontiers,* James Clifton, ed. (Prospect Heights, Ill.: Waveland Press, 1993): 276–289.

Theisz, R. D. "Acclamations and Accolades: Honor Songs in Lakota Society Today." *Kansas Quarterly* 13:2 (1981): 27–43.

———. "The Bad Speakers and the Long Braids: References to Foreign Enemies in Lakota Song Texts." In *Indians and Europe: An Interdisciplinary Collection of Essays,* Christian F. Feest, ed. (Aachen, Ger.: RaderVerlag, 1987): 427–434.

———. "Song Texts and Their Performers: The Centerpiece of Contemporary Lakota Identity Formulation." *Great Plains Quarterly* 7 (Spring 1987): 116–124.

Thiel, Mark G. "The Omaha Dance in Oglala and Sicangu Sioux History, 1883–1923." *Whispering Wind* 23:5 (Fall-Winter 1990): 4–17.

———. "The Powwow: Development of the Contemporary American Indian Celebration," Part 3. *Whispering Wind* 15:4 (1982): 7–14.

Thomas, Robert K. "Pan-Indianism." In *The American Indian Today,* Stuart Levine and Nancy O. Lurie, eds. (Baltimore: Pelican Books, 1970): 128–140.

Toelken, Barre. "Ethnic Selection and Intensification in the Native American Powwow." In *Creative Ethnicity: Symbols and Strategies of Contemporary Ethnic Life,* Stephen Stern and John Allan Cicala, eds. (Logan: Utah State University Press, 1991): 137–156.

Troutman, John W. " 'Tell Us More about Handling Poisonous Snakes': The Politics of Dance, Indianness, and Citizenship in Indian Country, 1900–1930." Paper presented at the annual meeting of the American Society for Ethnohistory, 2002. Copy in the author's possession.

Turley, Frank. "Ponca Fair and Powwow." *American Indian Tradition* 7:5 (1961): 180–181.

Wallis, Michael. "The Miller Brothers and the 101 Ranch." *Gilcrease Journal* 1 (Spring 1993): 6–29.

Weatherly, Suzanne. "Gathering of Nations." *News from Indian Country,* May 15, 2001, p. 4B.

Weltfish, Gene. "The Plains Indians: Their Continuity in History and Their Indian." In *North American Indians in Historical Perspective,* Nancy O. Lurie and Eleanor B. Leacock, eds. (New York: Random House, 1971): 200–227.

West, Richard. Foreword. In *Native American Dance: Ceremonies and Social Traditions,* Charlote Heth, ed. (Washington, D.C.: Smithsonian Institution Press, 1992).

Wissler, Clark. "General Discussion of Shamanistic and Dancing Societies." *Anthropological Papers of the American Museum of Natural History,* vol. XI, part XII (1916): 853–876.

———. "Societies and Ceremonial Associations in the Oglala Division of the Teton-Dakota." *Anthropological Papers of the American Museum of Natural History,* vol. XI, part I (1912): 1–100.

———. "Societies and Dance Associations of the Blackfoot Indians." *Anthropological Papers of the American Museum of Natural History,* vol. XI, part IV (1913): 359–460.

———. "Societies of the Plains Indians — General Introduction." *Anthropological Papers of the American Museum of Natural History,* vol. XI, part I (1916): v–viii.

Wooley, David, and William T. Waters. "Waw-no-she's Dance." *American Indian Art Magazine* 23 (Winter 1998): 36–45.

Wright, Muriel H. "The American Indian Exposition in Oklahoma." *Chronicles of Oklahoma* 24:2 (1946): 158–165.

———. "The Indian International Fair at Muskogee." *Chronicles of Oklahoma* 49:1 (1971): 14–25.

Yellow Robe, Chauncey. "The Menace of the Wild West Show." *Quarterly Journal of the Society of American Indians* 2:3 (September 1914): 223–225.

Young, Gloria. "Dance as Communication." *Native Americas: Hemispheric Journal of Indigenous Issues* (Fall/Winter 1994): 9–15.

Index

Hokeah, Jack, 131
Horse, Billy Evans, 13, 170
Horse, Cecil, 164
Horse, Jenny, 164
Howard, James H.
    nineteenth century dance societies,
        29, 32–33
    Pan-Indianism, 166
Hunting Horse, 139

Intertribal Indian Club of Tulsa
        Powwow, 1–2, 175–176
Iowa Tribe
    nineteenth century dance societies, 31,
        38, 41
Indian opposition to dances, 57–58, 60,
        70–72, 83–84, 164
I'n-lon-schka Society Dance, 21, 46, 48,
        52–53, 77, 157, 168. *See also* Osage
        Tribe; Red Eagle, Ed, Sr.
Iruska Society Dance, 49–52. *See also*
        Pawnee Tribe

Kasson, Joy S.
    dances and Wild West shows, 80–81, 94
    See also Moses, L. G.
Kavanagh, Thomas W.
    Comanche dances, 13–14, 20, 25,
        47–48, 171–172
    See also Foster, Morris; Nauni, Haddon
Kickapoo Powwow Club, 4–5
Kiowa Tribe
    fancy dancing introduced, 115–116
    nineteenth century dance societies,
        30, 38–41, 44
    O-ho-mah Society, 18, 25–27, 33, 35,
        48, 50, 53, 77, 103, 115–116
    Tiah-Piah Society annual dance, 2–4
Kotay, Ralph, 21, 25, 77, 166
Kracht, Benjamin, 6–7, 23, 165, 173

LaFlesche, Francis
    Omaha Hethu'shka, 40
Lassiter, Luke Eric
    conflict at powwows, 6–7
    importance of songs, 34, 174

Kiowa War Mothers, 24
O-ho-mah, 25–26, 35
powwow culture, 18, 53, 76, 104, 105,
        163–164, 165–166, 172, 173
    See also Foster, Morris; Kavanagh,
        Thomas; Meadows, William
Lefthand, Chester
    fancy dancing, 112, 114, 127, 131
Lonebear, Mary Belle Curtis
    Dogpatch Powwow, 129, 130
Lowie, Robert H.
    changes in nineteenth century Ute
        dances, 52
    nineteenth century Crow dance
        societies, 44
    nineteenth century Dakota dance
        societies, 31–32

Maker, Leonard
    Osage dances, 121
Marriott, Alice
    Kiowa dances, 116
Martinez, Tommy, 135
Mason, Archie, Jr.
    urban powwows, 157
Mattern, Mark
    description of powwow dynamics,
        7
Mausape, Eugenia
    Indian opposition to dances, 57
McDonald, Gus
    fancy dancing, 112–114, 153
    Haskell Powwow, 127
McKenzie, Parker
    American Indian Exposition, 140–146,
        154
Meadows, William
    Craterville Park, 66
    emergence of powwows, 115–117, 119
    nineteenth century warrior dance
        societies, 31, 37, 39, 41, 45, 46,
        53–54
    World War I and revival of dances, 74,
        105, 114–115
    World War II and revival of dances,
        105, 152